Media Strategies for Marketing Places in Crisis

To my parents, Sabiha and the late Avraham Avraham

E.A.

To my grandparents, Chaim (Werner) and Chawa (Livia) Ruebsteck

E.K.

Media Strategies for Marketing Places in Crisis

Improving the Image of Cities, Countries and Tourist Destinations

Eli Avraham and Eran Ketter

ELSEVIER

AMSTERDAM • BOSTON • HEIDELBERG • LONDON • NEW YORK • OXFORD
PARIS • SAN DIEGO • SAN FRANCISCO • SINGAPORE • SYDNEY • TOKYO

Butterworth-Heinemann is an imprint of Elsevier

Butterworth-Heinemann is an imprint of Elsevier
Linacre House, Jordan Hill, Oxford OX2 8DP, UK
30 Corporate Drive, Suite 400, Burlington, MA 01803, USA

First edition 2008

British Library Cataloguing in Publication Data
A catalogue record for this book is available from the British Library

Library of Congress Cataloging-in-Publication Data
A catalog record for this book is available from the Library of Congress

ISBN: 978-0-7506-8452-1

For information on all Butterworth-Heinemann publications
visit our web site at books.elsevier.com

Printed and bound in Great Britain
08 09 10 11   10 9 8 7 6 5 4 3 2 1

Contents

Acknowledgments

As we end the long journey of writing this book, we would like to thank all the partners who walked this path with us. First and most important we thank our families and friends for their endless patience and support along the way: David, Avishai and Ellen Avraham, and Ruthi, Michael, Benjamin, Nir and Ayelet Ketter.

While writing, we had many partners who assisted us in forming ideas and models, gathering case studies, giving good advices and honest criticism: Prof. Yoel Mansfeld, Prof. Peter Tarlow, Prof. Peter Schofield, Prof. Gadi Wolfsfeld, Prof. Amiram Gonen, Prof. Gabi Weimann, Dr György Szondi, Dr Hezi Israeli, Dr Anat First, Dr Tamir Shefer, Dr Jonathan Cohen, Mr Adam Ruskin and Mrs Aliza Yonas. We also thank our colleagues at the Department of Communication in the University of Haifa for their constant intellectual support and advice.

We offer our gratitude to The Floersheimer Institute for believing in the field of place marketing and for funding the first book, which eventually led to the current one. We are also grateful to the Office of the Rector and the Research Authority at the University of Haifa for their generous support of the writing, translating and editing of this book.

This book would not be the same without the immense assistance of two individuals: Mr Murray Rosovsky, our editor who successfully managed to alter highly complicated texts into accessible and easy-to-read manuscript, and Ellen Avraham, for the many hours she devoted during every step of the way. Her knowledge, ideas, writing ability and dedication improved our research and our book enormously. Last but not least, we thank our partners in Elsevier/Butterworth-Heinemann for sharing this dream with us and helping us to make it into a published book: Jane Macdonald, Sally North, Naomi Robertson and Hemamalini Rajendrababu.

List of figures

List of advertisements

Introduction

Living in the ever-changing world of the twenty-first century, crises have become a familiar problem for a growing list of countries, regions and cities. Popular tourist destinations such as New York, London and Madrid have suffered from terror attacks; the killer tsunami of 2004 swept the beaches of Thailand, India and Sri Lanka; epidemics of SARS, foot and mouth disease and other illnesses had a severe effect on tourism in the United Kingdom, China and Canada; and Hurricane Katrina destroyed one of the United State's fabled tourist destinations in 2005.

In the age of the World Wide Web, satellites, global TV networks and the global economy, crises such as these are widely covered in the international media and can empty out hotels, cancel flights and leave tourist attractions deserted overnight. On the other hand, in contrast to sudden unexpected crises, countries such as those of Africa, the former communist countries of Eastern Europe, Middle Eastern countries, as well as cities and regions in more developed countries, can gradually develop negative images as the cumulative result of a problematic past, peripheral location, neglected tourism infrastructure, high crime rates and social problems. In both scenarios – the sudden downturn in image resulting from a particular crisis and the development of a gradual negative image – an unfavorable image is projected in the media and has a correspondingly negative effect on the national and international tourism industry and on the place's economics, investments, commerce and its attractiveness to current and potential residents.

The growing competition between countries and cities over attracting investment, tourists, capital and national and international status means that, today, a negative image is more harmful than ever. Whatever the cause of the negative image, places perceived as dangerous, frightening or boring are at a distinct disadvantage. Many decision makers and marketers stand by helplessly, frustrated by their knowledge that in most cases, their city's negative image is not based on well-grounded facts. Given that stereotypes are not easily changed or dismissed, the challenge facing these decision makers is great. Analyses of many case studies show interesting examples of places that tried to change a negative image into a positive one, in order to bringing back tourists, investors and residents.

Although a great deal of knowledge about crisis communications has accumulated in recent years, very little has been written about strategies to improve places' negative images. The aim of *Media Strategies for Marketing Places in Crisis* is to discuss the various dimensions of an image crisis and different strategies to overcome it, both in practice and in theory. This book is based on the careful analysis of dozens of case studies, advertisements, public relations campaigns, press releases, academic articles, news articles and the websites of cities, countries and tourist destinations.

The target audience of this book includes urban marketers and designers; mayors, spokespersons, PR offices and managers of tourist destinations; decision makers in national level tourist bureaus; crisis communications experts; and teachers and researchers in several related fields such as marketing, public relations, tourism, media, advertising and urban studies. At this moment, decision makers from New York City to Rio De Janeiro and from Croatia to Phuket are willing to spend millions of dollars to create a strong and positive image for their place, to turn it into an attractive destination and desired place to live and to receive positive national and international media coverage, but are unsure of the optimal methods to achieve these goals. Basic knowledge such as the selection of the correct target audience, the decision about the right strategy to use and the pros and cons of different strategies can make all the difference. Similarly, destinations can downsize or even avoid the negative effects of an image crisis by knowing the proper techniques of handling the media and delivering the "right" messages during the crisis.

How does this book differ from other books? A careful survey of the market will find many books in the fields of advertising, urban crises, PR, marketing places and managing tourist destinations, but none of those books combine these fields while focusing primarily on marketing strategies for places facing an image crisis. The book's emphasis on the problem of negative images and how to overcome them makes it unique and a much-needed. It is important to say that this book is based on the strategic approach to public relations, stating that a change of image is ongoing, holistic, interactive and wide-scaled, requiring much more than a quick change of logo or slogan.

The book is divided into two parts, each containing several chapters. The first part of the book has five chapters that summarize the existing knowledge accumulated in the fields of place marketing, managing place public and media image, campaign conducting, consumer behavior, crisis management and crisis communication management. The second part of the book also has five chapters: Chapter 6 will introduce the preliminary analysis (CAP analysis) that place decision makers should conduct before choosing the proper marketing recovery strategy; Chapter 7 concentrates on media strategies that focus on the source of the message; Chapter 8 on media strategies that focus on the message itself; and Chapter 9 elucidates media strategies that focus on the target audience (SAP strategies).

The book concludes with a *multi-step model*, illustrating the proper choice of a strategy in altering an unflattering public image. The proposed multi-step model offers a detailed preliminary analysis, a variety of media strategies and other factors such as goals, timing, channels and techniques. The large number of media strategies detailed in the model offers a wide-range of solutions for every possible crisis.

Part One
Marketing Places, Media Campaign and Crisis Management

The first five chapters of this book, which constitute Part One, outline the concepts related to marketing places during image crises. Chapter 1 introduces and sets out in detail the field of place marketing. Chapter 2 discusses a place's image with the public and in the media and suggests ways to measure it by discussing types of images, means of measuring them, constructing images, levels of analysis and other such concepts. Chapter 3 analyzes campaign management, image management and the relevant factors involved in the place marketing process. This chapter also shows the link between place vision and place marketing, possible directions for place branding and ways of constructing public relations and an advertising campaign's strategies. Chapter 4 discusses the different aspects of consumer behavior and Chapter 5 summarizes present knowledge in crisis management and crisis communication management. An overview of the accumulated knowledge in the fields presented in Part One should furnish the reader with an understanding of our model for marketing places and the ability to implement it in an image crisis, as suggested in Part Two.

1 Introduction to place marketing and branding

Place marketing is a vast subject, and this introduction can highlight only some of its central concepts. Place marketing has become very popular since the early 1990s, in individual countries and internationally (Codato and Franco, 2006). On the latter level globalization has gained strength, with concomitant enlargement of transfers of investments, capital, human resources, knowledge and goods; the number of countries taking part in the global economy and global tourism is increasing, accompanied by a parallel process whereby worldwide transportation and communication have grown speedier, easier and cheaper. The barriers between East and West are fading and demand for international tourism is rising. On the national level, the need for place marketing has increased due to several factors such as smaller government budgets for local municipalities, greater relative independence of mayors and heads of local municipalities, residents' increasing concern for and involvement in their local quality of life and local governance and rising awareness among mayors and local leaders of place image and place marketing and their fundamental effect on different aspects of the place (Avraham, 2003a; Felsenstein, 1994; Hason, 1996).

These developments have created a climate of competition among different places around the globe for national and international status and for high-class residents, tourists, conventions, sporting events, entrepreneurs, investors, industries, businesses and global capital. For example, today **Glasgow** does not compete just with British cities such as Manchester or York, but with other cities worldwide, trying to win international tourism. Global competition for tourism and investment has always existed, but today visiting foreign parts or investing abroad is much simpler, cheaper and safer. Knowing this, more and more local and national leaders have become proactive in enhancing their place's attractiveness and improving its competitive edge. In many cities and countries, certain steps and changes have been implemented, the better to attract investors, entrepreneurs and immigrants. In addition to changes in the regulation of the economy and finance systems, efforts have been invested in the place's image because of its fundamental importance and contribution to its competitiveness. Confirmation of this process can be found in the work of Ashworth and Voogd (1990), who noted that "The perception of cities, and the mental image held of them, became active components of economic success or failure" (p. 3). Leaders of countries, regions and cities realize that a positive place image, combined with a successful marketing mix, is a powerful tool in competing for resources and other finance-related activities. A place's management patterns have been changed for the better by the significant elements of advertising, public relations, direct marketing and sales promotion (Felsenstein, 1994; Kotler et al., 1999a).

To improve the place's image, decision makers have to choose a suitable "package" for marketing the place competitively. The complexity of the process requires that this packaging be under the guidance of strategic marketing professionals. A proper package can ensure the place's economic vigor, reduction in its unemployment, growth in income from tax and other local activities, improvement of local services and infrastructure and residents' greater satisfaction with the authorities (Dunn et al., 1995; Felsenstein, 1994; Gold, 1980; Gold and Ward, 1994; Hason, 1996; Kotler et al., 1993, 1999a; Paddison, 1993; Pocock and Hudson, 1978).

Felsenstein (1994) identifies four economic strategies that can be used by local authorities:

1. Developing local economy by attracting large-scale industries;
2. Attracting small-scale businesses in the fields of private or public services;
3. Lobbying for national budgets;
4. Encouraging local businesses to expand their activities.

All these strategies have proven beneficial, but the following discussion will focus on the first two only, as they are the most relevant to our topic. Steps to implement them include incentives, tax benefits, loans and grants, improvement of infrastructure, opening new attractions and preparing land for development. All these measures are adopted to guarantee employment, economic comfort and high living standards for local residents. According to Felsenstein (1995), faulty development of a local economy results from an imbalance in the dual task that it requires: planning (changing physical and demographic aspects of the local market) and marketing (changing the local economy through advertising campaigns and attracting business and investors). Good planning for local economic development identifies problems, goals and objectives and proposes ways of action and viable alternatives. Good marketing identifies target markets and shapes techniques and strategies for place advertising and promotion. According to Felsenstein, officials responsible for local economic development spend too much time on marketing and not enough on planning because the former has a high public profile and great political importance and is an important tool to win favorable public opinion about the work of the local economic development department. Planning is a longer-term and more in-depth process, needing elaborate economic and architectural models; it takes place far from the public eye and its outcome will become generally known only several years later (by which time the current head of the local economical development department may well have moved on).

Definitions for place marketing

The conceptual foundation of place marketing lies in marketing theories, primarily the marketing-mix approach (Olsson and Bergland, 2006). Although place marketing has existed since colonial times, when colonial governments tried to persuade people to move to the newly conquered territories (Gold, 1994), the concept of "place marketing" (which some label "place promotion" or "city management") became popular in European urban literature only during the 1980s and a little earlier in the United States (Paddison, 1993). "Place marketing" has many different definitions in the literature; for example, according to Gold and Ward (1994), "...Place promotion [is] defined as the conscious use of publicity and marketing to communicate selective images of specific geographical localities or areas to a target audience..." (p. 2). This definition singles out the use of choice and desirable images in the marketing process and the active role of the target audience in accepting the marketing plan. Existing traits or components are selected and highlighted to make the place more attractive for this specific audience. However, this selectiveness means ignoring or even hiding some of the place's negative characteristics.

One very popular definition can be found in Short et al. (2000): "Place promotion involves the re-evaluation and re-presentation of place to create and market a new image for localities to enhance their competitive position in attracting or retaining resources" (p. 318). This definition describes the process of marketing a new place image as a means to preserve and draw on various resources. Ashworth and Voogd (1990) lay similar emphasis on resources, suggesting that place marketing is a process in which urban activities are adjusted to the needs of the target audience to maximize the place's socioeconomic functioning. European researchers (van den Berg et al., as cited in Paddison, 1993) emphasize in their definitions the promotion of various aspects of comfort and economic development in the marketed area, which satisfy the requirements of residents, investors and visitors, in what has been referred to as "the harmonious city." These researchers believe that promoting such aspects helps places compete with other places and remain in respectable positions in the international or urban hierarchy; they likewise focus on the need to work on the place's physical appearance as the key to a successful new marketing campaign. In any event, place marketing can be seen as a "refreshing" of urban or national identity or as the creation of new forms of identity (Dunn et al., 1995).

Studies in place marketing are based on two theoretical approaches: one connects place marketing and political economy, noting the transformation of a place's local government and the involvement of the business community in developing its economy; the other concentrates on the success of various marketing strategies (see list in Bradley et al., 2002; Short and Kim, 1993). Yet all the different definitions indicate that place marketing is a long and complicated process. Local decision makers, especially in cities, are concerned that launching a place marketing campaign is tantamount to admitting the existence of a problem in the way the place is managed. Local leaders are concerned that once a campaign is mounted questions might be asked, such as "What has been done so far to prevent the formation of the negative image?," "How blameworthy are the local authorities for the place's negative image?" or "Why should money needed for much more important goals be spent on costly advertising?" Such questions might discourage some local decision makers, generating a vicious cycle in which the place's negative image becomes worse, and no leader is willing to assume the responsibility of facing this challenge. Whatever the case might be, many researchers point to the difficulties and complexity of the place marketing process and the many variables involved in the process.

Nielsen (2001) refers to "place promotion," stressing the difficulty of the task especially in conditions of an image-related crisis: "Promoting a destination in normal circumstances is a difficult task, but promoting a destination that faces tourism challenges – whether from negative press, or from infrastructure damage caused by natural disasters or man-made disasters – is an altogether more arduous task" (pp. 207–208). In such circumstances, places have to tackle both the physical crisis in services and infrastructure and the intangible damage suffered by the place's image, a process that might take several years. In this book we address this complexity and the way different countries, cities and tourist destinations manage to overcome them.

Place marketing as social-public marketing

The set of tools used in place marketing originates in several disciplines. The three foremost of these are product marketing, marketing of services in the private sector and social-public marketing, each contributing its own techniques, methods, tools and concepts. As for which is the most suitable for marketing places, we believe that place marketing is mainly a social-public enterprise ("civic boosterism"). Still, it is firmly supported by the other two disciplines, especially in marketing tourist destinations, which is based more on services marketing.

Properly combining the definitions and methods of the three disciplines is not always easy. While the private sector defines financial profit as the desired outcome of the marketing process, the public sector is hard-pressed to define such clear and explicit goals, an obstacle that further impedes the marketing process. Another complexity in social-public marketing is that the simple motif of "Buy X and get Y" does not work in this case and the marketing process has to be more abstract and sophisticated (Gold and Ward, 1994). Lastly, cities and countries are not as flexible as products in the private sector; their construction takes a long time and their marketing focuses on long-term services rather than on short-term prerequisites. Note that place marketing embodies an inner conflict of sorts. It has a certain aspect of public policy – promoting a public product carrying a social benefit; but it is also affected by the free-market principle: a place must compete with other places, create business opportunities and use methods taken from the business field (Gold and Ward, 1994).

To resolve these complications a set of basic guidelines is needed. For social-public marketing to succeed, local decision makers must act democratically, not in an elitist or patronizing way; they have to cooperate in the process with the place's residents and other local players; the marketing plan should not be imposed on the market as a top-down decision but evolve bottom-up; and it should be based on the benefit to the general public rather than to the decision makers or their narrow interests. These guidelines apply not only to the actual marketing, but to processes such as decision-making, strategic planning, creating place vision, defining goals and choosing target audience to attract (e.g., residents, tourists, industry, investors,

conventions). From accumulated experience in the field, every decision is highly important and involves many debates and clashes due
to its possible future effect on the place (Paddison, 1993). For example, a decision taken in a certain city or state in the United States
to attract new residents who traditionally tend to vote Democrat
might change the place's political balance. Local Republican decision
makers therefore may well oppose such a marketing plan. Skinner
and Gould (2006) illustrate a similar situation with the difficulties
faced by the marketers of **Northern Ireland** when trying to define
the country's national identity in order to promote it. In this contro-
versy, each ethnic group tries to market Northern Ireland differently,
representing its own perception of the country.

Although each place marketing campaign is aimed at one target
audience, places commonly launch several campaigns simultaneously, trying to improve their image among several target audiences
such as potential residents, investors, exporters, importers, firms,
industrialists, visitors from other cities and tourists from abroad. The
place's image can be improved to suit each target audience, and
the common marketing goals are to make the place more attractive
for living, working, investing and spending leisure time; to support
the local tourism industry; to acquire capital; to improve social welfare; to make the place more important and central in the municipal,
regional, national and international hierarchy; and to improve the
place's image in general.

Parallel to marketing for outside audiences an inner marketing
process can take place, aimed at the place's current residents. Its
goal is to convince local residents that the local authority provides
a wide variety of high-quality services, serves residents, maintains
and improves the place's infrastructure, preserves and renovates old
buildings and establishes parks and commons. Another goal is to
create local pride and enthusiasm in local residents, involve them
in the place's vision, raise their awareness of the importance of the
tourism industry and increase their involvement in the place (Codato
and Franco, 2006). Additional importance of inner marketing arises
from the position of the place's residents in decision-making, within a
coalition of representatives of the local, regional or national authority,
entrepreneurs in tourism and industry and investors (Hason, 1996;
Kotler et al., 1993, 1999a).

Evaluating campaigns and media results

The growing popularity of place marketing leads inevitably to the
issue of a campaign's efficiency and its ability to attain the expected

goals. Measuring campaign results is an elaborate matter for various reasons (Kotler et al., 1993): first, different experts employ different evaluation methods. Second, even when experts agree on the method it is still hard to isolate the specific effect of the advertising or public relations campaign on the target audience. Nevertheless, several methods are used to assess the efficiency of a given campaign.

The simplest way to assess campaign efficiency is to run a pre- and post-campaign survey. The literature suggests two main methods: evaluating the effect on the target audience's approach to the place and evaluating the change in the actual place consumption. Both these methods also assess the target audience's response to the campaign itself. As an example of the first method, an advertising firm can take a sample of consumers from the target audience and ask them to evaluate the campaign on criteria such as the amount of attention it draws, creativity, persuasion, creation of awareness, the way it is recalled and whether the campaign has changed their opinion of the place. With these data the campaign creators can estimate how efficient the campaign is and in what way it should be amended (for further reading on the assessment of campaign efficiency see Kotler and Armstrong, 1989; Kotler et al., 1993; Nir and Rahav, 1993).

As an example of the second method, campaign creators should assess quantitative changes in the consumption of the place as regards immigration, tourism and business initiatives. In tourism, these apply to numbers of hotel vacancies and entries to local attractions and to services such as car rentals and restaurant occupation. In business initiatives, changes should be monitored in the number of companies moving into the place or in unemployment rate. In immigration, changes in the number of residents or other immigration trends should be assessed (Fenster et al., 1994; Kotler and Armstrong, 1989).

Another key to efficient evaluation of a campaign lies in the preliminary stage of setting goals for the level of awareness of a place, its desired image or its consumption. For example, if a pilot study found that current awareness of a certain destination among the target audience was 30%, the goal may be set to raise it to 60% within a year. At the end of that year any increase in awareness level can be gauged and also whether the campaign has achieved its goal. Note that elevated awareness does not always ensure an instant increase in the consumption of the place, but it is an important stage that every place must go through (Avraham, 2003a). According to Young and Lever (1997), the degree of complexity in assessing the campaign efficiency depends first of all on the goal-setting stage; since most local authorities do not start the campaign with clear quantitative or "measurable" goals, it is extremely difficult to assess campaign efficiency at later stages.

The question that began the discussion on whether place marketing can help places to improve their overall state is undoubtedly critical. Many places have employed different marketing initiatives, but only slight evidence of the campaign's efficiency can be found. The reasons for this include the high cost of high-quality surveys, concern by the place's leaders about being accused by the opposition of "spending public money to improve the mayor's image" and the tendency of professionals to keep the data to themselves out of personal and professional interests. The argument about the efficiency of campaigns also stems from their very high financial costs, naturally at the expense of resources for other fields under the supervision of the local authority such as social welfare, infrastructure and education.

Despite the lack of clear-cut evidence and the risk of political criticism, 93% of the local authorities in the **United Kingdom** were involved in some kind of marketing activity in 1995–1996, spending an average of £279,600 each (Young and Lever, 1997). A similar indication is given by Kotler et al. (1993), suggesting that 10% of all leading newspaper ads are used for marketing places. A survey by CNN in March 2000 found that the total expenditure on place marketing in the **United States** in 1999 was $538 million (Piggott, cited in Morgan and Pritchard, 2001). Considering the great amount of money spent on place marketing, the question of the efficiency of place marketing campaigns is gaining ever more relevance.

Like the argument over the effects of the mass media, the argument over the efficiency of place marketing campaigns embraces many contradictory opinions. While some research attests to their value, other studies conclude that these campaigns are a waste of resources. Young and Lever (1997) found that while the marketing campaign was very important for the place marketers, it carried only slight conscious importance for the place consumers. Consumers of an office project were more concerned with issues such as price, location, building quality, accessibility, infrastructure and proximity to their human resources. On the other hand, in a similar study Burgess and Wood (1988) found that a marketing campaign for the Docklands area in **London** exercised a major effect on small British firms. Many were directly influenced by the campaign and decided to move to the area. Note that small firms run a huge risk when moving to a new location, should it prove less successful than the previous one. To smooth the way, the place marketers should give firms' top management technical assistance and support in the move they are making.

Another interesting example of careful assessment of campaign efficiency can be found in a study by Avraham (2003a). In 1998, **Haifa**, a port city in northern Israel, launched a campaign aimed at competing with Tel Aviv, the city that serves as the economic center of Israel. The chosen slogan for delivering the message was "Haifa is better. It's a fact." In the campaign, statistical data were used to demonstrate the fields in which Haifa surpasses Tel Aviv, such as level of public education, spatial density and the size of parks and nearby forests. Soon after the campaign was launched a follow-up advertisement was presented illustrating the campaign's effect. The ad claimed that a recent survey showed that 49.3% of the residents of Israel thought that Haifa was better than Tel Aviv and only 30.9% held that opposite opinion. Although the survey did not present the distribution of opinions prior to the campaign, the follow-up advertisement gave the impression that the campaign for Haifa was very successful; half of the residents of Israel now thought that Haifa was better than Tel Aviv.

A success similar to Haifa's was achieved by **Serbia**. Following a campaign launched in 2000, the flow of tourists to the country increased dramatically, well up from the paltry few since the time of the civil war (Popesku, 2006). Similar examples of successful campaigns can be found in the study by Morgan et al. (2002). A failed campaign is exemplified in the case of **Jerusalem** in winter 2002. That year the city launched a campaign aimed at encouraging local tourism to the city. It soon ended, following reports from the local hotel association indicating that hotel vacancies had not been affected by the campaign (Ha'reuveny, 2002). This example, like many similar illustrations from around the world, indicates that campaigns do not always yield the expected effect.

Measuring the outcomes of public relations campaigns

In addition to the marketing campaign, place marketing is furthered by other techniques such as public relations (PR). The use of PR techniques is discussed in greater detail in later chapters; here we just mention that one of their main goals is to improve the place's image, and a common technique for this is to "encourage" journalists to write favorable news and columns about it. Launching a PR campaign aimed at improving a place's image is complex, as are the ways to measure its results. The most usual means of assessment is to count the number of media articles covering the place before and after the campaign (Kotler and Armstrong, 1989). This method also involves some problems, as no one knows for certain if the target audience has read, seen or heard about the articles or how they reacted if they did get the message. The ability to assess a PR campaign's efficiency is even lower than the very low ability to assess that of a marketing campaign.

One prime example of using a PR campaign to improve a place's image refers to **Miami**, Florida. In 1992–1993, several European visitors to the city, mostly from Germany, were murdered. The city consequently faced a severe image crisis, the number of visitors dropped and investors held back from opening new businesses there. A more detailed discussion of the techniques and strategies employed by Miami can be found in subsequent chapters; for now we only point to the great success of the PR campaign that was launched. It resulted in a significant enlargement of tourism to Miami, attracting in 1995 the same number of visitors as in 1992, before the crisis erupted (Tilson and Stacks, 1997).

An additional way to assess PR campaign effectiveness is offered by White (2006), who suggests focusing on what could have happened in the absence of PR resources. The organization should estimate the full potential damage that might have been caused and then calculate how much money was saved thanks to the use of PR techniques. For example, incorrect allocation of PR resources in the case of an image crisis at an American university can cause a sharp decline in the number of students, a decrease in the university's ability to raise funds and damage to the place's academic reputation. Proper use of PR techniques can diminish potential damage and save money, while improper use can end in a full-scale crisis and economic loss.

Why do places try to change their image?

One of the reasons for the growing popularity of place marketing in the last two decades is the ongoing effort by cities in Western Europe and the United States to transform from the industrial era to the post-industrial era. While industrial cities carry images of economic problems, pollution, negative immigration and social unease, post-industrial cities project images of clean streets, high-tech industry and residents with high socio-economic status. This expanding movement in the West is paralleled in Eastern Europe, where former communist countries are trying to improve their image to attract tourists and investors. In either case, Short et al. (1993) list the major reasons for improving a place's image:

1. *Trying to change the place's image for outside consumers*: This is the traditional civic boosterism of places that endeavor to attract tourists,

investors and immigrants. Underpinning this effort is the promotion of the place's name and image and replacement of the old perception. Morgan and Pritchard (1998) term this activity "image revolution." It is pursued by cities and countries alike, as they go in quest of a more attractive image.

2. *Promoting a post-industrial image*: Different actors and elements are present in many cities around the world who are interested in substituting the current industrial image with a post-industrial one. To achieve this, places improve their quality of life by cleaning up old industrial areas, rivers, beaches, lakes, forests and parks in order to deliver a message of change. In parallel, they try to attract clean industries and to strengthen cultural aspects. Examples are the cities of **Syracuse** in New York State, many cities in the north of England and **Glasgow** in Scotland. For years Glasgow's economy was based on shipbuilding, heavy industry, textiles and the chemical industry. Economic decline in these domains took place in recent decades, with resultant images of poverty, crime, heavy drinking and violence. During the 1980s Glasgow was transformed into a post-industrial city and creative campaigns heralded the good tidings. In consequence of this set of changes, together with a comprehensive process of physical improvement, Glasgow was selected as the European Capital of Culture for 1990 (Paddison, 1993).

3. *Rehabilitation, reconstruction and building of urban sections*: Physical changes made in the city can foster profound changes in a city's character, such as the generation of a vibrant, dynamic and fresh spirit. Such positive transitions can be promoted by creating urban spaces, preserving old buildings and rehabilitating neighborhoods. Aside from these expensive and elaborate processes, directing visitors, investors and residents to the reconstructed areas might not be easy, in light of past perceptions. Another difficulty may come from the current residents and business owners, wishing to avoid a change in their milieu. For example, in **Haifa** the local merchants in the city's downtown opposed a municipal rehabilitation project, concerned it might harm their businesses and encourage more customers to shop at the malls located in the suburbs. Whatever the case might be, a long-term marketing process can convince residents, investors, merchants and consumers that urban reconstruction is an important measure, with many positive byproducts, which they should all support.

4. *International rivalry and acquiring national status*: Places are marketed and their image is reconstructed so as to succeed in national and international rivalry to host exhibitions and sporting events such as the Olympic Games and attract global capital and international

firms. In addition, by cooperating with other places, improving their municipal functioning and creating fresh attractions, places can improve their national and international status. Different scholars and professionals use various methods to define the status of a city, a country, a region or a tourist destination. According to Short et al. (2000), a city's international status is determined by its financial centrality, the number of international firms and organizations with offices located in it, its business growth rate, the size of its population, its culture, telecommunications, transport, quality of life and international relations and its attractiveness as an immigration destination.

Another way of evaluating the status of cities is defined according to their political and social climate (political stability, international relations, low crime rate, freedom of speech and communication), level of health and education services, access to goods, transport services, cultural activity and natural climate. In a list published in 2002 and based on this method, **Zurich** was listed as the city with the highest status, followed by **Vienna**, **Vancouver**, **Sydney**, **Geneva**, **Frankfurt**, **Oakland**, **Copenhagen**, **Helsinki** and **Bonn** (*Ha'aretz*, 11 March 2002). Other lists rank cities by their crime rate, cost of living, quality of life and friendliness. The International Institute for Management (IMD) issues country or regional competitive power rankings, with many implications for testing country or regional status (Suyama and Senoh, 2006). Although different factors are used to determine a place's status, places ultimately use the same marketing strategies to create a positive image and improve their national and international standing.

Changes promoting place marketing processes

Why do the image of countries, tourist destinations, cities and regions change over the years? What kind of events can change a place's image for better or worse? As noted in the literature, many kinds of change can alter the place's image: in politics, in technology such as the shift from heavy industry to high tech, in changes in transportation technologies and infrastructure such as railroads and seaports and in consumer behavior and tourism trends such as the preference for eco-tourism. As a result, places can quickly become extremely attractive to audiences that previously ignored them. While many places gain from these changes, some suffer a decline in their status and ability to attract various resources, an economical recession, negative immigration from the place and a rise in unemployment and crime rates. On the other hand, places which become trendy enjoy a variety of resources, the entry of new industries, the building of new tourist attractions, growth of demand for real estate and a general improvement in the quality of life. In either case, for places to control the circumstances instead of being controlled by them, local decision makers have to constantly market the place, monitor its image and maintain its positive traits (Kotler et al., 1993).

Place branding and place positioning

Place positioning assists potential consumers to differentiate places and alternatives in the fields of tourism, business and immigration. According to Fenster et al. (1994), place positioning answers the question "What kind of place is this compared with other places?" in the consumer's mind. Every strategic plan for managing a place's image must determine that image for it. Place marketers try to influence the first association that pops into the target audience's mind on hearing the place's name. It may be one of crime, violence, danger, threat or homicide; or it may be one of fun, sun, white sand and blue-green lagoons. The common concept used to describe place positioning is the *unique selling proposition* (USP), and this is employed to create a distinct and positive image of the place in the mind of the target audience. This short discussion on place positioning can be summarized by a definition by Short and Kim (1993), describing place positioning as the active shaping of the place image in relation to competing places.

In recent years, the discussion on place positioning has merged with the discussion on place branding. A brand is a symbol (logo, color, shape, package, design), an object, a concept or a combination of them, aimed at identifying goods or services and distinguishing them from their competitors (Herstein, 2000). Suyama and Senoh (2006) offer an interesting specification for place branding named "brand-creating city," suggesting that the branding of a place can be divided into three categories: brand spirit, brand resources and brand personality. In marketing, the distinction between a product and a brand is quite clear: a wristwatch is a product, Rolex is a brand. Both the product and the brand satisfy the same basic needs (knowing what time it is), but the brand satisfies other needs too, such as attesting to economic capacity and lifestyle and also affecting one's self-image. The difference between a brand and a product is the "added value" a brand has over a product.

Designers try to make different brands distinct to make it easier for consumers to choose among the different ones available. The persuasion process in marketing a brand is not just aimed at common sense but also at the consumer's heart and feelings. According to Morgan and Pritchard (2001), "The battle for consumers in tomorrow's destination marketplace will be fought not over price but over hearts and minds – and this is where we move into the realm of branding" (p. 12).

Place branding has become one of the most popular concepts in the field of marketing places in general and tourist destinations in particular. The contemporary discourse on place marketing uses concepts such as brand design, brand values and identity, planning image strategy and managing the brand value. Many tourist destinations constantly seek ways to position themselves as a leading brand in a certain segment of tourism. Examples are brands such as "leisure capital," "shopping capital," "culture capital," "sports capital," "a city for kids/families" and "a romantic city." Aside from the places that have already undergone the branding process, many are still in search of the unique character they want to emphasize. Branding professionals suggest that whatever the chosen brand is, every project, activity, sight and attraction the place has to offer should support the preferred brand; the place's decision makers will give support to attractions and activities that promote the brand in budgets, infrastructure and marketing. As a result, the chosen brand will exert a comprehensive effect on the place and on the decision-making process in developing new tourist attractions, choosing new areas for development, building hotels or residency projects and renewing infrastructures. Every activity that supports the brand will be promoted and every activity that does not will be slowed down (Anholt, 2005).

Place branding is not easy, but those who succeed in it can expect a brighter future. Many places in the world offer the same products and the only way for places to survive in the competitive international market is by developing a unique identity. Like product branding, place branding is a combination of place characteristics and of added value, functional and non-functional. In the world of brands, the product image and positioning may be much more important than the place's actual characteristics. Place managers should emphasize the uniqueness of their place and how this place alone can satisfy a certain need for the target audience. The brand should include a slogan, a logo, visual material and colors that vaunt the brand's spirit and promote its marketing.

One interesting example of place branding is given by Morgan and Pritchard (2001), describing the branding process of **Israel** in 1993–1998 for British visitors. In the branding program, Israel was described as a destination for high-quality sea-and-sun vacations, offering a Mediterranean atmosphere together with a rich heritage and an exotic touch. Because many places offer vacations with sea, sand and sunshine, the campaign managers wanted to create a unique identity for Israel by emphasizing its multiple strengths. This branding process proved highly successful, yielding a steep rise in incoming tourism from England. Similar examples of countries, cities and tourist destinations that have undergone a successful branding process can be found in several studies (see Anholt, 2005; Codato and Franco, 2006; Henderson and Turnbull, 2006; Morgan et al., 2002; Suyama and Senoh, 2006). A partial list would include countries such as **Ireland**, **Australia**, **Britain** and **Spain** and cities such as **Turin**, **Osaka**, **Glasgow** and **Manchester**. In addition to places, other tourism services experience a branding process such as hotel corporations, tourist agencies, restaurants and car rental agencies. Herstein (2000) details the branding process of **Club Med** and illustrates the way vacation packages were adjusted for each market segment. Each package includes all the tourism services one might want on a certain vacation, at a fixed price, with emphasis on the high quality of services and the wide variety of leisure activities.

As we approach the end of this chapter it is important to note that while many experts praise and recommend a branding process, some contemporary researchers oppose it. According to the latter, branding is not a suitable solution for every city, country or tourist destination seeking a fashionable and speedy solution to their image problems. By this perspective, a branding process should generally be adopted by places intending to embark on a long-term process, involving deep strategic planning and comprehensive changes in place characteristics (Ashworth, 2006).

Summary

In this chapter, serving as an introduction to the field of place marketing, we have surveyed the causes behind national and international developments in the field and observed how the management of a place's image is an integral part of growing competition over status and resources. In a constantly changing world, places must monitor and improve their image continuously in order to keep attracting visitors, investors, entrepreneurs and residents. Its growing importance has made place marketing more professional in the last two decades. Many places are now experiencing branding processes, which take traditional marketing a step further by associating the place with a set of added values. As noted earlier, place marketing is part of social marketing and therefore involves a more comprehensive process on a variety of levels. The efficiency of a place marketing campaign or a PR campaign is thus extremely hard to assess and depends on many different variables. The next chapter focuses on one of the central concepts in place marketing: measuring a place's image among the public and the media.

2 Public images and media images of places

Place image is a central concept in several research fields, resulting from the hypothesis that the image of a country, city or a tourist destination has a marked effect on our actions and activities. Decisions such as where to live, where to travel, where to invest, where to study or which country to support in a conflict all result from the place's image. Place image has always been a central concept, but as post-modern theories have gained popularity the notion that a place's image may be even more important than the place's reality has become widespread, too (Morgan and Pritchard, 1998).

The discussion on place image so early in the book is essential as almost every PR or advertising campaign rests on the attempt to take an existing image and turn it into a better one. One of the first steps in every campaign is to measure and analyze the current image, choose a more desirable image, and take into account different variables that exert an effect on it. Such an analysis is fundamental because entirely different campaigns are required to alter different kinds of images. For example, places with a negative public image must focus their efforts on changing it, while places with a very weak image must concentrate on gaining awareness and then creating a public image. In any event, decisions such as choosing a slogan, visuals, format of advertisement, channels for delivering the message and communication strategies are based on the place's current image.

An example of the importance of the place's current image can be found in the branding process done by the Italian city of **Turin** (Codato and Franco, 2006). First, a national statistics institute was invited to conduct a study assessing the perception of Turin on the international level in economic and cultural terms. Next, the research results were used to fashion the new brand and to choose a logo, a slogan, visual imagery and a strategic communication plan.

When discussing a place's image, it is important to distinguish between the place's image among a specific target audience and the place's image in the mass media. Local and international decision makers, marketers and PR professionals believe that these two types are closely linked, so they spend resources, time and effort in creating a positive media image. This is generally believed to result in a positive image among the target audience. The opposite belief also applies: a negative media image will result in a negative image among the target audience. For example, the prime minister of **Slovakia** maintained in 1993 that the negative media coverage of his country had a powerful negative effect on foreign investment (Kunczik, 1997). Similar statements were made by spokespersons from **Malaysia** and the **Philippines** following the media coverage of local terror attacks and have been verified by academic research: Galician and Vestra (1987) found that bad news has a strong effect on the place's image.

A place's public image

The fundamental importance of the image has induced scholars from various disciplines to attempt to define it. According to Kotler et al. (1993) the image of a place is "the sum of beliefs, ideals, and impressions people have toward a certain place." These researchers argue that an image is the simplification of numerous associations and pieces of information related to a place and the cognitive product of the attempt to process large amounts of information. Boulding (1956, in Elizur 1987) takes a similar view, defining image as the sum of the cognitive, affective and evaluative characteristics of the place or an inherent perspective of itself. Boulding distinguishes the image of the place's residents from that of outsiders. He implies that place image is composed of four components:

1. Cognitive (what one knows about a place);
2. Affective (how one feels about a certain place);
3. Evaluative (how one evaluates the place or its residents);
4. Behavioral (whether one considers immigrating to/working in/ visiting/investing in a certain place).

Isolating these image components is possible only by academic analysis, as all are interrelated and affect each other. For example, if a certain person feels affection for a place he/she will presumably also find it attractive, its residents friendly and interesting and fun to live in/work in/visit. While Boulding chose to divide the image into several components, Elizur (1987) offered a more comprehensive definition, stating that an image of a place is the sum of all characteristics that come to mind when one thinks of the place.

Methods for evaluating a place's image

Many different methods may be used to evaluate a place's image among specific target audience, but the most popular are attitude surveys, various questionnaires, focus groups and in-depth interviews (Fenster et al., 1994; Kotler et al., 1993; 1999a).

Attitude surveys/questionnaires

A survey enables us to understand common attitudes to a subject, political party or place at a certain time (Yaziv, 1994). Surveys have several advantages and disadvantages that are described in the relevant literature, and they can be conducted in diverse ways such as regular mail, electronic mail, telephone and face-to-face. The decision on how a survey should be conducted is influenced by the characteristics of the target audience and of the survey itself. For example, an email survey is suitable for a target audience that uses the Internet frequently, and short surveys are more suitable for the telephone. The two major kinds of survey are the unstructured and the structured.

Unstructured survey (open-ended)

Unstructured surveys ask open-ended questions that elicit free and unbiased answers, without forcing the respondent to choose a ready-made answer, for example, *"What comes to mind when you hear the word 'Glasgow'? (not more than five associations)."* The obvious issue now is what can one do with the answers to this question? For example, if most answers state that Glasgow is "a beautiful city," is "clean," has "friendly people," is "cultural" and "welcoming," then the city has no problem with its image among that target audience. But if generally answers are that it is "crime-ridden," "polluted," "industrial," "unpleasant," "boring" and "dirty" the city must improve its image. In any event, the most common associations and their order in the answers should be examined. Running that one question through this simple analysis can provide a fast and straightforward indicator of the place's general image and of the common traits the place is known for. In the next step, local decision makers should decide how to deal with the findings and which marketing strategy should be employed to reverse the negative associations and bolster the positive ones.

Structured survey (close-ended)

In a structured survey, the respondent is asked to choose from a pool of ready-made answers. A close-ended survey can include questions evaluating the level of awareness of a place, its characteristics, satisfaction with its functioning and expectations of it. Questions can cover a large variety of fields, such as tourism, immigration and investment. For example, a survey questionnaire conducted by a tourist destination among a specific target audience can be distributed to people who intend to visit the place and to past and current visitors. The target audience can be asked whether they agree or disagree (with different levels of agreement or disagreement on a Likert scale) with various statements such as "**Croatia** *is a clean country,*" "*There are many tourist attractions in Croatia*" and "*Croatia offers a large variety of cultural events.*" Questions about the functioning of tourism services, the interaction with the place's residents and whether the cost of the visit was proportional to the experience can likewise be asked. Through questions of this kind the place marketers try to assess the perceptual/cognitive and affective components of the place (Brkic and Mulabegovic, 2006). These questions are aimed at understanding a person's perception of a place and his/her intentions regarding it (plans to immigrate, invest in it or travel to it) to assist the marketers in planning the future campaign. Another technique for assessing the place's characteristics is trait grading.

A. Trait grading   In the trait grading technique, the respondent is asked to determine how much each trait characterizes the place relative to other traits. In the following example, the respondent is asked to grade a list of traits from 1 to 10 regarding the characteristics of the city of **Cleveland** (1 – the trait greatly characterizes the place, 10 – the trait does not characterize the place at all):

Cleveland
_____ *is clean*
_____ *holds many cultural events*
_____ *has a wide variety of attractions*
_____ *is very impressive*
_____ *is fun to hang out in*
_____ *has tourism services of a very high standard*
_____ *is romantic*
_____ *is tourist-friendly*
_____ *is very easy to get around*
_____ *has reasonable prices for tourism services*

The respondent may also be asked to grade the place relative to other places, if the aim is to find out its status among competitors (Vandewalle, 2006).

B. Evaluating the place's characteristics   Another method for assessing a place's positive and negative characteristics is by asking the respondent to grade each trait on a 1–7 Likert scale. For example, it can be asked whether **Paris** is romantic or not, where 1 stands for "not romantic at all" and 7 stands for "very romantic." By such means, pairs such as safe vs. unsafe, boring vs. interesting, ugly vs. pretty and clean vs. dirty can be assessed (for more examples, see Kotler et al., 1999a).

A similar method for evaluating the place's characteristics can be found in travel magazines such as the *Conde Nest Traveller*, in which readers are asked to evaluate a list of characteristics at places they visited in the last 3 years: environment/ambience, people/friendliness, culture/entertainment, restaurants, fun/energy and so on. Possible responses are arrayed on a scale of excellent, very good, good, fair and poor. This technique can also be used in respect of airports, hotels, cruises and other tourist services.

C. Place grading   By this method respondents among the target audience are asked to grade the place in comparison with other places, as in trait grading. The marketers of **Greece**, for example, can assess their country's status in the Mediterranean area by asking questions such as: "*When you go on a family vacation, which of the following destinations you prefer to travel to:* **Cyprus**, **Croatia**, **Malta**, *Greece or* **Turkey**? *(Please grade the places on a 1–5 scale, in which 1 stands for the place you prefer best and 5 for places you are least interested in visiting.)*" Similar questions can be asked regarding places to invest in or immigrate to or regarding the place's safety, quality of life and cost of living, as against competing places. The place-grading technique can also be used in unstructured surveys, with question such as "*To which other cities can you compare* **Istanbul**?" or "*To which other countries can you compare* **Slovenia**?"

Surveys may also be used to understand the roots of the current image and the way it was formed among the target audience. Common sources of image forming are visits to the place, the media (such as watching a film or a television series shot at that particular place) or a friend who has visited the place. The surveys can be handed out to various groups such as people who have visited the place, people who have never visited the place, people who are interested in visiting the place, investors or other groups of people, depending on the campaign's objectives and the target audience. Other groups of people can be the place's residents, in surveys assessing the local residents' self-image. In this case, the survey must address issues such as changes the place has undergone in recent years, measures needed to improve the place's image, advantages and disadvantages of living in the place and residents' satisfaction with the local education system, local authority activities, cultural events and quality of life. In recent years, the techniques for conducting surveys have become increasingly sophisticated and now include online surveys on the place's website (see, e.g., the website of the city of **Dunedin** in New Zealand; http://www.cityofdunedin.com) and combine several research methods.

Focus groups

One of the most popular methods for assessing the place's image among the target audience is focus groups. This technique can also be supported by in-depth interviews with selected representatives of the target audience. Conducting focus groups is a very common technique, mainly in advertising. A group of 8–15 people is drawn from the target audience and they are asked to discuss in depth a certain subject, with the guidance of a discussion leader. For example, a group of British tourists aged 20–25 who have been to **Thailand** can be formed, and they can be asked whether they enjoyed their stay, what they liked and did not like during their visit, what can be done order to improve the experience and how they compare Thailand to other destinations. The focus group discussion is usually filmed and used to gain a better understanding of the place's image, the way the place functions and how it should be marketed.

Using focus groups for assessing place's image

An example of a study based mainly on focus groups concerns the city of **Be'er Sheva** in southern Israel. The researchers, who wished to pinpoint the reasons for negative migration from the city, tried to understand issues such as how the city was perceived, the level of satisfaction with municipal services and what the city's residents expected from it. The study used focus groups and in-depth interviews with three groups of population:

1. Residents who anticipated leaving the city, such as students, young adults and members of the upper-middle social class aged 34–45;

2. Residents who had already left Be'er Sheva for its environs;
3. Residents who had already left Be'er Sheva for **Tel Aviv** and its environs.

From the focus groups' comments and interviews, the researchers were able to map the reasons for the negative migration and to plan a counter-campaign for the city (Fenster et al., 1994). The study found that all three groups held the same perception of Be'er Sheva: a depressing provincial town, desert-like, boring, gloomy and unattractive. In response, the researchers analyzed the characteristics that were mentioned and suggested how the city's positive traits could be promoted, how the negative traits could be eliminated or made positive and how the city's general image could be improved.

While focus groups are usually used for assessing a place's image, they can also be used in a sudden image crisis. For example, following the 9/11 terrorist attack, the air-travel industry in the **United States** used focus groups to learn how people felt about commercial flights. One group was formed in **New York City** and another in the state of **Ohio**. From these groups, it became clear that customers wanted to know that things were being done to make traveling safe again (White, 2006). In this case, the main advantage of using focus groups was that it assisted the campaign managers to identify what precisely the target audience was concerned about. Once the issue is identified, it is much easier for campaign managers to choose an effective message for the campaign, which is more likely to solve the problem.

Interviews with experts

In parallel to surveys and focus groups, various experts, key stakeholders, current and previous CEOs and spokespersons, investors, journalists who cover the place, industrialists, tourist operators, tourist agents, marketing and PR professionals and urban designers can be interviewed. These interviews can serve as a major source of data regarding the way the place is perceived, its disadvantages and how they can be removed. Informants can enrich the interviewer with their experience in marketing the place, the difficulties they had to face with different audiences, the solutions they tried and different partners with whom they cooperated in order to promote the place. Recent examples of place proponents who interviewed experts as part of their marketing process can be found in Byrom (2006) and

Skinner and Gould (2006), who interviewed experts with the aim of marketing **Northern Ireland**.

So far, we have offered several ways to explore a place's image. The choice of the optimal research method is very complicated, depending on factors such as the place's previous image, its characteristics, the target audience's characteristics, resources and the campaign objectives. In any event, the best way to analyze a place's image is by combining several complementary research methods. Accordingly, the findings of a focus group or in-depth interviews can assist in creating a comprehensive and useful survey covering all relevant issues. On the other hand, the focus groups can be used to gain a deeper understanding of issues found essential in the surveys. Note too that surveys and focus groups are very costly, and this might discourage local decision makers from conducting a wide-scale image assessment.

Types of image: from a rich image to a stereotype

Kotler et al. (1993) argue that a place's image can be positive and attractive, negative, weak (as in the case of peripheral locations that are not well known), mixed (when the image includes both positive and negative elements) or contradictory (when the place has a favorable image with one population and a negative image with another). Place images can also be classified as "rich" or "poor." A "rich" image means that we know a lot about the place, usually from different sources and also from personal visits and knowledge; a "poor" image means that we know very little about the place, and what we do know usually comes from only one source of information (Elizur, 1987).

Scott (in Elizur, 1987) refers to rich/poor images and offers a graphic star-shaped model, aggregating different place attributions. According to the *star model* (Figure 2.1), each cognitive trait forms a

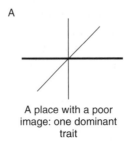

A place with a poor
image: one dominant
trait

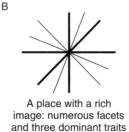

A place with a rich
image: numerous facets
and three dominant traits

Figure 2.1   The star model.
Source: Elizur, 1987

straight line, intersecting with all the other traits of the same image. The sum of all different traits creates the shape of a star: the more lines a star has, the richer the image it represents. But not all traits have the same effect: some lines in the graphic model are very salient while others are almost invisible.

In the star model, a place with a rich image will be portrayed by a multi-armed star (illustration B). A poor image will be represented by a star with only two or three arms (illustration A). The star model illustrates clearly that by marketing different perspectives of a place a poor image can become a richer one. The star model also suggests a way to handle stereotypes: the more dimensions a place has, the less the audience will focus on the problematic aspects. Intensive marketing of an attractive facet can become the dominant part in the place's image (i.e., a very salient arm on the star) and in that way overcome the previous perception, in the case where it was not over-dominant.

Two kinds of place images may be differentiated for target populations: open and closed. Open images allow the addition of more characteristics, whereas closed images are not likely to have new characteristics added, at least not characteristics that differ from the core image. Such images are also known as "stereotypes": simplified attitudes or beliefs about a place that are not examined thoroughly and are difficult to change (Elizur, 1987; Gold, 1980). Once a stereotype is formed about a certain place it is very difficult to change since much effort is required to make the target population amenable to a new and different image (Kunczik, 1997). An illustration refers to **Chicago**, which was the center of organized criminal activity in the 1920s and 1930s. Nowadays local authorities complain that wherever they go in the world Chicago is still spoken of as a center of crime and violence, even though its actual crime rate is one of the lowest among large American cities (Tal, 1993). Many people still seem to remember Chicago as a city of crime; its reality has changed but the stereotype persists. In another case, Burgess (1982) notes that local municipal leaders in **northern England** believe they must still combat stereotypes persisting from the nineteenth century concerning their way of life.

Factors influencing place's public image

Many different factors influence a place's image or perception held by outsiders. Many people have images of different places, and these vary in different countries and cultures. According to Kunczik (1997), the construction of a place's image is a lengthy socialization process with different socialization agents, such as the home environment, school, the literature and the media.

Successfully changing a place's public image requires analysis of the factors that construct the image. Many researchers (see Avraham, 2003b) have addressed this issue and found numerous factors to be involved. These include the nature of the place's population (e.g., race) and its size (big city or small peripheral town), status, political power (a national center such as a capital city), crime rate, socio-economic status and employment situation; number and character of national institutions located in the place (e.g., prestigious universities); location (in the country's core or periphery), historical background; advertisements and brochures about the place, movies and television series filmed in the place; type of media coverage (highlighting criminal activity and social problems or cultural events and other positive news); entertainment options, tourist or cultural value, physical appearance; and many other factors (see list in Avraham, 2003b; Kunczik, 1997). The widespread nature of these factors prevents discussion about all of them, but without doubt place marketers will be interested in gaining a profound understanding of the specific factors that they believe affect their place's image more than others. We advise emphasizing these particular factors, using the methods noted earlier such as surveys, focus groups, in-depth interviews and interviews with experts.

The second part of this chapter considers the effect of two major factors on a place's public image: films and media news. A deep understanding of the role of the media in shaping places' images is essential for a grasp of the media strategies applied by places to improve their image, as listed in Part Two of this book.

Place image in the mass media

People construct place images and cognitive maps according to the kind of information they receive from various sources; many marketers believe that accurate information results in more precise perceptions (Gold, 1980; Kariel and Rosenvall, 1978). The role of the mass media in this process is crucial. While people usually become aware of occurrences in their immediate environment from direct contact with the events, they learn about events that occur in more distant places primarily from the media. Information about a faraway place is not considered crucial to most people so they do not attempt to locate first-hand sources to verify what happens there (Kunczic, 1997). Hence the "reality" that the media transfer from distant places is conceptualized as their "objective" or "true" reality by those who do not live there (Adoni and Mane, 1984; Burgess and Gold, 1985; Gold, 1980; Pocock and Hudson, 1978; Relph, 1976). In our discussion of places' images in the media, we distinguish images projected by films and television shows from those projected by the news media.

Place image in TV series and films

Many researchers have written about the effect of television shows and films on the image of countries, cities and tourist destinations. Most people have not visited many of the places, so one of their main sources of knowledge of the world is what they see in films and television (Weimann, 2000). Numerous examples exist of places that have been negatively affected by television shows, especially those that focus on police officers, homicide detectives, violence, poverty and social problems. One unusual example of such an effect is a complaint by **Rio de Janeiro** city officials claiming that the episode of *The Simpsons* which "took place" in the city portrays it as unsafe, violent and dirty, overrun by rats and monkeys, where tourists are kidnapped for ransom (*Yediot Acharonot*, 10 April 2002). Similar examples can be found in the study by Avraham (2003a) where he presents several cities and neighborhoods that have been adversely affected by their presentation in television shows as places where crime, social instability and economic distress are rampant.

Movies can exert a similar effect on a place's image. One prime example is the movie *Midnight Express* (1978), in which a young American is caught trying to smuggle drugs out of **Turkey** and is thrown into a barbaric prison. The film caused grave and long-term damage to Turkey's image, portraying the country as violent, terrifying, poor and dirty, with no respect for basic human rights (Kotler et al., 1993). A more recent example of such a damaging film is *8 Mile*, staring the rapper Eminem and set in **Detroit**. It tells the semi-autobiographical story of Eminem, focusing on the hard times he experienced as a kid growing up in a trailer park in the city. The movie describes Detroit as a poor and crime-ridden place, associating the city with images which repel visitors. According to a local paper, "*8 Mile* makes Detroit look like a prison ass" and "If you've never visited and 8 Mile is your first impression of the city, you'll never want to" (http://www.metrotimes.com).

Films, however, can also have a very positive influence on a place's image. For example, the **New Zealand** Tourism Board estimates the worldwide effect of the first *The Lord of the Rings* movie as the equivalent of a $41 million promotional campaign. In addition to promoting the country's image, the trilogy's great commercial success resulted in 10% increase in tourism every year since 1998 (Hudson and Ritchie, 2006). In addition, 10% of the tourists who travel to New Zealand do so to visit the film locations; **Wellington**, New Zealand's capital, is estimated to earn approximately $160 million from film tourism (*Ha'aretz*, 2 December 2003).

Among the many places which gained their international reputation as a result of films are **Paris's** Montmartre Quarter, due to *Amelie* (2001); **northeast England** due to the *Harry Potter* films; **Australia** due to *Crocodile Dundee* (1986); the islands of **Phi-Phi** and **Phuket** in Thailand due to *The Beach* (2000); **Lake Como** in Italy due to *Ocean's Twelve* (2004); and **Boston** due to *Good Will Hunting* (1997). In Part Two of this book, we will shed more light on the use of films as marketing strategy to reverse a place's negative image.

Place image in the news media

While films or television can contribute greatly to a place's positive or negative image, most places concentrate their efforts on obtaining positive coverage in the news media because of their enormous popularity and their major role in shaping public opinion (Weimann, 2000). The following passages detail different images projected by the media, examine relations between news media and places and analyze the factors affecting a place's media coverage.

Types of place images

A close analysis of how countries, cities and tourist destinations are presented in the media reveals four types of places' images (Manheim and Albritton, 1984):

1. Places that receive much negative coverage
2. Places not covered by the media except in a negative context, usually related to crime, social problems, natural disasters, etc.
3. Places that receive much positive coverage such as cultural events, tourist activity, or investments
4. Places largely ignored by the media but when noticed they receive primarily positive coverage.

Naturally, local and national decision makers would prefer the third kind of media coverage for their city or country, winning a good amount of positive media attention. As a result, many local leaders are indeed willing to spend much time, resources and effort on achieving positive media coverage.

The "multi-dimensional image" and the "one-dimensional image" of a place in the news media should be distinguished. Similar to the findings of our analysis of different kinds of public images, places with a multi-dimensional image in the news media are those that receive coverage for a wide variety of subjects and events that occur in them, such as politics, economics, social events and cultural developments. Places with a one-dimensional image are those that only receive coverage when events of a certain nature take place there, such as crime or disasters. When a place is labeled by the media as one in which only a certain type of activities and events occurs, it becomes a symbol of such events, and other activities and events do not get covered (Shields, 1992; Strauss, 1961).

Measuring images of places in the news media

Research that has dealt with the coverage patterns of places in the media views the subject in two dimensions: quantity and nature (Avraham, 2003b; Manheim and Albritton, 1984):

1. The *quantity dimension* refers to the amount and visibility of coverage the place receives in the news media. Factors examined include details such as the number of reports or photos of the place, on what page or in which section the articles appear, the article's size (in the press) or the length of the report (in TV news) and so forth. It is only natural that spokespersons and PR experts want the place they are working for to be the first item in the newscast or the newspaper headline, together with colorful pictures that catch the reader's eye. But as we know, not only the amount of media coverage but also its content is important; this aspect is illustrated in the second dimension: the nature of the media coverage.

2. The *nature dimension* refers to several factors: which subjects are most frequently covered from the place (such as crime, poverty, social and community events, culture, sports or violence); the ways the place is described in the reports; who is represented as being responsible for the events that are covered; who is quoted and who is the source of the information reported; what is the tone of the stories or photo captions (Avraham, 2003b; Dominick, 1977; Graber, 1989; Larson, 1984; White, 2006). In this dimension, there are studies that treat the nature of coverage "beyond the numbers." This body of research focuses on more subtle levels in which the

spirit behind each news item or article is monitored. Such studies look for stereotypes, generalizations and myths which appear in the coverage of certain places and embrace a more general theme regarding the place's identity (Avraham, 2003b; Shields, 1992; van Dijk, 1988a). Examples of such statements are: "This is the city with the best museums in the world" or "This city is the place for those who like romance." Because of the powerful effect of statements like these, many researchers try to locate and reveal such themes.

Another case is the use of generalization, where a notion about one place is projected to other cities, the whole region or the entire country. For example, "**Lugano**, *like other cities in Switzerland, is spotlessly clean and offers a very high level of tourism services.*" On the other hand, generalizations might be very harmful for the place's image, for example, "*In **Ghana**, as in most countries in Africa, doing business can be very dangerous.*" In this case, many countries get tagged with a negative stereotype implied from one single case. In a quantity study, information on the nature of the media coverage may get lost, information which in some cases is much more meaningful than the number of news items published in a given time period. In addition, it is recommended to analyze the place's image over a long time period and try to monitor the changes in the place's media representation, especially the negative ones. For places which have suffered a sudden crisis, a common technique is to monitor the place's media coverage before, during and after the crisis (White, 2006). Most places conduct a study assessing the quantity dimension, the nature dimension, or both, but some places choose to employ the techniques of iconography and culture studies. These techniques focus on the visual aspect in the place's media representation or on other visual material such us advertisements and analyze their content in various ways (Gold, 1994).

Journalists as "image creators"

Over the years, many researchers have studied the power and the effect of the media on the social, political, economic and cultural spheres. Hoare (1991) argues that newspapers' mass circulation makes them a powerful, aggressive agent and that they translate this power into decisions regarding what to cover (or not to cover), what significance will be given to various stories and what will be the direction or judgment of the events. Other researchers have argued that newspeople's influence lies in their role as "gatekeepers," who have the power to decide what events become news and therefore determine what the public will read, hear or see (Shoemaker, 1991; Tuchman, 1978; Walmsley, 1982). Whatever the case may be, it is a well established fact that the media construct our reality regarding the events happening around us by creating distorted images of people, issues, organizations and places (Adoni and Mane, 1984; Avraham, 2003b; Cohen and Young, 1981; Weimann, 2000).

According to Tuchman (1978), news is socially constructed through well-recognized frameworks that are influenced by the routines through which reporters gather, filter and judge information (Crane, 1994; Shoemaker and Reese, 1996). News production is not merely a process of gathering information, writing, editing and reporting on major events in different places (Fishman, 1980; van Dijk, 1988a). Cultural, social, economic and professional constraints affect the news production process (Hackett, 1984; Hall, 1977; Tuchman, 1978; van Dijk, 1988b). Therefore at the basis of the social construction of reality lies the claim that the news is not an objective means of portraying reality but a means to construct this reality (Tuchman, 1978). The news production process creates a singular version of "reality" through the amplification, sensationalization and polarization of ideas and images within a limited, well-defined range (Waitt, 1995). The news creates and reinforces labels for people, events and situations (Avraham, 2000b, 2003b; Davis, 1990; Wolfsfeld et al., 2000).

News content reinforces existing attitudes and beliefs towards place, issues and people in three ways: selective exposure, selective perception and selective memory. When an individual has no information about a distant place that he/she has never visited, the media provide basic information that constructs that place's stereotype and image (Dahlgren and Chakrapani, 1982; Gold, 1994). The images of places, people and issues are based on knowledge, and the more knowledge a person has, the more accurate his/her perception of the place or issue generally will be (Gold, 1994; Kariel and Rosenvall, 1978). The Media-Dependency Hypothesis predicts that the media's influence on perceptions of social reality decreases when a person has personal experience related to the covered phenomenon (Perry, 1987). That is, we know more about places we are close to (whatever the form of "closeness"), and this knowledge increases the importance of these places in our eyes, compared with other places about which we know little (Gould and White, 1986). An individual learns through the media what significance he/she should ascribe to different places, people and issues with which he/she has no contact. It is because of this power, Walmsley (1982) believes, that the media is an effective instrument of social control.

Countries' and cities' coverage patterns in international and national media

Research on places' coverage patterns in the news media has taken into account both the international and national levels. The international level deals primarily with the coverage patterns of countries in the international news media. This level of analysis concentrates on the "imbalanced" news exchange between developed and developing nations that began after World War II (Kim and Barnett, 1996). The second level of analysis is the national level, which deals with the coverage patterns of cities and regions in the national news media. Studies on this level have found, for example, that the most frequently covered regions in the national American media were those of **New York City**, **Washington, DC**, and **Los Angeles**, whereas other cities are virtually ignored. Most "important" news, those stories dealing with politics, culture and the economy, came from these three cities. Coverage of small towns was mostly limited to reports about disasters, strikes, crime or the courts, while their political, economic and social situation was rarely discussed (Brooker-Gross, 1983; Dominick, 1977; Graber, 1989). In **Israel**, as in the United States, the coverage of peripheral regions in the national media is significantly different from that of the nation's center (Avraham, 2003b).

Several researchers have made considerable contributions to the study of pattern coverage of places. Among them, Strauss (1961) and Gould and White (1986) argue that a location's image can be examined only through comparison with other locations. Comparisons of different locations are based on quantitative measures (more, less) or on criteria for the contrast between or the similarity of the locations compared. When the metaphor used is "development," places are described in the context of the point they have reached in the life cycle. "They" are modern, more (or less) settled, more (or less) advanced than "we" are. Thus, the ways in which the media choose to cover certain regions lead to the formation of "us" and "them" identifications (Anderson, 1998; Avraham, 2003b; van Dijk, 1988a). As a result, "proof" of the developmental level of different regions is provided by the selection of events that receive coverage (Avraham, 2003b; Dahlgren and Chakrapani, 1982; Strauss, 1961).

Media, stereotypes and places with image crisis

"Symbol," "stereotype," "label" and "reputation" are the main concepts used when examining place image in the media. When a location is labeled as a place where certain types of events and activities occur, it becomes a "symbol" of these activities. As a result, other events in this location are not covered (Shields, 1992). Strauss (1961) defines this phenomenon as "reputation" and argues that the tendency to speak stereotypically of cities persists so that even if changes in the real-life situation of these cities occur, they are not reflected in their media coverage patterns (Elizur, 1994; Graber, 1989). Shields (1992) adds that the myth created regarding a certain place can persist for years, whether it is favorable or not. As soon as events are covered that serve to describe certain groups' behavior patterns, their image is created accordingly. According to Epstein (1973), editors' and reporters' stereotypes become self-perpetuating when their past experiences influence their choice of future stories to cover.

The connection between place images in the media and newsmakers' use of stereotypes has been documented by researchers. Relph (1976) claimed that images of places in the media are transferred through what he called "opinion makers" and distributed by journalists via use of stereotypes. Usually the mass media reflect stereotypes that already exist in society and the public, but give them much broader distribution and a means of continuity from generation to generation (Gans, 1979; Gould and White, 1986; Pike, 1981). Elizur (1994) commented that the centrality of television in our lives during the previous decade had increased the creation of stereotypes of places. Stereotypes and distortions result when television news covers crises in distant places through short, highly superficial reports that lack both background and commentary.

Factors affecting places' news media images

Avraham (2003 a,b) argues that policy makers in localities who want to analyze their place's news media image must ask four basic questions:

1. What are the place's characteristics?
2. What is the editorial policy on the place's media coverage, and who are the newspeople who cover the place?
3. What are the components of the socio-political environment in which the media operate?
4. What public relations efforts are made on behalf of the place to build the desired image in the news media?

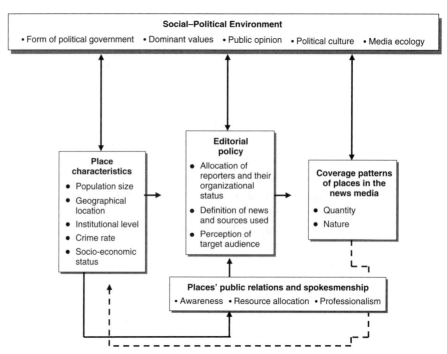

Figure 2.2 An integrated model of factors constructing coverage patterns of places in the news media.
Source: Avraham, 2003b

Answers to these four questions figure in an integrated model (Figure 2.2) that provides important information about the place's image as represented by the news media and the factors affecting it. The model also explains how such images can vary over time and as circumstances change.

Place characteristics

Places differ from each other in many aspects, including population size, geographical location, crime rate, socio-economic indicators, national institutions and services they provide. Do these varying place characteristics cause a difference in the quantity or nature of the coverage in the news media?

Population size
Population size is one of the frequently examined characteristics. Do places with large populations receive more coverage than those with small populations? Several researchers argue that the majority

of coverage in the American and Canadian media is about big cities (Brooker-Gross, 1983; Kariel and Rosenvall, 1978). News items are mainly about people, and one of the primary conditions that helps convert an event into "news" is the number of people affected by the event. Avraham (2003b) also found a connection between the size of city's population and the amount of coverage it receives. In heavily populated cities, a wide variety of events occur, so the larger the population of a place, the greater its chances of receiving more coverage in the news media.

Geographical location

Regarding the geographical location characteristic, do cities close to the place where the media organizations' editorial boards are located receive more coverage than more distant ones? The geographical location of a newspaper or TV station affects their level of interest in and attention to other cities (Womack, 1981). Usually nearby places receive much more coverage than faraway places (Pocock and Hudson, 1978). The media decision makers believe that their audience is interested in events which occur close to home and might affect their life (Hoare, 1991). Many other studies also support the hypothesis that geographical location has an effect on coverage patterns of places (see Johnson, 1997). Adams (1986) examined the coverage of earthquakes that occurred around the world in the American media. He found that the events' distance from New York was one of the factors that explained the amount of coverage they received. In sum, the closer a place to the location of the media organizations, the better its chances of being covered. Thus, if we are discussing coverage of places in the national media, cities that are closer to the place where the national media organizations operate (usually the capital) have better chances of receiving media attention (Avraham, 2003b).

Crime statistics

Another characteristic that affects coverage patterns is the crime statistics of the place. Crime is one of the most popular subjects covered by mass media organizations. A number of studies have shown that there is often no correlation between the actual crime statistics of a place and the number of reports on crime in the media (Avraham, 2003b; Jerin and Field, 1994). Some places have become symbols of crime. The problem is that if crime news is the focus of a place's media image, there is a tendency not to cover socio-economic developments or other positive events in the place (Avraham, 2003a, 2003b; Shields, 1992; Tilson and Stacks, 1997).

Number and nature of central/national institutions
Another characteristic that might affect the coverage of a place is the number of central institutions on the national level found there. By "central institutions" we do not mean institutions that exist in every city such as the city hall or a local court, but national institutions such as the parliament, the Supreme Court, the stock market or the federal bank. Generally it is difficult to distinguish between cities' images and the important institutions that they host. Gans (1979) argued that such institutions give the cities that host them news value (Shoemaker and Reese, 1996). Because the people who work in such institutions are familiar to the nation's citizensand the decisions made in them affect the entire country, newspeople believe it is important to cover them regularly.

Editorial policy and the place coverage

In addition to the specific characteristics of a place, there is a need to examine the policy of media organizations on the coverage of that place and the background of the newspeople that cover it. By "policy" we mean the decisions made by the media organizations as to the coverage of a certain place. Examples include the decision whether or not to allocate reporters to cover the place, if the place's residents are considered a target audience of the media organizations and how to define news from the place. Many studies have shown that decisions such as these, along with the personal background of the designated reporters, exert a powerful effect on the image of places in the news media.

Allocating reporters to cover the place
The decision to allocate reporters to a place is a major factor in how much coverage that place will receive in the news media; wherever there are reporters there is news. After the editorial board's decision to designate a reporter to a specific place, there is often an attempt to justify this decision by publishing a large share of the stories filed by that reporter (Kariel and Rosenvall, 1978). The location of the editorial board also affects places' coverage; Dominick (1977) and Graber (1989) found that the cities most covered in the American media were those that contain many national media organizations, primarily **New York City** and **Washington, DC** (Epstein, 1973). This was found to be the case in other countries too (Avraham, 2003b; Hoare, 1991; Kariel and Rosenvall, 1978, 1981). The largest number of reporters is located in these places, a fact partially responsible for

these central places being dominant in national news. In addition, journalists who live and work in these central places tend to cover them in much more positive ways than other cities (Avraham, 2003b; Kaniss, 1991).

Target audience

Another decision made by editors is who should be considered their target audience. Editors must carefully select and focus on their target audience and their wishes, because a mass medium will survive only if it succeeds in satisfying its audience's needs (Shoemaker, 1991). As mentioned, the editors have a long-held belief that readers have more of an interest in what occurs where they live or close by than in distant places (Hoare, 1991; Kariel and Rosenvall, 1981; Womack, 1981). Despite the argument of the contribution of the mass media to the "no sense of place" (Meyrowitz, 1985), local audience in every place is still interested in their immediate environment (Kirby, 1993). Accordingly editors will concentrate on covering a greater number and variety of events in the places where the perceived target audience is located. In the national press, the coverage of places depends on the geographical distribution of the readers. For example, a British national newspaper that views its target audience as readers from **London** and the south will cover the northern part of the country differently from the manner of the same kind of newspaper that sees its target audience as readers from the north (Hoare, 1991). We can expect that the north-based newspaper will present a more positive and rich image of this area while concentrating on the events occurring there and emphasizing the implications of national development for this area's citizens (Avraham, 2003b).

Place's news definition

How do journalists learn what type of news stories to file and from which places? The training of reporters is a socialization process in which they learn what sort of events the news organization prefers to turn into news (Waitt, 1995). When journalists see what types of items make news from a particular place, they learn what their editors are looking for. Since they are usually interested in advancing within the organization's hierarchy, they tend not to "rock the boat" and continue filing stories that fit the accepted pattern of reporting (Avraham, 2003b). When a certain place is defined by the newspapers as a site of crime, violence and disorder, newspeople tend to use the police and courts as the main source of information about events occurring there (Wolfsfeld et al., 2000). However, when a place is defined as a site of cultural events, tourism or national news, the media organizations use very different sources to learn about events there. As mentioned, a place of the latter type is considered to have a rich image in the media, while the former kind has a one-dimensional media image. In this way, the types of sources utilized by journalists determine the coverage patterns. As a result, a conservative approach is taken by the media organizations, with a replay of the familiar, proven formulas of reporting about the same places and subjects (Shoemaker, 1991; Shoemaker and Reese, 1996; van Dijk, 1988).

Newspeople's personal background and social–ideological distance/proximity

After discussing the policy of the media organizations, the next step is to examine the effect of the newspeople's background on the place's media image. Many researchers have explained coverage patterns of places or groups according to the proximity between the residents of a particular place and the journalists and editors covering it (Galtung and Ruge, 1965; Gamson and Wolfsfeld, 1993; Jakubowicz et al., 1994; van Dijk, 1996). Decisions on defining the target audience, the news definition of a place and the allocation of reporters are mostly determined by social–ideological proximity. Inhabitants of a place who are socially and ideologically similar to the newspeople will be considered part of the target audience, the news definition of their city will not be only negative and one reporter or more will be allocated to cover them on a regular basis. Such proximity can be based on ethnic, racial or religious identity. For example, in a study on the Israeli media, Avraham (2003b) found that places considered to be in close social–ideological proximity to the media's decision makers received wide and positive coverage. The reverse was also found to be true: places far from the media decision makers received scant or negative coverage.

One of the most important elements to examine when looking at issues of proximity of this type is ethnic origin of the newspeople (Adams, 1986). van Dijk (1988, 1996) maintains that in Western countries, white journalists work within the dominant ethnic consensus and this is reflected in the media content/journalist discourse when they cover places comprised primarily of minorities. This discourse contains the creation of "us" and "them," using labels, stereotypes and prejudice (Fair, 1993). It can be anticipated that journalists from within the minority group would cover such places differently because of their familiarity with the culture and the reality described, resulting in less stereotyping and prejudice. Wolfsfeld et al. (2000) found that the coverage patterns of demonstrations in Israeli-Arab cities were affected by the fact that the cities were covered by Jewish journalists and editors (Avraham, 2003b; First and Avraham, 2004).

In addition to the newspeople's ethnicity, other individual characteristics may affect their coverage of a place, including their birthplace, their familiarity with the place, the location of the reporters' immediate family members and their level of education, values and outlook (Johnson, 1997; Shoemaker and Reese, 1996). For example, we could expect that the image of **northern Britain** in the national press would be different from the existing image, had most of the journalists and editors been born in that area. Their familiarity with the north would be greater, they would have many sources there and they would most probably see things from the northern point of view. All of these factors would be likely to lead to different coverage patterns.

Socio-political environment

The third question to be addressed concerns the socio-political aspect of news coverage. By "socio-political environment" we mean the context in which the media operate and interact with different actors. Journalists and editors always operate within a certain socio-political context which affects the ways they collect and report events. This context encompasses the central values of their society and the political culture and the political arena (Johnson, 1997; van Dijk, 1996; Wolfsfeld, 1997). Changes in these components may affect the coverage patterns of places or groups. For example, although there is still room for improvement in the media's coverage patterns of minorities, there is no doubt that there has been a positive change in the last few years. This change stems from changes in the socio-political environment (Lee and Solomon, 1990; Wolfsfeld, 1997) and illustrates the point that journalists are influence by the social context.

As presented in the integrated model, the socio-political environment affects all the other factors involved in the construction of the city's media image. Thus, the influence of a specific factor on the media image can vary depending where and in which society the media operate. For example, in the **United States**, where crime is much more of a political issue than in other countries, it can be expected that a place's crime statistics will be central in its coverage patterns. As a result the place's media portrayal – positive or negative – is basically determined by the crime statistics. Because of the dominance of crime coverage, all other events and developments are marginalized by the newspeople (see Tilson and Stacks, 1997).

The connection between coverage of places and the socio-political environment has been examined in various studies. Avraham (2003b) found that the coverage of peripheral cities in **Israel** was affected by the fact that the nation's elite felt threatened by people from these cities after the 1977 parliamentary elections. Another example is given by Dunn et al. (1995), who claim that the image of industrial cities had symbolized prosperity and power in the past, while now, in the post-industrial era, it symbolizes pollution, recession and crisis. Other studies have shown that the image of settlement groups in the Israeli national media was affected by changes in the central values of society, the political culture and public opinion (Avraham, 2003b; Herzog and Shamir, 1994). Changes in the political culture can cause changes in the interpretation of any given group, place or event. For example, Yochtman-Yaar and Ben-Rafael (1987) found that the media image of kibbutzim (collective agricultural settlements) had become more negative in recent years because of the growing individualism in Israeli society. The cases portrayed in each of these studies illustrate that images of places may change in response to changes in the socio-political environment. For this reason the represented model is dynamic.

Public relations

The fourth question addresses the public relations efforts of places. In the previous sections, we saw that many types of factors can affect, positively or negatively, the image of a place in the news media. So far we have seen that a place's image is determined by factors over which, for the most part, the place has no control. Places cannot control the socio-political context, the editorial decisions or most of their characteristics. This does not mean that a place cannot influence its own media image. It can do so by public relations and promotional efforts. These may help the place's policy makers to overcome factors that may cause the media to ignore it or report negatively on it, such as a small population size, large distance from media centers, small number of institutions or reputation as a source for crime news.

There are three different components of the public relations efforts of places: awareness, resource allocation and professionalism. The only public relations efforts that have the potential to be successful are those in which all three exist (Avraham, 2003b):

1. *Awareness*: The first component is awareness among the local government decision makers of the importance of media image and of the fact that their actions and behavior affect the image of their place in the national media (Walker, 1997).

2. *Allocating resources*: However, this awareness is not enough; to succeed, they need to allocate sufficient resources to operate their public relations effort such as an adequate budget, skilled people and equipment (Wolfsfeld, 1988, 1997).
3. *Professionalism*: The third component is professionalism. Even if a place's decision makers are aware of the need for public relations and are willing to allocate resources, their public relations efforts will fail if the people responsible for implementing them are not professional (Burgess, 1982). Avraham (2003b) found that many cities appoint spokespeople for promotional purposes, but due to their incompetence they are not able to help create a positive city image in the news media.

Nevertheless, in the last few years there has been a marked increase in awareness and willingness to improve the local public relations professionalism, resulting in a number of publications in which authors give advice on how to create a positive media image for a place (Bjornlund, 1996; Stoner, 1992; Walker, 1997; Wheeler, 1994). This awareness has also resulted in the hiring of a large numbers of employees; in **Britain**, for example, nearly a thousand public relations professionals worked in local government in 1994 (Harrison, 1995).

Having discussed the individual elements of the model, it is now important to emphasize how they interrelate. Each factor can affect other factors' influence on the image. For example, city size and number of national institutions affect the editorial board's decision to designate reporters to cover a city, a fact that positively affects the amount of the city's coverage. A great deal of coverage – resulting from large population size and reporter allocation – does not automatically mean a positive news media image of the city, because the nature of coverage depends on the city's news definition and its public relations efforts. The interrelation between the factors is also represented by the dotted arrow between a city's image and its characteristics on the chart of the model. This arrow indicates that an entrenched image, positive or negative, becomes an integral part of a city's symbolic characteristics. A city's positive media image can attract a larger population, increased investments and economic development and more institutions (Avraham, 2003b).

Summary

This chapter focused on the concept of place image and the distinction between the place's image among the target audience and its mediated image in the media. Aware of the link between these two images, many local decision makers invest a great deal of resources in improving their media image. Another important distinction is that between different kinds of images, and this chapter outlined factors shaping this image and several methods for assessing it. We highlighted places beset by an ongoing image crisis and the role of the media in constructing it. Although the place's image among the target audience differs from that in the mass media, it is highly recommended that both be analyzed as the basis for launching public relations and advertising campaigns to reverse a negative image and make it positive.

3 Image management and campaign

In the previous chapter, we discussed the concept of place image, ways of measuring it and ways to analyze the place's image as it is represented in the media. This chapter focuses on techniques to improve a place's image and on choosing the most appropriate media strategy. As noted earlier, changing a place image is not a short-term, single, cosmetic act but rather a long-term, holistic, comprehensive, deep-rooted and strategic act. A successful change in a place image is contingent on a lengthy process and the investment of time and other resources, cooperation with marketing professionals and local residents and constant checking of achievements, goals and objectives targeted.

Changing images, changing reality

It seems natural to ask what steps local authorities should take to improve their place's image and market a more positive one. Space limitations prevent a detailed description of all the stages of decision-making and implementation of marketing campaigns (for such elaborations, see Kotler et al., 1993; Morgan and Pritchard, 2001; Short et al., 1993). Still, two approaches or scenarios should be distinguished. First is the strategic approach: changing a place's image while changing its actual reality. By this method the place's problems are resolved first, and only then is the place marketed (Beriatos and Gospodini, 2004). The second approach is the cosmetic one: attempting to change the place's image without changing anything real; the place's problems are not solved or managed but the local decision makers try to portray it in a positive light.

According to the strategic approach the change must be implemented in stages: first diagnosis, followed by building a strategic vision and finally planning the next action needed to realize the predetermined vision. Another action in the pre-marketing stage is inspection of local services, attractions and infrastructures, in order to determine how well they meet the needs of residents, visitors, businessmen and local companies. If the level of the basic services offered by the place is extremely low, a marketing campaign can hardly succeed, and in most cases it is a waste of effort and resources.

Several case studies in marketing places have shown that prior to embarking on a campaign, local decision makers must understand that for it to succeed money has to be spent on developing new facilities, attractions, parks and recreation areas, as well as on improving the quality of life and the place's attractiveness for investments, business and new immigrants. The nature of the attractions to be developed depends on the type of crowd the place is interested in drawing (Dunn et al., 1995; Kotler et al., 1993, 1999a; Short et al., 1993). For example, a place that wants to bring in families with young children should invest in building or improving its schools, kindergartens and parks; if it wishes to attract senior citizens, it is advised to invest in senior complexes, golf courses and shopping malls. The same principle applies to attracting tourists, where different kinds of tourism (sea and sun, historical–cultural, etc.) demand construction, development and investment accordingly.

Actors in managing a place's image

Factors involved in initiatives to market places with negative images commonly include private entrepreneurs in business, real estate and tourism, in addition to local decision makers. Their main motive is the sense that the place's negative image is not justified and that with proper marketing strategies, the external public will learn to appreciate the place. Residents and local decision makers in a place with a negative image are usually well aware of it. They encounter the negative perceptions in friends, relatives and colleagues who live elsewhere. To change this problematic situation, in many cities and towns residents join forces with local decision makers from the private and public sectors to undertake a wide-scale image makeover. As we have seen, such cooperation can raise large sums of money required to hire marketing professionals and to launch PR and adverting campaigns.

Examples abound of successful cooperation between private firms in business or tourism and local or national organizations and authorities to alter their place's image. Usually the organizations and firms involved are hotels and travel agents, national tourism offices, local authorities, aviation or transportation companies, construction and real-estate firms and local residents. These firms cooperate to finance and implement the marketing plan and to increase long-term investments in the place and improve its attractiveness. One prime example of such successful cooperation in launching a marketing campaign is the case of **Wisconsin**, United States. There, representatives of the state's department of tourism, several cities and towns, hotels and catering services, tourist attractions, the state university and local industries all worked together to market the state (Kotler et al., 1993).

In recent years, many countries, cities and tourist destinations have established a Destination Marketing Organization (DMO), responsible for all marketing initiatives. The DMO collates and coordinates all messages, events, campaigns and other promotion efforts. In addition, some places establish a Town Center Management (TCM), "which involves development, management and promotion of both public and private areas within town centers, for the benefit of all concerned" (Wells, in Coca-Stefaniak et al., 2006). Two examples of places that set up similarly titled marketing organizations are the city of **Manchester**, which formed a "Destination Marketing Team," and the city of **Osaka** in Japan, which formed the "Osaka Brand Committee" (Suyama and Senoh, 2006).

Starting the process of changing the place's image

Kotler et al. (1999a) list four groups that are the most active in place marketing: (1) local actors (public and private sectors), such as mayor, city manager, tourist bureau, individual citizens, travel agencies and hospitality industries; (2) regional actors, such as regional economic development agencies, county and state government and regional tourist boards; (3) national actors, such as political leaders, inward investment agencies and national tourist boards; (4) international actors, such as embassies and inward investment agencies. Of all these elements, one of the most significant is the involvement of local residents. It is essential that not just the local elite or national governmental machinery control the marketing and branding of a certain place; its residents dispose of a large body of knowledge about its characteristics, and they can assist in the marketing plan's creation and implementation alike. It is true that coordinating different organizations, firms and individuals, from both the public and private sectors, is not easy, mainly due to different interests, viewpoints and agendas. On the other hand, the greater the degree of coordination, the more likely is the marketing plan to succeed.

The process of changing a place's image starts differently in different places. In some places, groups of residents tried to move the local authority to promote change, while elsewhere it was senior executives in tourism or construction who realized that the place's current image prevented tourists and immigrants from coming there. Whatever the case, many places start by hiring a marketing consultant firm, which can suggest to the place the basic tools and methods needed, recommend which target audience to focus on, determine the existing level of infrastructures and services offered and estimate the cost of the place's marketing process. On the other hand, some local decision makers outline the general recovery plan themselves, according to their intuitive feelings and sporadic inspections. Similar differences in approach may also appear at the execution stage of the marketing strategy. Some local authorities hire a PR and advertising specialist to escort them through the marketing process, while other places choose to allow the local spokesperson to plan and direct their efforts.

Strategic image management

Different places can market themselves in different ways. One of the most recommended means of running a successful campaign is *strategic image management* (SIM). This is a continuous process of researching a place's image among target populations, clarifying its advantages, examining the factors influencing its image and making changes over the years, handling image-related crises and delivering relevant messages to different audiences (Kotler et al., 1993, 1999a). The main advantage of this strategy is that the involvement of many different bodies in the marketing campaign requires coordination in planning, implementing and following the marketing program. Marketing, promoting and advertising are geared to several goals. Dealing with potential investors, tourists or entrepreneurs is an ongoing process that does not end with securing a one-time investment or establishing a single tourist attraction (Felsenstein, 1995).

The successful changing of a place's image begins with examining its existing image among the target audience, since this image constitutes the foundation on which the marketing campaign should be built. Places with a positive image need campaigns that reinforce it, while negative images need campaigns to improve them. Weak images need campaigns that focus first on enhancing awareness of the place and only then on constructing the desired image (Avraham, 2003a; Manheim and Albritton, 1984).

Image construction is not an easy process, and several different studies have suggested various strategies: the place's uniqueness needs to be identified, positioned and marketed in a way that reflects what is unique about it and how it differs from competing places. Special attention must be given to ensuring that all campaign messages are geared to underlining the unique image chosen by all the participating bodies. The campaign should not try to cover too many target audiences; rather, it should have a succinct, consistent message. Every agreed step should be followed, and the various assorted components such as advertising, public relations, promotion and direct marketing should be well coordinated (Avraham, 2003a; Dunn et al., 1995; Kotler et al., 1993, 1999a; Morgan and Pritchard, 2001; Short et al., 1993; Young and Lever, 1997).

Place vision

One of the most interesting advances in place marketing in recent years is the use of place vision as a framework for the marketing process. Local decision makers in Europe, the United States, Canada and Australia work together with residents, entrepreneurs and executives of hotels and factories to formulate a vision for the future of their place, where they live and work. The participants envisage how they would like the place to be in 5, 10 or even 20 years, and what actions should be taken for this vision to come to life. For example, the UN has proposed an alternative model for democracy in local government, already implemented by more than 5000 local authorities worldwide. One tool suggested by this model is a town meeting, where various factors involved in the place are invited to take part in municipal discussions and in forming local policy (*Ha'aretz*, 23 January 2002). This policy is often expressed as a vision, including a theoretical element stating how things should be and a practical element outlining the strategies and objectives on which action should be taken. Supporters of this model assert that only cooperation of the public sector, the business sector and the place's residents can bring social and economic problems to an end and usher prosperity into the place.

Formulating a vision, as many places have already realized, is a sophisticated task, demanding careful administrative guidance and allocation of resources. For example, when the **Tel Aviv** municipality wanted to create a new vision for the city, they involved more than 800 residents in the process. The residents were divided into small groups, and each group focused on a different field such as education, transportation, culture and economy. Each group wrote a vision for its field; the visions were then merged into a city vision, embracing the desirable objectives to be realized (http://www.tel-aviv.gov.il).

Toronto Unlimited: a case study of residents' inclusion

In November 2004, the city of **Toronto**, Canada, embarked on a major process of brand developing. The goal of the "Toronto Branding Project" was to develop a fresh way of communicating the city's distinct identity to the rest of the world as a foremost tourist and business destination. The 13-month brand developing process was based on 4500 responses to a local survey and 230 in-depth interviews with different decision makers and leaders in tourism, leisure, convention business, academics and the public sector. In an interview, Toronto's mayor explained the reason for this protracted and expensive project: "The open dialog with residents and decision makers helped us to understand what makes Toronto special, unique and better than other cities in the world, in the perspective of those who live and work in the city. The new brand must be relevant for both local residents and tourists and outside investors" (Harel-Dor, 2005). In addition, 14 focus groups were conducted in Canada, the United States and Great Britain. This $4 million project was undertaken to build the Toronto brand from the inside out. According to the president of the branding firm, "The task was not to impose a position on the city, but rather to reveal the true essence of Toronto." In June 2005, the brand developing process was complete, and the city's new brand was launched: Toronto Unlimited. Five new icons were born, representing music, food, film, festivals and the arts, all used for the branding campaign (http://www.city.toronto.on.ca, http://www.torontounlimited.ca).

City vision on the World Wide Web

Once the city vision has been formulated, many places publish the text on their websites to be available for the place's residents and also for potential immigrants interested in the place and its future plans. Here are some examples from various places' official websites.

Wroclaw: The city of Wroclaw in Poland has gone very far with its city vision, with objectives, guidelines, activities and plans for the next 25 years. During that time span local decision makers intend to accomplish existing short-term objectives, define new ones and re-evaluate the long-term objectives and the process of achieving them. The Wroclaw website seems to show that local decision makers

Plate 1 South Africa – Cosmopolitan meets Vogue
South Africa associates itself with leading international fashion brands
Source: Courtesy of South Africa Tourism

Plate 2 South Africa – It's (Im)possible (Logo)
South Africa using the strategy of counter-stereotype branding
Source: Courtesy of South Africa Tourism

Plate 3 South Africa – Alive with Possibility (Logo)
South Africa using the strategy of counter-stereotype
Source: Courtesy of the International Marketing Council of South Africa

Plate 4 New Zealand – Best supporting country in a motion picture
New Zealand understands the effect of movies on its image and associates itself with the
success of The Lord of the Rings
Source: Courtesy of New Zealand Tourism Board

Plate 5 Louisiana Rebirth (Logo)
Louisiana employs patriotic feelings for its marketing
Source: Courtesy of Louisiana Office of Tourism

Plate 6 Washington, DC – The American Experience (Logo)
Washington, DC using the strategy of patriotism and nationalism
Source: Courtesy of Washington, DC Convention & Tourism Corporation

**Born in Israel,
Used in USA**

All of the following were developed in Israel:

Cell phone technology

Microsoft Windows NT®
operating system

AOL Instant
Messenger®software

Intel Pentium MMX®Chip

Heart Attack Blood Test
Diagnoses By Phone

PC anti-virus software

"Gut cam" Ingestible
pill video camera to
diagnose cancer

Blue-light, skin damage-
free acne treatment

Radiation-free, breast
cancer diagnostic test

FireWall®internet
security software

Drip irrigation technology for
farmers to conserve water

Large-scale solar electricity
plant in Calif. Mojave desert

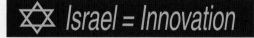

Israel = Innovation

Plate 7 Born in Israel, Used in USA
A Israeli patriotic corporation demonstrating its appeal to American target audience and
expanding the country's image
Source: Courtesy of Blue Star PR

THERE'S MORE TO JAPAN THAN BUSINESS

From neon-lit cities to the tranquillity and peace of Mount Fuji. From a culture thousands of years in the making to a world of tomorrow. There's so much more to Japan than just business.

Similarly, when you fly Japan Airlines, whether it's for business or pleasure, you will discover an atmosphere of total relaxation that r eflects the very best of modern and traditional Japan, where nothing is too much trouble.

JAL is perfectly placed to fly you to any destination in Japan, thanks to its double daily non-stop flights to Japan from London and its domestic network serving up to 63 cities. Plus, you can experience the real Japan with our specialist division, Jaltour, who boast an in-depth knowledge and unrivalled experience in creating unforgettable holidays to suit all budgets.

With Japan Airlines and Jaltour, there has never been a better time to explore the beauty and mystical qualities of Japan.

Telephone JAL on 0845 7 747 700 or Jaltour on 020 7462 5577
www.uk.jal.com or www.jaltour.co.uk

Plate 8   There's more to Japan than business
Japan trying to expand its image
Source: Courtesy of Japan Airlines

Estonia. Positively transforming.

Plate 9 Estonia – Positively Transforming
Estonia acknowledging its problematic image in the past but promises a better future
Source: Courtesy of the Estonian Tourist Board

Plate 10 Philly is more fun when you sleep over (Logo)
Philadelphia is trying to change the way it is being consumed
Source: Courtesy of Greater Philadelphia Tourism Marketing Corporation

NY

LA

DC

Plate 11 Kansas City – NY, LA, DC, KC
Kansas City associating itself with leading metropolitans
Source: Courtesy of Kansas City Area Development Council

Plate 12 Polish Plumber
Poland: the use of ridicule to shatter stereotypes
Source: Courtesy of Polish National Tourist Office

Plate 13 Polish Nurse
Poland: the use of ridicule to shatter stereotypes
Source: Courtesy of Polish National Tourist Office

have acquired a profound understanding of how inspiring and productive a city image can be (http://www.wroclaw.pl).

Renton: The city of Renton in Washington state, United States, is a prime example of a place that underwent an organized process of decision-making and research and produced a 5-year plan for promoting the city. Renton's vision was formulated through the cooperation of residents, businesses and schools. It states that the city is obligated to "provide a healthy, welcoming atmosphere where citizens choose to live, raise families and take pride in their community; promote planned growth and economic vitality; create a positive work environment; and meet service demands through innovation and commitment to excellence." Renton's business plan is aimed to promote citywide economic development and neighborhood revitalization, manage growth through sound urban planning, meet the service demands that contribute to the livability of the community and influence decisions that impact the city. In short, Renton's vision could be condensed into a single sentence: "A world-class city where people choose to live, work and play" (http://rentonwa.gov).

Hamilton: Many places around the world have settled on 2020 as the target year for accomplishing their vision. One of them is the city of Hamilton in Ontario, Canada. Its main objective is to make Hamilton "a place where social, health, economic and environmental issues are jointly considered as we make decisions. In Hamilton, we look after the environment, look after each other, and create safe and healthy places to live, work and play" (http://www.vision2020.hamilton-went.on.ca). In this vision, Hamilton municipality holds itself responsible for various spheres in the life of the city and its residents, trying to create a sustainable community.

Porirua: A fine example of a place that has experienced the strategic process of marketing, including future planning, vision and residents' inclusion, is the city of Porirua on New Zealand's North Island. Trying to improve the city's image, the municipality decided to work together with local businesses, merchants and executives from the fields of hospitality and recreation. The principal concept of the joint effort was the creation of events and festivals that would be supported by all businesses in the city and would serve them all.

The city's website (http://www.pcc.govt.nz) sets out the Porirua City Strategic Plan for 2000–2010, as worded by residents and local decision makers. The community's vision starts by declaring "Porirua City is an exciting place full of life, color and fun. It has energy and a heart." It goes on to elaborate the city's present and future characteristics and to outline eight major strategic goals that it hopes to achieve by 2010. Being aware of its striking effect on visitors, residents and immigrants, one of Porirua's eight major goals is to form a positive image. The website lists the reasons for launching a marketing campaign, the desired outcomes and the media messages that have been used. The city's strategic plan also includes information such as the key people responsible for accomplishing the goals, the schedule and short-term and long-term objectives.

Marketing strategies – from theory to practice

Three preliminary steps necessary before a marketing campaign is launched are defining the campaign objectives, defining its target audience and recognizing the place's characteristics.

Defining the campaign objectives

In preparing a campaign, one first needs to know who its target audience is and what the campaign's objectives for this public are. For example, the target audience may be the place's residents, potential tourists or immigrants, entrepreneurs without any knowledge of the place or residents of nearby cities. The place marketers should define the objectives they set themselves in the campaign accordingly. Objectives may include increasing awareness of the place, conveying information, reminding the target audience about a certain place or convincing them to go and live there, visit it or invest in it (Kotler and Armstrong, 1991).

(a) *Informing*: This campaign is intended to inform the target audience of the establishment of a new city, residential project, industrial area or tourist destination.
(b) *Convincing*: Campaigns of this type are intended to convince the target audience of the preferability of a certain place over its competitors or to make it more preferable. It attempts, for example, to persuade immigrants to move to a certain city or decision makers in industry to invest in a specific location. These campaigns also try to change negative perceptions of the place and to elevate it in both consumption and image.
(c) *Reminding*: This objective is obtained when the campaign keeps consumers aware of the place. This kind of campaign is used mostly by familiar places that already have a strong and positive image, but wish to remain in the target audience's set of options.

Defining a campaign objective is greatly influenced by the place's existing image with the target audience and by what the place has to offer them (Gold and Ward, 1994). An informing campaign is most suitable for new cities or destinations or for those that have undergone a major change. For example, in recent years, some areas in **Italy** that were not considered tourist destinations started marketing themselves by means of informing campaigns. Campaigns aimed at convincing are most beneficial for places that have strong competition, as in the sea-and-sun tourism market. Places that launch campaigns aimed at reminding are usually already well known to the target audience. For example, both **Spain** and **Turkey** have used advertisements bearing only the country's name, intended to remind the target audience of them as tourist destinations.

Defining the target audience

Defining the target audience carefully is very important before launching a campaign, as different audiences require different campaigns. Even with the same campaign objective, such as marketing a sea-and-sun destination, campaigns will differ widely if addressed to tourists in their early twenties, families with young children or organized groups of senior citizens. Place marketers have to segment the market and analyze the place's image, values and fields of interest for every individual market segment. Usually deep analysis of all possible segments is very costly, so it is best to focus the research on just some of them and gain a deep understanding of those audience. The choices of target audience and campaign objectives are fundamental decisions and will affect the timing of the campaign launch, its language, its marketing mix and the choice of media strategy.

The place marketing literature contains some interesting examples of the ways places choose a specific target audience and the preferred image they want to promote in it. Several researchers describe work done to discover the particular image held by a specific public; examples are the image of **Greater Manchester** as a "short break" destination among alumni of the University of Salford (Fallon and Schofield, 2006), the image of **Osaka** among habitants who live in commuting distance of the city (Suyama and Senoh, 2006) and the image of **Israel** for upper middle class Londoners (Morgan and Pritchard, 2001).

In sum, to reach the target audience and convince it to prefer a certain place, marketing professionals have used diverse techniques such as distributing brochures, creating advertisements for different media, hiring a spokesperson and a PR office and publishing a newsletter. To market the place successfully, marketing experts try to

single the place out among its competitors and to market its uniqueness. As shown in Chapter 2, it is important to note that the campaign
messages are a direct result of target-public research: what is their
image of the place, what are their sources of information regarding
the place, which place characteristics are they familiar with and what
are their intentions regarding the place.

Recognizing the place's characteristics

Many marketing professionals maintain that to launch a successful
campaign one must have a deep understanding of the product one is
marketing. Often, getting to know the product is the best way to find
the key element that will later serve as the campaign's anchor. By this
reasoning, place marketers have to be familiar with place characteristics such as population size and demographic data such as average
income, age, education and race. Marketers should also be familiar
with such characteristics as the local real-estate market, local economy and business, business supply and demand of human resources,
tourism to the place, health and community services, leisure and
recreation, attractions, natural resources, crime rate and education
services. Once these characteristics are assembled, campaign managers will be better able to select those that should be highlighted in
the campaign (and those that should be kept out of sight) and those
that should be improved; they will also have a better idea of how
this improvement might affect the place's image.

Familiarity with the characteristics of other places competing for
the same resources is essential as well. For example, satellite communities around **New York City** endeavor to attract the same firms
as the metropolis does; to succeed, they must perceive their relative
advantage compared with NYC or to other nearby communities. In
other cases, places need not be in physical proximity to compete
for the same resources: **Morocco** and **Croatia**, for example, vie for
the same holidaymakers. In any event, place marketers should be
familiar with the decision-making process of the target audience,
their criteria for choosing a certain place instead of others and which
of the place's characteristics are most relevant for their decision-
making. The consumers' decision-making process is discussed in
greater detail in the next chapter.

SWOT and post-SWOT analysis

Place evaluation, as mentioned, is a fundamental element in every
marketing plan. The elementary starting point for place evaluation

is *strength, weakness, opportunity and threat (SWOT) analysis*, namely the process whereby places learn to identify these four aspects. Strengths are place characteristics that improve its competitive edge; its weaknesses are characteristics that harm it or its image; opportunities, if used wisely, can improve the place's competitive advantage; and threats are characteristics potentially dangerous for the place or its image. Each cluster of characteristics identified can be major or minor, changeable or fixed, human-made or nature-made (Kotler et al., 1993).

One important distinction between the four categories is that strengths and weaknesses are related to the place's internal environment, and opportunities and threats are related to its external environment. An exception to this distinction is that a strength that has not wholly realized its positive potential will also be marked as an opportunity, and a weakness that has not exhausted its full negative potential will be marked as a threat. For example, if a certain place has some great natural resources, but they are not maintained, operated and marketed properly, this characteristic will be marked as both a strength and a weakness. Similarly, some place characteristics can be both an opportunity and a threat. For example, if coexistence between two ethnic groups is successful, it can serve as a major opportunity for attracting visitors and residents from both groups to live together in harmony. But if coexistence deteriorates into ethnic conflict, this can constitute as a major threat, causing a negative climate of fear and persistent tension.

SWOT analysis may vary on account of its target audience. For example, young adults tend to perceive big, crowded and hectic cities as positive characteristics, while families with children tend to perceive these attributes as negative. Accordingly, each SWOT analysis is done in respect of a clear-cut target audience; a different target audience might require a series of adjustments. The more similar two target audiences are, the more similar their SWOT analyses will be (Seaton and Bennett, 1996).

From this angle, SWOT analysis enjoys a few key advantages: first, it promotes familiarization with the place and its characteristics. Second, using the perspective of the target audience helps not only in grasping the way they perceive the place, but also in understanding what they are and their likes and dislikes. Third, probing for potential threats and opportunities is a creative process, widening the perspective by which the place is perceived; it may result in the development of new attractions on the one hand and forming a crisis management plan on the other.

The SWOT analysis complete, it is time to descend to a deeper level of analysis, using the *performance/importance matrix*. This is a practical application of the SWOT analysis, integrating the place's strengths and weaknesses and the target audience's needs and demands. The goal of the performance/importance matrix is to direct place marketers' focus onto what should be highlighted in the process and what physical changes should be carried out at the place (for more details, see Kotler et al., 1993).

The campaign components

To brand a place and deliver the desired message to the target audience, campaign managers must tackle many components that comprise the campaign. Most important are the place's logo and slogan and the visual symbols used. Each of these components contributes to the campaign's success or failure, and accordingly should be handled with utmost care.

Place's logo

When a city is undergoing a marketing process it might need to change its symbols to match the new image. For example, industrial cities moving into the post-industrial era often have symbols that are no longer relevant to the city's new spirit and a logo change is required; so it was with **Syracuse**, New York. This city was striving to move toward the post-industrial era but had a logo showing chimneys, an industrial landscape and smoke, which was incongruent with the new image. After lengthy debate a new logo was adopted, depicting a modern skyline of skyscrapers, open skies and a lake (Short et al., 1993). Another example is the case of **Seattle**, Washington, a city whose greatest assets are its high-tech industry and the magnificent wild nature surrounding the city. In its new logo, the letters "SEA" had turned into a watching eye and the "at" had become the symbol "@," highlighting the city's two main advantages. The influence of a place's "new era" on its logo can be found in various countries; for example, a peripheral region in **Israel** that attempted to attract high-tech employees added the symbol "@" to its logo, to suggest that it was technologically advanced.

In his study of logos and symbols of cities in Israel, Avraham (2003a) found that most logos are very much alike, using the same motifs such as flowers, trees, stars, cog-wheels and buildings. Similarly, towns on the sea commonly display motifs of boats, waves, sun, water, stars and nature. Many places use geometrical shapes such as triangles, arcs and circles – shapes and motifs that in most cases have no symbolic meaning and do not promote the place's image. Some of the logos studied indeed proved highly creative, but they are not much help in distinguishing those places from their competitors. To fulfill the logo's potential as a meaningful marketing tool it should be unique, cohere with the new image the place is trying to project and use the place's distinctive characteristics (Gabor, 2006). While some logos can support the place's image and assist in its marketing, some logos may actually harm the place's image, as evident in the following examples from the research of Avraham (2003a). In one case, a town near **Jerusalem** that wanted to position itself distinctly from the famous ancient city, in fact used the symbols of Jerusalem in its logo. Similarly, a small town that wanted to brand itself as a high-tech center used traditional images of fields, trees and an agricultural landscape.

From Spain to "Espana"

Following the death of Franco in 1975, **Spain** resolved to "transformed itself from a backward, inward looking dictatorship into a sophisticated, outward looking democracy without losing its essential Spanish character and personality" (Olins, 2001). The branding process was supported by Joan Miro's bright and lively "Espana" painting as a national logo and as a symbol of the nation's post-Franco optimism. The logo was also accompanied by the slogan "Spain – Everything under the Sun." Another important aspect supporting the new identity was the hosting of the Barcelona Olympics in 1992, bringing the Espana brand into people's awareness.

Place's slogan

Like any other commercial product, many places use slogans to promote the place and increase its salience among the target audience. The slogan generally carries the essence of the place, trying to condense the marketing campaign into a pithy phrase. For example, the slogan chosen to support a campaign which described **Thailand** as a land of amazing people, amazing experiences and amazing landscapes was "Amazing Thailand." Similarly, **South Africa** used the slogan "South Africa – It's (Im)possible" to project the unlimited possibilities that exist now in the country after the collapse of apartheid.

One of the prime examples of a slogan used to foster fondness for a place is the well-known "I ♥ New York." A good slogan may serve for many years and through several different campaigns; it can lay out a destination's vision, reflect its spirit and create enthusiasm and momentum. Formulating a slogan depends on the target population and on the campaign goals, but the slogan must also be at least somewhat congruent with reality (Kotler et al., 1993). After using the slogan "I ♥ New York" for over 30 years, New York City is now in a search of a new one. Recently, the city came up with two new slogans: "Made in NY" and "The World's Second Home," for which it has already applied for a trademark. The new slogan, when it is chosen, will be attached to more than 200 products and services, all associated with one of the most successful brands in the world (*New York Times*, 17 February 2005).

"Malaysia, Truly Asia"

As noted earlier, a destination undergoing a change has to replace its slogan with a new one that will serve as an auxiliary tool for the new brand. **Malaysia**, a country which was once associated with poverty and cheap labor, has recently undergone a comprehensive branding process. As part of its marketing plan, Malaysia chose two slogans: "Malaysia, Truly Asia," which sought to offer an authentic visitor's experience and "Made in Malaysia," emanating a sense of quality, excellence and innovation (Sya, 2004).

From their accumulated marketing knowledge, many campaign managers now understand that a good slogan is a powerful marketing tool that can reflect the place's vision, create enthusiasm and be identified with the place for many years. Again, like a campaign, a slogan's wording is influenced by the target audience's characteristics and the campaign goals and has to be based on reality rather than fantasy. If a certain slogan spuriously promises golden beaches, turquoise lagoons and a unique experience for the visitor, tourists who go to the place will be disappointed and the place's image may be gravely damaged as a result.

"Made in NY"

After using the slogan "I ♥ New York" for over 30 years, New York City is now in a search of a new one. Recently, the city came up with two slogans: "Made in NY" and "The World's Second Home," for which it has already applied for a trademark . The new slogan, when it is chosen, will be attached to more than 200 products and services, all associated with one of the most successful brands in the world (*New York Times*, 17 February 2005).

Mark Twain once said, "I didn't have time to write a short letter, so I wrote a long one instead." By the same reasoning, finding a winning slogan is sometimes more complicated than writing the entire campaign. For example, the slogan "**Tel Aviv** – A 24 Hour City" was chosen out of 120 competing entries (Rosen, 2000). In his above-mentioned study of slogans used by cities in Israel, Avraham (2003a) found that most slogans highlight the place's uniqueness, but without elaborating what makes it so special compared with other places. One atypical example found in that research was the slogan for the city of **Holon**: "Holon, Great for the Kids." This slogan, supported by a logo of a young child, tells us about the city's branding plan as a "city for kids" and reminds the target audience of what makes Holon unique (Shir, 2006). This branding was supported by the construction of several facilities especially for children such as museums, parks, a media and art center, a theater and year-round music, film and drama festivals.

Australia, a different light

In 2000, **Australia** won worldwide recognition thanks to the successful Sydney Olympic Games. Since then, local decision makers have felt that Australia needs to refresh its brand due to the decline in the number of tourists visiting. According to the Australian tourism commission, the need for a new brand, differentiating Australia from other countries competing for the tourists' attention, was clear (http://www.tourism.australia.com). The fresh branding occurred in 2004, under the new slogan "Life in a Different Light," accompanied by a new visual icon, a signature line that was to be inserted into all of Australia's advertising campaigns. The signature line would also have a distinctive orange color and a new logo of a kangaroo jumping against the background of the sun. The new campaign was aimed at linking up light, land and life in Australia and involved a series of several television advertisements hosting world-renowned Australians.

Places' visual symbols

Many campaigns for different places use in addition to logos and slogans unique visual symbols such as monuments, interesting buildings, gates, sculptures, towers, bridges or forts, which have become identifying symbols of the place and part of its image. Some examples of world-famous visual symbols are the Eiffel Tower in **Paris**, Big Ben in **London**, **San Francisco**'s Golden Gate Bridge, Red Square in **Moscow**, the Great Wall of **China** and the Guggenheim Museum in **Bilbao**. The main advantage of visual symbols is their ability to convey messages quickly and efficiently; for example, it is enough to show a picture of the **Sydney** Opera House for the target audience to know that it is Sydney or Australia.

Using the right visual symbol to promote a place is not always a simple matter. For example, there was a long and interesting debate in Israel regarding the visual symbol representing **Jerusalem** and its effect on the city's image. According to Tal (1993), the focus on the Muslim Dome of the Rock is problematic as Israel seeks to represent Jerusalem as a Jewish city. The upshot was Israel's choice as its visual symbol of the Tower of David, whose name alone is more appropriate for representing Jerusalem as the most important place for the Jewish people.

Techniques for delivering campaign messages

Campaign managers have several options for delivering the campaign's central messages. The choice depends on the campaign's goals and timing, the target audience of the place and of its rivals, available resources and many other factors. The most common techniques are advertising, direct mailing/marketing, sales promotion and public relations.

Advertising

Advertising is the most popular tool for place marketing. According to a CNN poll, $538 million was spent on marketing locations in the United States alone during 1999 (Piggott, 2001, cited in Morgan and Pritchard, 2001). According to the World Tourism Organization (WTO), governments spend $350 million annually on destination marketing (Morgan and Pritchard, 2001). Advertising is based on purchasing space in the media and using it to deliver messages to target populations. Though very costly, advertising affords the campaign managers maximum control over the delivered message, the target audience and the timing of the publicity. Yet advertising has several disadvantages, such as consumers' tendency not to trust ads and to doubt their credibility. Every day the average consumer is exposed to thousands of advertisements, so the effectiveness of each of them is questionable (Ries and Ries, 2004).

In addition to "regular" advertisements, some newspapers carry special supplements in which places that want to advertise themselves can buy several pages or even the entire issue. Examples may be found in newspapers such as the *Economist* and the London *Times*, in which many countries buy special supplements to attract investors and entrepreneurs (more examples may be found in Kunczik, 1997). Examples of supplements to attract tourists or visitors to a country, a city or a tourist destination are readily found in tourism magazines such as the *Conde Nast Traveler*. As an illustration, the May 2006 issue included special advertising sections for tourist resorts, hotels, cruise operators and such places as **Peru**, **Colorado**, the **Virgin Islands**, the **Bahamas** and the **American Caribbean**. Some of the special advertising sections were only a single page, but countries such as **China** and **Mexico** bought eight-page advertising sections.

Direct mailing/marketing

This method involves directly addressing target populations through mail, personal meetings, telephone or electronic mail. Target audience is sent brochures, maps, photographs and information pamphlets in the hope that they will become interested in investing in or visiting the place. Through direct mailing, place representatives directly address potential investors, tourists or residents and try to convince them to see what the place has to offer without the use of middlemen. One of the biggest disadvantages of direct mailing/marketing is the investment of many resources in single individuals, which can prove extremely costly when used for large audience. On the other hand, the use of direct mailing/marketing enables the place marketers to address each potential customer personally and to respond to his/her specific needs. In addition to sending information pamphlets and brochures, many places use direct mailing/marketing to deliver other items that might improve their public image: flags, key rings, pins, DVD films of the place, New Year greeting cards, stickers, magnets, maps, pictures and postcards from the place, information on events there, word games, newsletters, calendars and so on.

Sales promotion

By this technique limited-time bonuses are extended to encourage the target audience to consume the place and the services it offers tourists, investors or residents. Some of the more common examples of sales promotion are tax benefits for companies and factories that are willing to relocate to the place within a specified time frame, various sales and property tax exemptions, reduced prices in local hotels, free training for workers in relocating companies, inexpensive land for investors and benefits for relocating residents.

Public relations

One of the classic definitions of public relations is given by Kotler et al. (1993, p. 169): "Public relations is the effort to build good relations with the organization's publics by obtaining favorable publicity; building up a good public image; and handling or heading off unfavorable rumors, stories and events." Public relations are a key ingredient in place promotion and its major tools are press connections, event publicity and lobbying. Despite the importance of implementing these tools simultaneously, here we focus on public relations only as they concern the news media and the effort to portray a place positively. Public relations efforts are primarily undertaken by a place's spokesperson/press officer or by an external public relations firm.

It is generally accepted that when a PR expert succeeds in getting a good story in the news media it has a positive effect on the place's image. PR is considered less expensive and more reliable than advertising. PR's relatively low cost is due to its not needing to purchase expensive media space, and its high credibility is due to the readers' assumptions that the article (based on a PR news release) was written by a neutral journalist with no specific interest in the reported item (Kunczik, 1997). In other words, a recommendation to visit a certain place – appearing in a news article – is perceived as more sound when it comes from a journalist than when it appears in an advertisement sponsored by the place promoted.

The positive aspects of PR notwithstanding, this technique has several disadvantages. There is fierce competition among places, organizations, firms and other commercial companies over limited media space, especially when regarding their desire to gain positive media coverage. It is also very hard for the campaign organizers to control the message that is eventually delivered and the time of its publication. Some places found that the use of PR can backfire, when journalists were invited to cover a positive story but they eventually focused on the negative aspects of the story or of the place (Avraham, 2003b).

In general, PR people work on both the good and bad sides of their place's media image. Their effort is to promote the place's positive side, yet it is important to mention that they also work to prevent or mitigate the fallout of negative news published about the place. This negative news may be about violence, crime or social problems, which might cause the place to be perceived by the general public as dangerous or dirty, a place seething with unrest or suffering stagnation or a long crisis. On top of working with the media, PR experts also consult local decision makers about their media appearance, researching and collecting data of the place's image, producing events and festivals and lobbying (the work of PR experts is elaborated in the following chapters). Places' PR efforts are crucial, particularly at times of sudden crisis such as crime/violence waves, terror acts or natural disasters. In these cases, the places receive broad national media coverage that can create a perception – in the national and international public – of a dangerous place.

Marketing places on the World Wide Web

In recent years, the Internet has become a key tool in the marketing and promotion of countries, cities and tourist destinations around the world. As online marketing is not in the focus of this book, we will limit the discussion of marketing on the Internet to a few key comments. Today the Internet offers thousands of place websites containing information for visitors, investors and immigrants. Information is provided on tourism services such as hotels and tourists attractions, education services such as schools and universities and also employment, sanitation and sports and cultural events. Some websites have maps, pictures, virtual tours, a visitors' guide, the place's vision, links to websites of local partners such as hotels, tourist destinations and firms and virtual aspect of the place.

The Internet offers multiple advantages: designing a website is often less costly than advertising or buying media space, the Internet makes the place available for a variety of target audiences and it enables the place to constantly deliver a great quantity of updated information. Websites can be updated easily for low maintenance costs and using user-friendly software. Messages on websites can be changed frequently and it is easy to track the number of site visitors. Taking advantage of its two-way nature, the Internet encourages feedback in various forms, including online surveys and a direct "contact us" email. The web allows place decision makers to ask their target audience various questions and probe public opinion when choosing a new logo, symbol or slogan. In addition, many places have turned their websites into their central communication route with local residents, serving as a means to increase civil activism, involvement in the place's life and improving residents' image of the place (Avraham, 2003a).

Choosing a medium and a technique for delivering campaign messages

The use of these four techniques must be coordinated, and the messages delivered to the public must be similar. Marketing and public relations campaigns are complementary and have to be mutually supportive. For example, when a marketing campaign attempts to attract investors to a place through advertisements and brochures, in the PR campaign spokesmen and advisors should tell the media about investors hurrying to the place, about conferences for new investors and about the various benefits offered to prospective investors.

To maximize target audience exposure to the campaign, it should be advertised in the medium that the target audience consumes. Every campaign manager has a large variety of newspapers, magazines, radio stations, television channels and Internet websites to choose from. The campaign manager can likewise choose to produce brochures and information pamphlets, DVD films of the place or any other kind of advertising material. If, for example, the campaign's target audience is executives, an experienced campaign manager will first find out which papers they read, which websites they visit, which radio stations they listen to and which television programs they watch. Based on the message components and their complexity, one should first choose a medium (such as newspaper, Internet, radio or television) and then make a more specific choice regarding a certain magazine, a selected television or radio program or particular website. The most effective medium for delivering complex messages is the printed press, while for messages that are more emotional and less complex radio or television is recommended. Other factors affecting the choice of medium and technique are the campaign's objectives, the target audience's preferences and the available resources.

Summary

This chapter described the way to change a place's image. This is a lengthy, complicated and expensive process, hence it requires the coordination of many factors and resources and the assistance of professionals. To advance from the stage of drawing up a strategic plan for changing the place's image, it is advisable to start by defining the campaign's objectives and the target audience and analyzing the place's characteristics, preferably through SWOT analysis. The campaign components include the place's logo, slogan and visual symbol; proper management of each component can help or even promote the place's image. In the last part of the chapter, we noted several techniques used for delivering campaign messages, whose use depends on the campaign's objectives and resources and the target audience's characteristics.

4 Consumer behavior

Launching a campaign for a city, state or destination is directly influenced by the target audience and by the advertiser's aim: to get people to visit, invest or move to a certain place. To accomplish this and attain the campaign's goal, the behavior, needs and motivation of the target audience must be thoroughly understood (Avraham, 2003a; Swarbrooke and Horner, 1999). Without such understanding, reaching the campaign's goal will be difficult or indeed impossible in certain cases. In this chapter, we further discuss the motivation behind place consumption and the process of choosing places for visiting, investment and immigration.

Introduction to consumer behavior

Understanding how potential customers make decisions regarding which places to visit, invest in or immigrate to has long been of interest to tourism industry professionals and place marketers. They seek answers to several crucial questions such as "What do people look for in a destination they visit?," "Why do consumers prefer one place over another?," "Which factors affect the ways people construct place images?" and "What do people expect to gain from investing in or moving to a place?" To answer these questions, a large body of research examined the demand and satisfaction in place consumption. It is now obvious that decisions taken about place consumption are the outcome of a long, complicated and highly involved process, especially when regarding investment or immigration. Discovering the criteria behind the decision-making process is a highly elaborate task, involving a variety of factors, motivations, considerations and pressures, which can be conscious or unconscious. Moreover, the decision-making process is lengthy, and from the moment one hears of a place, a long time may elapse before he/she visits or otherwise "consumes" it. In a time of crisis, the decision-making process is much more problematic because the potential consumer feels a threat to his/her personal security and cannot be sure that the visit, investment or relocation will be a positive move in light of the adverse circumstances.

Models of decision-making processes

Swarbrooke and Horner (1999) describe several consumer behavior models that provide simplified versions of the relationship of various factors that influence consumer behavior. The models, according to the researchers, were developed and describe consumer behavior with the intention of trying to control the behavior patterns.

The consumers' decision process prior to consumption of a product can be illustrated in various ways. A classic model is offered by Kotler and Armstrong (1989) as consisting of five fixed phases. Those authors dealt with consumption of a product; we have adopted their model to address the consumption of a place:

1. Acquiring awareness of the place;
2. Accumulating knowledge of the place (cognitive component);
3. Preferring it to other places (emotional component);
4. Choosing to consume the place;
5. The actual place consumption.

A more modern model reduces these five phases to a three-way stimuli–response model, suggested by Kotler et al. (1999b):

1. *Marketing stimuli*: A certain product enters into the consumer's awareness.
2. *Buyer's decision process*: The consumer processes the new information together with other pieces of information and with his/her own personal preferences.
3. *Buyer's response*: The consumer makes his/her decision regarding the product. If it is affirmative it includes choice of dealer, purchasing time and purchasing amount.

In any event, to accomplish the campaign's goals, the advertisers behind the campaign must be aware of all these phases and track the potential consumer throughout. To maximize campaign efficiency, advertisers must constantly pinpoint the phase at which the target audience is situated. For example, if the target audience is already aware of the place, nothing is to be gained by continuing to elevate awareness; it is better to concentrate on promoting the place's consumption. As a direct result, advertisers will try to understand the different criteria, needs, dreams, aspirations and perceptions affecting the decision-making of tourists, investors and immigrants.

Information sources

While the first phases of decision-making usually involve an active search for information, the final phases constitute a more limited and personal process. For places to be a part of this process they must supply fast, reliable, appealing and updated information. In the age of global competition, competition for the consumers' attention is constantly intensifying, forcing advertisers to launch expensive and sophisticated campaigns in quick succession.

To make up their mind, the target audience uses a number of information sources: (1) *personal sources* such as friends, relatives and neighbors; (2) *commercial sources* such as campaigns, salesmen, professional advisors and trip planners; (3) *public sources* such as the mass media or narrowcasting journals; (4) *experiential sources* such as visiting the place (Kotler et al., 1993). Although commercial sources are the most available, consumers usually prefer personal sources. A recommendation from a friend or a relative is in many cases deemed more trustworthy than a slick brochure covered with a place's Photoshop-made sunset.

Consumer involvement in the buying decision

Sometimes the buying process is not done by a single individual but involves several people, playing different parts. According to Kotler et al. (1999b), a buying decision can consist of several roles:

- *Initiator*: The person who first suggests, thinks of or identifies the need for a certain product or service. For example, a wife suggests to her husband that they go on vacation.
- *Influencer*: A person whose opinion or advice serves as a meaningful factor in the decision. For example, one of the spouse's parents has just returned from a great vacation in **Aruba** and they warmly recommend going there.
- *Decider*: The person who ultimately makes the buying decision. For example, the husband decides that the vacation destination will be a particular resort in **Jamaica**.

- *Buyer*: The person who makes the actual purchase. For example, the wife pays for the vacation with her credit card.
- *User*: All the people who use or consume the product or service purchased. For example, the husband and wife who are going on vacation.

Even in the business field, making a hotel reservation or booking a flight may involve the mediation of secretaries, logistics coordinators and other administrative staff. In any case, for many decisions the decider, the users and the influencers are distinct people who should be addressed differently. As a result, locating the people who hold key positions in decision-making processes is vital for getting the campaign across (Kotler et al., 1999b). But reaching single individuals – who are involved in the process – and persuading them to make the "right" decision is not easy; the buyer's decision process, for example, is mediated by interpersonal variables such as age, gender, education level, marital status, personal preferences and more (Shaw and Williams, 2002). The marketer needs to understand which factors will affect the buyer's decision-making: the climate? the cost? the kind of events that the place hosts? Furthermore, there are different types of consumer behavior, of which Shaw and Williams (2002) identify three main types. The first is the *impulse buyer*: a consumer with short planning horizons, often attracted by last-minute deals. The second type is the *repeat buyer*: the tourist who tends to go back to the same destination on every vacation. The last type is the *meticulous planner*, who has long planning horizons and makes well-considered decisions.

As noted earlier, tourism, investment and immigration involve different decision-making processes. For example, the choice of a vacation is influenced by criteria such as climate, attractions, price and distance; the decision to immigrate is influenced by work opportunities, educational system, transportation and lifestyle; the decision to invest is affected by real-estate prices, availability of human resources, tax rate, infrastructure and proximity to markets; the choice of convention center is influenced by local facilities, their size, price and availability and other external factors such as local attractions and level of personal security (Avraham, 2003a). This long list of assorted criteria obliges advertisers to acquire a deep understanding of consumer behavior and of the different elements involved in the decision-making process. Below we analyze the factors and the criteria that enter into the target public's decision to consume places for the purposes of immigration, tourism and investment.

Place consumption for immigrants

How do people decide where to live? In every country, there are hundreds of cities, towns and villages to choose from and the variety is enormous. One reason this question is hard to answer is that the factors influencing the decision are constantly changing. For example, for many years citizens of Western countries preferred to live in high-rise buildings in the heart of big cities. Today many of those people prefer small or medium-sized towns where they can live in a private house with a big garden and within commuting distance from central metropolitan services and opportunities. On the other hand, people who left the big cities for the suburbs are returning to city centers, which are undergoing a massive process of regeneration; old neighborhoods downtown are being turned into hip and colorful quarters with gourmet restaurants, trendy cafés and many art galleries (Gonen, 1995).

Parallel to the decision-making process of the potential immigrants, advertisers and marketing professionals constantly try to follow up on these considerations, not always successfully. Following the immigrant's decision-making process is complicated for two main reasons: first, public preferences tend to change over the years, and these changes force the marketing professionals to follow up on trends and adjust their marketing strategies accordingly. Second, not all sectors of the population adhere to the same decision criteria. For example, ethnic immigrants tend to live close to people who share their background, and a residence project for those groups must be marketed in its own particular way, highlighting specific relevant motifs by, say, using the immigrants' mother tongue, telling them who the neighbors are and focusing on other familiar facets to make them feel at ease. The different needs and desires of the diverse elements in the population have to be addressed differently by the marketing campaign.

Whatever the case may be, choosing a place is a matter of social trends and, even more so, the general stereotypes about the place's image, as discussed in Chapter 2. Most places have good/positive or bad/negative stereotypes, and some of them have already been transformed into a myth or symbol. Such stereotypes are extremely hard to change and they can have an enormous impact on people's impressions, sometimes more than actual reality. People from the higher social classes tend to prefer places with a positive image, while places with a less favorable image tend to be associated with the lower social classes. This tendency creates two vicious cycles: in one, places with positive images continue to attract high-class residents, which reinforces the positive images. In the other cycle, real-estate prices fall in places with a negative image, which then attracts low-class residents, thus damaging the place's image even more. Accordingly, place differentiation is actually a social differentiation: the place is not just a geographical location for its residents but also a symbol, indicating the different opportunities one can enjoy. In the social context, location of residence is a status symbol, a label and an important component in the resident's perception of himself/herself (Birnboim-Karmeli, 1994). To conclude, we now know that besides the rational considerations in the decision-making process, many factors are at work on the emotional level, both conscious and unconscious.

Trying to understand why people prefer one place to another, we might first focus on the benefits one gains by living in a certain place. Avraham (2003a) studied a series of cases analyzing the criteria influencing migration decisions within Israel. For example, a survey done by a large city found the following factors (in order of their importance): socio-economical level of the city's residents, quiet environment/prestigious era, good educational system, large variety of entertainment, proximity to the workplace and proximity to friends and family members. A list of opposite factors was found in interviews with people who migrated out of **Jerusalem**: high real-estate prices (41%), lack of proper employment (16%), family reasons (13%), decline in quality of life (6%), the religious character of the city and more (*Ha'aretz*, 11 November 2002). In their research on residential mobility, Tsfati and Cohen (2003) state that "intentions to move or actual relocation were predicted by life-cycle factors, race, socio-demographic factors and aspirations of social mobility, crowding and other indications of housing, families ties, duration of current residence, tenure, mobility history, and various forms of neighborhood participation" (p. 713).

Concrete and non-concrete benefits

Another perspective for understanding the factors behind the decision-making process is given by Fenster et al. (1994). These authors note two kinds of influencing factors: concrete and non-concrete benefits.

Concrete benefits

There are three kinds of concrete benefits: functional benefits, saving-driven benefits and experiential benefits.

- *Functional benefits*: These focus on the place's actual functioning level: lifestyle, education, welfare and diverse opportunities for accommodation, entertainment, employment and more. All these benefits are highly functional and they encompass the everyday quality of life in the chosen place.
- *Saving-driven benefits*: These focus on savings in time, effort and money resulting from living in a certain familiar place. The main effect of the saving-driven benefits lies in the decision against immigrating and for staying in the same place. They include proximity to friends, family and social infrastructure and convenience in consuming the same habits and environment.
- *Experiential benefits*: These focus on the sensuous pleasures a place offers its residents, for example, esthetic, cultural, culinary and entertainment experiences, as in cities such as **New York**, **London** or **Paris**.

Non-concrete benefits

The more abstract benefits one gains from living in a place are known as non-concrete benefits. The literature distinguishes two kinds: social benefits and psychological benefits.

- *Social benefits*: When a consumer selects a certain product, especially in choosing a place of residence, it can also be seen as a statement of his/her lifestyle, personality and the values he/she upholds (Morgan and Pritchard, 2001). One important aspect of social benefits is the potential for social interaction with desired social sectors. For example, one major motive in moving to a highly exclusive neighborhood is the wish to live among people similar to oneself or people one would like to be similar to. A person who moves to a highly exclusive neighborhood delivers a message about his/her socio-economic status. Showing that one lives in an exclusive place serves as ego-enhancing motivation. Campaigns accordingly work on this motivation and promote these affirmative feelings, intimating that only a certain kind of person may reside in a certain kind of place. This rule also holds for places with an image crisis; living in a place associated with poverty, crime and violence can lower the residents' social status and even harm their future social possibilities (Avraham, 2003a). To summarize, living in a highly exclusive neighborhood or city allows its residents to identify with the social group or class into which they would like to be absorbed. A survey by an Israeli construction company found that for a relatively significant percentage of their customers, the prime consideration in choosing an apartment was their future neighbors' social class (*Yediot Acharonot*, 28 August 2002).

- *Psychological benefits*: As with social benefits, the psychological benefits of living in a certain place are the effect of the place's social aspects on the resident's self-esteem or image. For example, moving to a highly exclusive neighborhood improves the new resident's self-esteem, filling him/her with positive feelings of success and achievement. While the social benefits gained from living in a certain place are projected outside the residents' social environment, the psychological benefits are internal, aimed at the self-image and self-esteem (Fenster et al., 1994).

Naturally, people want to immigrate to a place that maximizes both their concrete and their non-concrete benefits. Knowing this, many place marketers try to highlight those particular benefits to attract their target audience. Through these campaigns the potential consumer can clearly see how relocating to a certain place will maximize his/her benefits, promising a better future.

Place consumption for investment

Investors, businessmen and entrepreneurs will prefer to invest where the chances of profit are the greatest. Accordingly, a set of preconditions must be satisfied by any place that wishes to attract investments: well-trained employees, proximity to markets and raw materials, reasonable taxation, a certain level of infrastructure and so on. Usually the potential investor first chooses the general area for the new factory or investment and only then selects the specific location. Burgess (1982) found that business managers preferred to get brochures focusing on business and financial aspects first, then a more general brochure. According to this researcher, managers and investors seek specific information such as real-estate prices, property taxes, benefits from the local municipality, access to air and sea ports, access to railroad and other major transport routes, high-quality human resources, parking space and the place's general image. Possessing this information can be very useful for place marketers.

In a survey, the Israeli Manufacturers Association found that most factories in **Israel** were dissatisfied with the level of municipal services they received (Manufacturers Association of Israel, 2002). Another survey conducted among executives of high-tech companies revealed that the most fundamental factors in the placement of a company office were real-estate prices and high-tech infrastructure.

Other factors, in order of importance, were municipal benefits, parking space, the place's image, high accessibility, high-quality environment (clean, esthetic and quiet), flexibility for further development, proximity to business-related services such as banks and business districts, proximity to employees' residential areas, proximity to similar high-tech companies, a friendly and active local administration, proximity to financial centers, proximity to the headquarters of big leading companies and proximity to universities or other research institutes. Among these factors, proximity to the employees' residential areas exerted only a minor effect on company relocation (*Ha'aretz*, 3 May 1998). Furthermore, every type of industry has its own scale for the relevant locating factors, depending on the industry's characteristics. For example, heavy industry depends mainly on raw materials and their shipping costs, so proximity to export and import routes will serve as a major factor in the choice of a place. By contrast, the prevalent goods required for high-tech companies are software or hardware, so proximity to main transport routes serves only as a minor factor. Moreover, the priority of these factors can easily change according to circumstances. For example, in times of recession or other financial difficulties, the importance of property tax levels increased dramatically (*Ha'aretz*, 13 January 2003). All in all, these survey results can assist both local decision makers and place marketers when trying to attract investors, businessmen and entrepreneurs (Bornstein, 1995).

Place consumption for tourism

Unlike many other purchases, consumption of a vacation is more of an experience than buying a good. It also usually involves long-term planning and large amounts of money, without getting any "real" material product in return: what one gets is an intangible experience. Another characteristic distinguishing the purchase of vacations from other goods is the distance – while in most fields customers aspire to minimize distances, the travel element is an important part of the vacation product (Shaw and Williams, 2002).

Push and pull factors in tourist motivation

The literature discerns two kinds of factor at work in the tourist's motivation: *pull factors* and *push factors*. The latter determine the need to travel, and the former guide the choice of a specific destination by satisfying those needs. Push factors for tourism are the outcome of a number of causes, including a wish to break the routine, feelings of alienation and a sense of purposelessness, ego-enhancement motivation (vacation as a means to strengthen social status) and peer pressure to take a vacation. Ryan (1997, in Shaw and Williams, 2002) adds another dimension to the ego-enhancement motive – a tourist's self-perception may include all the various places they visited. In this perspective, one factor determining tourists' motivation is how well the place's image integrates with their self-perception. A different perspective is suggested by Kent (1995), whereby push factors can be arrayed on a continuum. At one extreme are people who perceive their home as their spiritual center and regard tourism as a way to take a break by getting out of this center. In contrast, there are people who consider their home an inadequate environment and perceive their spiritual center to exist in a more authentic milieu.

Another concept proposed by Kent (1995) is *holiday goals* – a set of explicit objectives to be achieved during a vacation. Naturally, holiday goals are the ultimate outcome of push factors. By contrast, the destination's pull factors will guide the tourist's choice by dovetailing with his/her psychological needs (Shaw and Williams, 2002). Pull factors are the sum of all different dimensions in the destination's image, serving to attract visitors. For example, if the main push factor for a certain individual is the need to take a relaxing break, the main pull factor for this customer would be the triple S: Sea, Sand and Sun. Accordingly, a grasp of the target public's push factors can assist destinations in creating better campaigns by emphasizing the relevant pull factors. For example, the five main fields of interests for cultural tourism are crafts, traditions, history of the region, architecture and local food (Ritchie and Zins, 1978, in Shaw and Williams, 2002). By highlighting these fields in a campaign one can easily appeal to this target audience.

Case Study: marketing an inexpensive vacation in Sinai

In a study by the Israeli tourism company Tzabar in 1997, researchers probed the vacation habits of Israelis traveling to the Sinai Peninsula. Finding that 43% of visitors to Sinai slept in sleeping bags, tents or bungalows, Tzabar launched a campaign offering inexpensive three-star rated hotels in Sinai (*Ha'aretz*, 29 December 1997). Tzabar's understanding of the target public's behavior helped it to maximize the campaign's efficiency by offering the most suitable product for its potential clients. This case illustrates that by learning the target public's needs and motivations the place marketers can devise more effective campaigns.

Holiday opportunity sets

Kent (1995) identifies six sets of opportunities in the process of holiday choice. These are divided into two groups of three sets. The first group illustrates simply the technical aspects of decision-making. It consists of the *perceived opportunity set* – the range of available holidays that the customer is aware of; the *attainable opportunity set* – the range of holidays that the customer can afford; and the *realizable opportunity set* – the range of available holidays that the customer is aware of and can afford. Note that the opportunities set varies with different customers as a result of diversity in their economic status and their awareness of holiday destinations. The other group of three illustrates the psychological aspect of decision-making. It consists of the *consideration opportunity set* – the range of holidays suitable for attaining the customer's holiday goals; the *choice opportunity set* – a combination of the two preceding sets – which represents a range of holidays which are attainable, available and conform with the holiday goals. Last comes the *decision opportunity set* – a small set of suitable holidays from which the final choice is made.

The opportunity sets are a simplification of a long and complicated process, but they might be helpful in illustrating the different phases involved in choosing a destination. They underline variables such as awareness of different destinations and the vacation goals. However, they omit important variables such as emotional viewpoints, stereotyping of the destination and other subconscious factors (Ashworth and Goodal, 1995).

Evaluating a destination

Kent (1995) offers yet another perspective for evaluating destinations over a range of alternatives. The destination evaluation model is constructed of two independent processes: discursive processing and imagery processing. In *discursive processing*, the potential consumers identify the attributes they consider important in a vacation and then evaluate the destination according to the absence or presence of those attributes. For example, a potential customer who wants the "triple S" vacation (sea, sand and sun) may evaluate destinations according to their climate, quality of seaside resorts and the like. In *imagery processing*, the potential customers form an imaginary picture of how they will experience a specific destination: the way they will sunbathe on the beach, the people they will meet at their hotel and other such situations they will be in. An important aid for imagery processing is the destination's brochures, helping potential customers to put themselves "in the picture." The sum of the two processes is a most helpful tool in evaluating destinations and serves as an important element in the decision-making process. For more information on methods of evaluations and different ways to measure the potential tourist's destination image, please see Chapter 2 above.

Summary

The focus of this chapter has been consumer behavior and the various factors affecting the decision-making process in choosing a place to live, visit or invest in. Place marketers can avail themselves of different models to understand the consumers' decision-making process and to improve their marketing strategy. We should note here once again that place consumption is an extremely elaborate process, involving various factors, different players and many kinds of benefits which the consumer seeks. The models outlined here, together with the marketing strategies described in the following chapters, can serve as powerful tools for successful marketing.

5 Crisis and communication management

Following the discussion of place marketing, place image and consumer behavior, different aspects of crises and ways of handling them are now to be considered. Current literature offers an extensive discourse in the field of crises in general and the role of the media during crises in particular. This chapter sets out the major concepts, strategies and techniques to manage, control and overcome crisis situations. From the accumulated knowledge of the field it is by now well known that the media play a key role in the crisis life cycle, so understanding media routines, media decision-making and media effect on stakeholders has become an essential part of crisis management. In some cases, media effect on crisis situations is so marked that it has been claimed that the crisis was actually created by the media (White, 2006) and its desperate quest for "bleeding events." In any event, it is now apparent that the media's role starts well before the first signs of the crisis emerge and end long after the smoke has cleared.

The aim of this chapter is to review two related concepts: crisis management and crisis communication management (also known as "crisis communication"). The discussion of the crisis situation will help us to gain better understanding of the ways a city, country or tourist destination can prepare in advance for future crises, act during a crisis event and recover from it. Crisis situations are often dangerous and unexpected; the content of this chapter should provide an overview of the different aspects of crisis and this improved understanding can be a fundamental element in the critical moments of an actual real-life crisis (Coombs, 1999; Glaesser, 2006; Mansfeld and Pizam, 2006; Smith, 2002).

As noted in earlier chapters, this book addresses two kinds of crisis: sudden crisis and crisis as the cumulative result of ongoing, long-term problems. This chapter is mainly concerned with the sudden crisis; in this case the place goes through the full crisis life cycle.

By contrast, places suffering from the ongoing crisis have already undergone the first phases of the crisis and now either still face the crisis or are proceeding through the lengthy post-crisis era. In either case, understanding the full crisis life cycle is beneficial for both handling future crisis and overcoming a current one.

The nature of crisis

The first part of this chapter discusses the nature, definitions and types of crisis and the crisis life cycle. Following the introduction to crises, the first part illustrates two methods used for handling a crisis situation: crisis management and crisis communication management. The second part of the chapter opens with an integrated model, linking the different concepts discussed in the first part: crisis life cycle, crisis management and crisis communication. The presentation of the model is followed by a detailed specification of the way crisis management and crisis communication management are implemented through the different stages of a crisis event.

What is a crisis?

A brief examination of the daily news indicates that many destructive events occur every day; homicide, robbery, natural disasters, corruption and other afflictions crowd local and international television channels, newspapers and Internet websites. When faced with bad press resulting from such catastrophes, a place's local decision makers must continually ask themselves whether the negative events are merely routine incidents that may or may not damage their place image or if they have an image crisis on their hands. An additional, crucial question is at what point place marketers need to begin managing the crisis and how they can prevent potential damage.

It is important to answer these fundamental questions and to understand what a crisis is, before moving on to a discussion of crisis preparation and management.

"Crisis" has a variety of definitions given by various scholars (Ritchie et al., 2003). According to systemic approaches, a crisis is "a critical change in an important variable that endangers or destroys either parts of or the entire system" (Glaesser, 2006, p. 12). The systemic approaches offer a general definition, emphasizing the occurrence of a change in institutions, companies, groups or places that threatens to break the current equilibrium or routine. A similar definition is offered by Coombs (1999), suggesting that crises are unpredictable events that have the potential to create negative or undesired outcomes. This definition emphasizes the threat of the crisis event disrupting or affecting the function of an entire organization. This emphasis is also given by the Pacific Asia Travel Association in their *Crisis Management Manual*, published in 2003. The manual defines a crisis as "any situation that has the potential to affect long-term confidence in an organization or a product, or which may interfere with its ability to continue operating normally" (p. 2). From this perspective, the core of the crisis is its threat to the trust and confidence of the stakeholders and the public in a specific place or organization.

Glaesser (2006) suggests a comprehensive definition for crisis:

A crisis is an undesired, extraordinary, often unexpected and timely limited process with ambivalent development possibilities. It demands immediate decisions and countermeasures in order to influence the further development again positively for the organization/destination and to limit the negative consequences as much as possible. A crisis situation is determined by evaluating the seriousness of the occurring negative events, which threaten, weaken or destroy competitive advantages or important goals of the organization/destination.

(p. 14)

In summarizing several other key definitions, Glaesser combines different variables relevant to crises in a country, city or tourist destination: unexpectedness, time limits, unpredictable future, the need to estimate the damages and the risk of losing the place's competitive edge.

Types of crisis

The occurrence of a crisis can be the result of a wide variety of situations and events. To take some recent examples, **Hong Kong** suffered a crisis caused by epidemics, **New York** suffered a crisis as a result of terrorism, **Croatia** due to war, **Nepal** because of political unrest and **New Orleans** through natural disaster. The literature proposes different crisis classification in accordance with different crisis features. Various scholars have categorized crises by their duration (short, long), their geographical scale (local, regional, national or international) or the scale of the damage they do to lives and property. One common classification that is very relevant to the field of place marketing is by cause. This classification, offered by Glaesser (2006) and by Mansfeld and Pizam (2006), suggests a list of five possible crises every place should be prepared for:

1. *Crime*-related events such as robbery, rape, murder or kidnapping;
2. *Terror*-related events such as bombing of public places or plane hijackings;
3. *Political unrest* events such as violent demonstrations, uprisings or riots;
4. *Natural disaster* events such as earthquakes, forest fires, extreme heat/cold wave, hurricane or tsunami;
5. *Epidemic*-related events such as SARS, AIDS or foot and mouth disease.

This typology is available to local decision makers who are interested in knowing what possible crises they should be prepared for and in accumulating knowledge for managing them.

The crisis life cycle

Even though crises are unexpected by their nature, crisis evolution is an identifiable process that can be predicted. Different scholars have demonstrated that crises are composed of fixed stages, which form the crisis life cycle. Because these different stages require different responses, understanding the crisis life cycle is useful for applying the right response to the given stage (Coombs, 1999). Another reason for the importance of being familiar with the crisis life cycle is that it diminishes their unpredictability. Since crises tend to evolve quickly and in an unexpected manner, familiarity with their life cycle can help in predicting their course.

Researchers divide the crisis life cycle differently. One basic definition is offered by Gonzalez-Herrero and Pratt (1996), who demarcate four phases: birth, growth, maturity and decline. This division corresponds with a biological model, describing the crisis life cycle as parallel to that of the living organism, which quickly expands and then fades away.

A similar schematic model for the crisis life cycle and management is suggested by Coombs (1999), who offers a three-staged process. In the pre-crisis stage, organizations engage in the prevention of, and preparation for, possible crises. This stage includes acts such as signal detection, developing crisis portfolios and the creation of positive relationships with the media, target audience and key stakeholders. The second stage is managing the crisis event itself. This stage is divided into three sub-stages: crisis recognition, crisis containment and business resumption. The third and final stage in Coombs' model is post-crisis, where organizations verify that the crisis is really over and prepare themselves for future events. Although this model is comprehensive, other scholars have suggested more detailed models.

One of these is suggested by Mitroff and Pearson (1993), who divide crises and their management into five stages:

1. *Signal detection*: All places are inundated with a constant flow of signals. The main task is to distinguish between the first signs of a real crisis and the "noise" emanating from day-to-day business.
2. *Preparation/prevention*: Once a crisis signal has been detected, experts on the crisis management team start making the proper arrangements for it. In addition, the expert team should work to prevent the looming crisis.
3. *Containment/damage limitation*: Not all crises can be prevented. When a crisis does occur, the main goal of this phase is to manage, limit, contain and control it and ensure the welfare of guests, visitors, residents and employees.
4. *Recovery*: Although physical crises are usually solved relatively quickly, the resulting image crisis can last for a much longer period. The recovery phase is frequently the longest and contains several levels: recovery of infrastructure, restoring tourism and improving the place's image.
5. *Learning*: Once recovery is more or less accomplished, it is time to learn lessons from the recent crisis, refresh the crisis management portfolios and prepare for managing the next crisis.

In Coombs' (1999) terminology, the two main stages highlighted by Mitroff and Pearson (1993) are the pre-crisis and the post-crisis. From their perspective, the pre-crisis stage includes signal detection, preparation and prevention, and the post-crisis stage includes recovery and learning.

Similar to the detailed model offered by Mitroff and Pearson (1993), Glaesser (2006) identifies two major phases in the crisis life cycle: crisis prevention and crisis coping. *Crisis prevention* is the proactive anticipation of potential crisis and can be described as two independent processes. The first of these is *crisis precautions*: the theoretical and practical development of risk management and crisis management strategies. The second process is *crisis avoidance*: the ongoing evaluation and identification of potential risks. The aim of this process is to maximize the place's reaction time and to make it possible to contain a potential crisis before it swells into a full-blown crisis.

The second phase in this model is *crisis coping*, which begins once a crisis is identified; its aim is to limit the consequences and bring the crisis situation to an end. The model proposed by Glaesser (2006) makes detailed reference to the crisis and pre-crisis stages, but it lacks a specific reference to the post-crisis stage. Yet this stage carries an extremely important meaning for places, as it serves to restore the place's favorable image.

To summarize and unite the different models into an overall concept of the complete crisis life cycle, we propose later in this chapter an integrated model for the crisis life cycle and its management.

Crisis management

In the past, crises were perceived as *force majeure* – events occurring as an act of God without any way to prevent or control them. When a crisis erupted, the role of the specialists was limited to objective advice on how to deal with the particular unexpected event until it passed. This traditional paradigm in crisis management was a reactive, single agent and limited to the time of the crisis. The present paradigm evinces a broader perspective: the modern practice of crisis management is a proactive, comprehensive and long-term process involving a number of agents from different fields and using a multidisciplinary approach (Specht, 2006).

One definition of the modern paradigm is given by Glaesser (2006): "Crisis management is the strategies, processes and measures which are planned and put into force to prevent and cope with crisis" (p. 22). According to Glaesser, crisis management is the constant practice of avoiding and containing crisis. Unlike the traditional paradigm, which focused on the coping stage, this definition emphasizes the role of planning and prevention as being of equal value in the management processes. The term "crisis management" implies that crises are no longer uncontrollable incidents but events that can be directed, modified and managed. The phrase crisis management is composed of two words which together mean to control, run and operate a sudden extraordinary event. Behind the need for "management" is the active perception that a crisis, like any other complex occurrence, can be controlled and affected. The shift from "handling a crisis" mindset – which dominated the field in the past – to the contemporary "managing a crisis" concept is not just semantic, but rather represents a new paradigm of professional knowledge. The paradigm of crisis management is the direct outcome of the accumulated experience of crisis experts, public relations managers and senior executives who have successfully overcome various crisis situations.

The comprehensive process of crisis management involves many different factors absent from the traditional paradigm of handling a crisis: acts of prevention, acts of preparation, the well-in-advance creation of a crisis management team, preparing risk management and crisis portfolios, training spokespersons and employing general image management techniques. Additionally, the modern paradigm emphasizes partnership with the community as a means for the successful resolution of the crisis. In other words, the resolving process should be undertaken in cooperation with the community and not as an effort external to the community (Specht, 2006). In keeping with the concept of partnership, the organization delivers the important message that it is an integral part of the community and it shares the same duties and rights as everyone else. As noted in Chapter 3, partnership with the community is also a key process in mitigating the negative image of places suffering from an ongoing crisis.

Crisis communication management

The media are well known for their preference for negative news. From the early days of printed journalism, it was clear to editors that stories covering sensations, human suffering, violence and crime were the best way to get passersby to buy the evening paper; this understanding persists even today (Caspi, 1993). In the past, crises caused the same damage as they do in contemporary times, but today the intensive media coverage of crises exerts a marked effect on the course of events, specifically on the decision-making process during the event. In earlier times, an audience far from the heart of the crisis had only partial, mediated and distorted knowledge of it. Once, several weeks or even months would elapse until the public got the relevant information, and when the information arrived it was already out of date. Today, the modern audience is immediately aware of any crisis, its course and its results, regardless of its physical location. In the age of global television networks and especially the Internet, the media have made the world a global village, instantly supplying up-to-date pictures of events taking place virtually anywhere on the planet.

Many scholars have researched the role of the media during crisis situations, leading to a variety of models and definitions, including "reputation management," "issues management," "crisis communication management" and "image restoration," While the accumulated body of knowledge in the field of crisis communication shares many similar concepts, it also contains numerous contradictions among different researchers (Beniot, 1995; Coombs, 1999; Dougherty, 1992; Gonzalez-Herrero and Pratt, 1996; Mansfeld and Pizam, 2006; Smith, 2002; Tarlow, 2001, 2006). Although the field of crisis communication management has been widely covered, most researchers choose to focus on one aspect of crisis communication management, resulting in a lack of an overall perspective on the subject. One researcher who does offer such a holistic approach is Fearn-Banks (1996), who defines crisis communication as the "Communication between the organization and its public prior to, during, and after the negative occurrence" (p. 9). According to this definition, crisis communication is an ongoing process in which the place or organization is constantly communicating with the public. A more detailed view of crisis communication management and its various aspects can be found in the integrated model for crisis management, illustrated in the second part of this chapter.

Applying crisis management and crisis communication management

The second part of this chapter opens with the presentation of an integrated model of crisis management and crisis communication. This is followed by a discussion of the different measures, techniques, procedures and methods listed. Although not all the concepts of crisis management and crisis communication management can be discussed in the present framework, this chapter portrays the major conceptions in crisis and communication management, illustrating the frame of the management process.

As we navigate this maze of concepts and definitions, we propose an Integrated Model of Crisis Management and Crisis Communication Management. The model (Figure 5.1) summarizes and unifies the bodies of knowledge in the fields of crisis, crisis management and crisis communication management. This integration is based on the four stages of a crisis's life cycle – precaution, planning-prevention, crisis coping and post-crisis – and uses these stages to illustrate the different aspects, techniques and activities applied in crisis situations. The perception behind the integrated model is that crisis management and crisis communication management – or image management and place management – are all parallel, ongoing processes. That is, an organization or a place which is managed by a strategic approach will always take simultaneous actions of crisis communication management and of crisis management, whether it is under an actual threat of crisis or not.

A key point in the comprehensive perception of a crisis is that identification and active intervention in the early stages of the crisis life cycle can affect the crisis's development, by restraining and managing it. As a result, the phases of precaution and prevention, at both the organizational and communications levels, are just as important

Crisis life cycle	Crisis management	Crisis communication management
Precaution	Positive organizational environment; open communication between employees, executives and stakeholders; balanced and proper use of organizational resources; health and safety measures; cultivating and motivating human resources	General image management as part of the place's management; media relations; allocating resources for PR; creating rapport with the media; community relations and social contribution
Planning-prevention	Preparing emergency response and action plan; forming crisis management team and special assistance team; risk management; signal detection	Training spokespersons; preparing ready-made media messages; issue management
Crisis coping	Staffing the crisis management center; operating medical team, logistic team, security team and victims' relief team; investigating the cause of the crisis	Crisis communication techniques such as quick response with one, simple message; using a single spokesperson; transparency and creating empathy
Post-crisis	Rehabilitation of infrastructure; re-establishing work routines; compensating victims; debriefing; updating crisis portfolios	Media strategies for improving negative image; activities to change the negative image; debriefing; impression recovery

Figure 5.1   Integrated model for the relations between crisis life cycle, crisis management and crisis communication management

as managing the crisis itself. One of the most important stages is post-crisis, at which time the place's image is restored. As a result, this book focuses mainly on the stage of place recovery, in which media strategies are employed to battle the image crisis and restore a positive image. Following is a discussion of the various components of each stage in the crisis life cycle.

Precaution

In accordance with its name, during the precaution stage most actions taken by organizations and places have nothing to do with a specific crisis situation but mainly concern preventive measures. From the perspective of crisis management, various actions taken at this stage emphasize the creation of a positive, stable, open and safe organizational and work environment. This environment should not be limited to the organization's employees but should extend to its executives and stakeholders, customers and the surrounding community. By creating this positive and supportive environment, the organization can prevent many possible crises such as failures in communication, health and safety issues and negligence.

From the perspective of crisis communication management, this ongoing stage is used to create a strong and favorable image for the place or organization; this is brought about through activities such as social contribution, community relations, allocating resources to PR and creating good media relations. By employing *general image management* techniques, the place maintains its public image and creates a type of "positive credit" that can reduce the effects of future negative events or possible crises.

One key factor in general image management is the creation of good media relations. Experts maintain that good media relations can decrease or even prevent damage caused to a place's image as a result of a crisis event (Lahav, 2004). According to Avraham (2003b), *media relations* is the sum of efforts made by spokespersons and PR experts of organizations or places to establish close relations with journalists and editors based on rapport, trust and mutual understanding. The creation of good media relations is to the advantage of both the organization and the media: as for reporters, their job will become easier if they can be certain that the information they get from the organization is reliable and relevant, and that other reporters have not obtained better or more information. On the other hand, it is easier for spokespersons and PR specialists to deliver their messages through a reporter or an editor with whom they have established rapport and who understands their point of view. At times of crisis or other emergency situations, the value of media relations increases dramatically for both sides.

During a crisis situation negative information will naturally find its way to the media. If good media relations exist, the reporter is more likely to ask for the organization's comments and to take the organization's perspective on the crisis into consideration. This window of opportunity will allow the organization's spokesperson to explain the context in which the negative incident has occurred and to clarify what the organization is doing to repair the damage. Having the opportunity to explain the organization's viewpoint on the perceived crisis exerts a fundamental effect since this may contain or even end the crisis event (White, 2006). In any case, media relations are created because both reporters and spokespersons understand the necessities, considerations and constraints of the other side and try to help each other through a sense of common purpose (Lahav, 2004).

Good media relations are extremely helpful for an organization's spokespersons, yet research has proven that if media relations are poor, communication with the media can be very complicated, especially during a crisis event. In his research on the coverage of places in the national media, Avraham (2003) found that good media relations had a positive effect on the coverage of specific places. Places' spokespeople who invested in creating close relationships by inviting editors to visit their place, assisting reporters in their work and sending a constant stream of reliable information enjoyed better media access in times of crisis and non-crisis alike.

Planning-prevention

In the second stage of crisis management, the place's main goal is to prepare for future crises and to try to prevent them before they get out of control. The main tasks in the planning-prevention stage are the preparation of risk management, an emergency response and action plan, which are parallel to the components of issue management, and the creation of a communication response strategy.

Emergency response and action plan

Being aware of the possibility of an unexpected, unusual and undesired threat that might strike any city, country or tourist destination, many places prepare ahead with an emergency response and action plan (ERAP) for any possible scenario. Because crises tend to be unstable situations that develop quickly and require an immediate response, a ready-made action plan can be priceless (Benoit, 1997). Many experts believe that having a prepared plan is one of the main things distinguishing places that might overcome the crisis much quickly from those that might suffer from it for many years. The creation of an ERAP is based on risk management estimation (Mansfeld and Pizam, 2006). *Risk management* is the detailed inspection of every possible scenario and its short-term effect on various actors and factors such as residents, the tourism industry, media, investments and infrastructure.

After a detailed list of potential hazards is compiled, the next step in fashioning a crisis management strategy is to form a team of "crisis experts" that will cover the various aspects of every potential crisis. A crisis management team (CMT) is a group of cross-functional professionals who can prove helpful when a crisis situation has to be resolved (Coombs, 1999). The crisis management team should include various experts that can help a place, organization or institution handle every possible situation: these are PR specialists, spokespersons, security inspectors, public health experts, hotel managers and other local decision makers. In addition, there should be a special assistance team (SAT), an operational arm subject to the CMT which handles the logistic aspects of the crisis (Glaesser, 2006). Once the CMT and the SAT are formed, an updated contact list, whereby the management of the place can find anyone at any time, should be drawn up and made as widely available as possible. The contact list should be arranged in order of priority according to who should be called first and in what circumstances. It is also helpful to ensure that everyone on the list knows that they hold key positions in case of a crisis, and who else is on their team. In addition to experts, the contact list should include other people whose help might be required such as the heads of different municipal departments, members of state and federal agencies and rescue teams (Dougherty, 1992).

After both the CMT and the risk management estimation are ready, it is advisable to assemble the expert team and devise the ERAP itself by discussing every possible scenario from all relevant angles and to conclude with a written response and action plan. The process of forming the coping strategy is lengthy, but eventually every place should have detailed portfolios for every possible crisis scenario. The ERAP should refer not only to the crisis, but also to all levels of the place including resources, employees, management, consumers, visitors, residents, competitors and governmental authorities (Mitroff and Pearson, 1993). In addition to the coping strategy itself, each portfolio should include relevant background data and the means of contacting other relevant professionals whose help might be required in the specific case.

Issues management

While the common concept for the assessment of future crises by the crisis management method is called "risk management," the same concept is referred to as "issue management" by the crisis communication expertise. The literature suggests different definitions for *"issues management"*; Smith (2002) defines it as "The process by which an organization tries to anticipate emerging issues and respond to them before they get out of hand" (p. 22). Smith suggests that every place or organization should actively look out for potential situations that constitute matters of concern and bring them rapidly under control.

While Smith has a broad view of issues management, other scholars focus more on the context of crises and preparation for their occurrence. According to Gonzalez-Herrero and Pratt (1996), the issue management process "should be concerned with any issue that may have any impact on the organization's well being" (p. 85). A similar and more detailed definition is given by a group director in the global PR firm Ogilvy:

An ongoing process of aligning corporate behavior with stakeholder expectations. Issues become issues when this alignment is missing. But through a process of identifying issues early, prioritizing them, and closely monitoring their evolution, issues can be managed – either by changing the company's behavior or its stakeholders' expectations, or both.

(Winkler, 2006)

In keeping with this definition, Ogilvy PR developed an eight-step program for issues management. Each step is arranged around a guiding question:

1. What issues could arise because of the client's industry or its scale?
2. Which of these issues could cause significant damage to the client's reputation or business operations if not managed effectively?
3. How is this issue evolving, on a monthly or even daily basis?
4. How can we anticipate the course of this evolution and devise an action plan?
5. What steps can we take to change the course of an issue's progression?
6. If the issue developed into a crisis that threatened the company's ability to conduct business, how would we react?
7. Did we respond effectively to the issue, preventing its emergence as a crisis? What lessons were learned?
8. Has the issue lessened in severity over time? Is it still a concern moving forward?

The sum of these eight proposed guiding questions creates an inclusive perspective of each issue and enables managers, experts and professionals to acquire a proper estimation of the potential risk.

To conclude, management of issues can be considered an integral component of reputation management, which helps prevent damage to institutional or place image or to diminish it. A fundamental part of the issues management process is the development of proactive strategies to attempt to change or control an issue as it evolves and is reported in the media. The evolution of issues should be monitored closely by organizations, and the decision to develop a proactive strategy should be made when issues reoccur in the media and are legitimized by journalists (White, 2006).

The preparation of communication response strategy

While the process of issue management focuses on identifying, controlling and preventing potential hazards, this stage has a preparation component as well. With this component, the organization develops a contingency plan for any issue identified in the process of issue management and sets a proactive policy on that issue (Gonzalez-Herrero and Pratt, 1996). As part of the contingency plan, the organization has to prepare a *communication response strategy*, including decisions such as the kind of messages that should or should not be delivered during a time of a future crisis, target audience, channels for delivering the message and who will be the spokesperson. Additionally, the organization should prepare ready-made media messages that can be used in the event of crisis situations.

Crisis coping

Crisis coping is a highly complex task from the perspective of crisis management. At this stage, a wide variety of measures are taken to contain the crisis, reduce its scale and bring it to an end. Among these actions are staffing the crisis management center and operating the special assistance team, medical team, logistics team, security team and victims' relief team. Much can be said about the details of this extremely intricate stage, but we leave this discussion to the dozens of books written on the subject.

From the perspective of crisis communication management, the parallel process to crisis coping is *crisis communication* – the proactive process of communicating during the time of a crisis. As in the preceding stages, a correct, professional and proactive use of communication can ease the perception of the crisis and prevent long-term damage to the place's image. On the other hand, places that do not succeed in gaining control of the crisis coverage and delivering the right messages might find themselves facing a long-term image crisis.

A key concept in crisis communication is the "golden hour." According to Rob Shimmin, Managing Director of Ogilvy Public Relations, the golden hour is "The time between when you control the story and when other parties take the story, shaping the crisis and the public's perceptions of your company." The golden hour is the time when one gains control of the crisis or it goes out of control. One of the best ways the place can gain control is by delivering honest, detailed and reliable information and proving itself to be the best source (Liss, 2002).

Communication response strategies

Once a crisis occurs, many spokespeople try to decide how their place or organization should react. The choice of the most suitable communication response strategy depends on the type of crisis, the place's characteristics, the target audience and other circumstances. According to Stocker (1997), the basic response strategy includes three or four steps: express regret that the situation has happened, act to resolve the situation, ensure the situation will not happen again and if necessary offer restitution to the injured parties.

A more complex pattern of action is suggested by Coombs (1999), who identifies seven communication strategies that can be used in response to a crisis: attacking the accuser, denial, excuse, justification, ingratiation, corrective action and full apology. To distinguish different crisis situations, Coombs presents two dichotomies: whether the crisis is internal or external and whether the crisis is intentional or unintentional. Once the crisis type has been identified, Coombs specifies five guiding questions for further characterization of the crisis:

1. *Evidence*: Is there substantial evidence that the crisis occurred?
2. *Damage*: Is the damage that was caused minor or major?
3. *Victim status*: Has the public suffered from the crisis and does it perceive itself as a victim or not?
4. *Performance history*: Does the organization have a positive or a negative general image based on past performance?
5. *Crisis-response strategy*: What is the most appropriate way to react to the crisis?

In Coombs' model, the answers to the five guiding questions, together with the identification of the crisis type, are the key for selecting a suitable communication response strategy.

Crisis communication

Although its image is one of the organization's main assets, its vulnerability to crisis situation is substantially high. According to Benoit

(1997), the potential damage caused by crises situations can be mini-mized through the use of *crisis communication techniques*. This is based upon two underlying assumptions: crises are a substantial threat to an organization's image and the use of crisis communication can protect or repair the threatened image (Huang, 2006).

Coombs (1999) suggests that effective use of crisis communica-tion should include two key elements: information and compassion. By providing a constant flow of reliable information, the organiza-tion prevents the media from filling in the blanks with speculation and misinformation. On the other hand, giving too much informa-tion could create the impression that the organization carries full responsibility for the crisis and that the crisis situation could have been prevented. While conveying information is related to decreas-ing damage or preventing additional damage to the organization's image, showing compassion is related to restoring a favorable image. By implementing supportive activities for the crisis victims, the orga-nization can easily improve its reputation by a measure involving very little or even the complete absence of a downside. In the field of tourism, Ritchie et al. (2003) emphasize the different roles of crisis communication as a means of recovery: "Crisis communication and marketing is important to provide information to key publics and to help tourism destinations limit the impact of a crisis as well as help them recover from incidents by safe-guarding the destinations image and reputation which is of immense value to tourism destinations" (p. 203).

Crisis communication techniques

One major aspect of crisis communication is the crisis communication techniques, a set of practical procedures applied to control the story at any given time. Coombs (1999) isolates four basic principles of crisis communication:

1. *Respond quickly*. Develop two-way communication with the media to reduce misinformation and help get your message through.
2. *Speak with one voice*. By being consistent with one spokesperson, the organization can develop its key messages and discourage the use of unofficial spokespeople.
3. *Openness*. Allow high availability to the media, willingness to dis-close information and honesty.
4. *Express sympathy* to the victims.

As elementary as these basic guidelines are, many researchers and professionals concur with them. The field of crisis communication techniques is mentioned more frequently in the crisis management literature than any other topic (Coombs, 1999).

Summing up the work of many scholars and PR experts, we note some basic practical suggestions that are easily implemented in communication during a crisis:

- *Keep it simple.* No matter how complex the situation is, keep your message short and simple so everyone can remember and understand it.
- *Stick to your message.* Bring all questions back to your crisis media message and repeat it. A *crisis media message* is a short text answering three basic questions: (1) what went wrong; (2) how it will be fixed; (3) how we can ensure it will not happen again.
- *Provide as much information as possible.* If the media get the feeling that you are hiding something they will go and get the facts themselves, or even worse, start speculating.
- *Empathize.* The first communication about the crisis should include information about the victims, and what is being done to help them.

Spinning a crisis using empathy

When two French tourists who were sunbathing in **Miami** Beach were accidentally run down during a police chase, the tourism director immediately got involved personally, showing his concern for the victims. A flight was arranged for the grieving parents right away; the tourism director met them personally at the airport and spent the evening with the family at the hospital. As a result of the tourism director's involvement, the focus in the next day's newspapers was an emotional personal story rather than an article on police negligence.

- *Remember Machiavelli.* "Give good news over time, bad news all at once."
- *Create personal relations with the journalists.* During a crisis the role of media relations is more important than ever. Help journalists with accommodations, refreshments, printed data and every other possible assistance. Let them feel comfortable, safe and welcome.
- *Update your employees.* Your workers are an important asset and you should keep them updated with the information you want them to know. Instead of letting them count on the media or rumors,

update them constantly with your version of the story, using your organization's website or internal newsletters.

- *Update your website.* A place's website is a unique method of communication, allowing the place to control the flow and content of outgoing news. To keep your website a relevant source of information update it frequently, in both crisis and non-crisis times.
- *Spotlight positive aspects in the crisis.* Based on the proactive method, instead of letting the media search for stories to fill airtime, try to feed the media with the stories you want to be told. For example, look for positive human-interest stories, such as local residents assisting victims.

Although being very diverse, the thread connecting all these guidelines, suggestions and techniques is the perception of crisis communication as an active process. In this process, the aim of the techniques is to enable places and organizations to deliver their side of the story and to take control over the crisis event.

Sources: Coombs (1999); White (2006); World Tourism Organization (2006); http://www.satte.org; http://www.brandchannel.com.

Post-crisis

In every crisis, there is a post-crisis stage, starting once the smoke has cleared and lasting months or even years after the physical crisis has faded. From the crisis management perspective, much effort is invested to restore and rehabilitate the place's facilities and infrastructure. The aim at this stage is to re-establish work routines and to operate the place regularly. In addition to the physical acts, strategic actions of learning and debriefing should be undertaken to implement the lessons learned from the recent event. The emergency response and action plan should be revised and updated, in readiness for the occurrence of a future crisis.

In parallel to restoring infrastructure, restoring a place's positive image is a long and elaborate task. A traditional Far Eastern adage asserts that "Every problem is a treasure," implying that a place can also gain from a crisis situation. If a place or organization overcomes the problem that caused the crisis, it will eventually become more enhanced and stable than it was before. Although crises have a destructive potential, they can help places identify weakness and improve internal communication, management and functioning during the difficult times and facilitate preparedness for future crises (White, 2006).

In the post-crisis stage, a place should monitor the cause of the event and make sure the crisis is past; it should continue to pay attention to the victims and express concern for their suffering, evaluate how the crisis plan worked and how it can be improved and develop a long-term media strategy to restore its public image (Gonzalez-Herrero and Pratt, 1996). Additionally, initiatives need to be taken in this stage in order to regain the trust of stakeholders, employees and the public.

In the field of public relations, a series of proactive steps is taken by tourist destinations, cities and countries to deliver the message that it is "business as usual" and all facilities and attractions are open and accessible to the public. Apart from the regular flow of PR items, events such as festivals, exhibitions and visits of celebrities, journalists and other opinion leaders are relayed, supporting the restored image (Avraham, 2004; Avraham and Ketter, 2006). Furthermore, many places choose to launch full-scale campaigns aimed at allaying the negative image and restoring a favorable one. A detailed discussion over the use of media strategies to improve a place's negative image can be found in the second part of the book.

Case study in crisis communication management

The case of the Travel Industry Association of America following 9/11

Following the terror attack on the World Trade Center in **New York City**, the Travel Industry Association of America (TIA) had to come up with an immediate response. In a matter of hours, a travel industry recovery coalition was formed, with representatives of 26 sectors of the US travel and tourism industry. The outcome was a 10-week counter-offensive plan, with two major goals: to ensure safe, secure travel, and to restore travelers' confidence.

The first step of the plan was the choice of one message and its delivery to the media. The chosen message was "Travel is a fundamental American freedom." Following that, the TIA provided the media with spokespeople, facts, figures and other materials to satisfy media hunger for news and to fill television airtime with the single chosen message. The second step of the plan was to mount a national newspaper advertising campaign. From two focus groups, held in **New York City** and **Ohio**, it became clear that customers wanted to know that things were being done to make traveling safe again. In the patriotic spirit of those days, the advertisement was based on the media strategy of patriotism and nationalism (see discussion in the next chapters): "America was founded, expanded and made great by travelers. And nobody can take that away from us. Not now. Not ever." The message in the next ad in the campaign was "It's your country. See it. See America" (SeeAmerica.org is a non-profit, non-commercial consumer website that links to every travel industry organization in the United States). This advertisement was a template that members of the TIA could download from their websites and wrap around their advertisements. In addition to the ad campaign, the Veterans' Day holiday was announced as "See America Day," encouraging people to start traveling again.

The next step on the recovery campaign was a television advertisement featuring President Bush and actual travel industry workers. This campaign was taken to international trade shows, aiming to spread the news, and to major local TV stations, localizing the message. At this point the TIA undertook a new initiative in partnership with the US Postal Service. The Postal Service released a new series of stamps called "Greetings from America" that featured a stamp for each state. The release of the new stamps was accompanied by a sweepstake on the See America website, offering a free 1-week dream vacation in each of the 50 states.

In sum, the TIA crisis management plan can be reduced to four succinct points:

1. "Develop a strategy and message and stay with it.
2. Engage the entire industry and government too.
3. Leverage your resources so everyone can participate.
4. Move quickly and take control of the situation – you cannot afford to wait and let it control you." (p. 154)

Source: (Koehl, in Deuschl, 2006).

Summary

In this chapter, we have analyzed the concepts of crisis management and crisis communication management, as well as their everyday practice in places and organizations. Both concepts were discussed in accordance with the four stages of the crisis life cycle: precaution, planning-prevention, crisis coping and post-crisis. The perspective used in this discussion was of the modern paradigm for crisis management, describing those processes as holistic, ongoing, comprehensive and active. From our discussion, it is clear that the concepts of crisis management and crisis communication management are strongly related to each other. Both concepts are well elaborated in the proposed model and followed by a set of guidelines for their implementation by any city, country or tourist destination.

Part Two
From Theory to Practice

In the first part of this book, we discussed relevant theoretical knowledge in the field of place marketing, such as place branding, public image, strategic image management, consumer behavior and crisis management. Now it is time to shift from theory to practice and see what actions should be taken by place marketers to improve a place's negative image during or after a crisis.

The second part of this book consists of five chapters. First, in Chapter 6, we will introduce the factors that should be taken into account when analyzing the crisis and choosing the proper marketing recovery strategy. The following three chapters present different strategies implemented by cities, countries and tourist destinations to alter negative images. Chapter 7 elaborates on media strategies, focusing on the source of the message; Chapter 8 sets forth media strategies that focus on the message itself; and Chapter 9 elucidates media strategies that focus on the target audience. To wrap it all up, Chapter 10 introduces a concluding model which illustrates the decision-making process in the choice of a media strategy for improving a place's image.

6 Preliminary analysis: crisis, audience and place characteristics (CAP)

Every marketing process for any product or service starts with a preliminary analysis of the product's characteristics, values, advantages, disadvantages, life cycle, competitors, the market in which it is active and the public that might consume the product. Such an analysis is done by place marketers, who must familiarize themselves with the place they are marketing. The process usually includes several visits to the place in order to understand the experiences, values and feelings it radiates. At the same time, a grasp is gained of its spirit and atmosphere, and valuable information is gathered on such matters as its residents, climate, business opportunities, attractions and choice of recreational activities.

As noted in earlier chapters, there are several kinds of crises and each requires its own handling and marketing recovery strategy. To determine the correct strategy to apply, a preliminary analysis of the current crisis situation is recommended. The purpose is to gain better understanding of the negative events and to use this understanding to choose the most suitable recovery strategy.

For in-depth understanding of the given crisis, this chapter offers an easy-to-use preliminary analysis, as illustrated in Figure 6.1, of three groups of characteristics: crisis characteristics, audience characteristics and place characteristics (CAP). The preliminary analysis, we believe, is a powerful tool for evaluating the crisis situation and serves as a guideline when choosing media strategies to overcome the image crisis.

Crisis characteristics	Audience characteristics	Place characteristics
1. Geographical scale 2. Origin of casualties 3. Stage and duration 4. Type of threat and scale of damage	1. Proximity to the place 2. Type and size 3. Knowledge of crisis and place 4. Sources of information 5. Social–political environment	1. Power and status 2. Resources available 3. Location 4. Life cycle 5. Regime and leadership

Figure 6.1   CAP analysis

Crisis characteristics

When assessing a crisis, the first thing we should analyze is the crisis characteristics. Crises, as we know, differ greatly. Some are caused by terror attacks on tourist destinations, others by a sudden plague; certain crises cause enormous damage and thousands of casualties, and others have no casualties; there are prolonged crises and short-lived ones. With all these variations different recovery strategies are obviously necessary. To refine crisis analysis we suggest an examination of each of these characteristics: geographical scale, casualties, duration and damage wrought.

Geographical scale

There are two major levels on which to define the physical boundaries of the crisis – the international and the national. On the international level, it is advisable to examine which countries are affected; on the national level, the regions/cities/resorts struck by the crisis should be noted. In the case of a limited-scale crisis, one direct result of this quick examination can be the use of a media strategy called "limiting the crisis' geographical scale." In such a case, the country marketers inform tourists that the crisis is limited to a certain region in the country, and it is still safe to visit other regions. The crisis' geographical scale is an important factor, and a place's location at the heart, or on the periphery, of a crisis area can affect the choice of marketing recovery strategy.

Origin of casualties: local or foreigner?

Another issue arising from the geographical location of a crisis is the nationality or the origin of the casualties. When the victims of a crisis are tourists – especially from first-world countries – the crisis will have wide-scale media coverage; when the victims are locals from third-world countries, the crisis is more likely to receive limited coverage. The amount of media coverage, as we have mentioned, may affect the perception of the crisis severity, unfortunate as this may be. Studies in media coverage found that the international media have a "scale of blood" according to which the odds of a crisis in a third-world country winning media coverage increase as the number of foreign casualties rises. Beirman (2006), for example, asserts that the **Philippines** has suffered from terrorism since the early 1990s but only "attacks against foreign tourists have raised the media profile of this problem" (p. 254).

In any event, not just the presence of foreigners matters, but their nationality as well. For example, if several visitors from **Ethiopia** are injured by a terror act in **Somalia**, it is unlikely that the incident will be covered by the international media. Over the years, the international media organizations seem to have adopted the perception that the blood of North Americans and Western European citizens is worth more than the blood of citizens of the third world. According to Adams (1986), the measure of news coverage for a dead West European is 3 times that of a dead East European, 9 times that of a dead Latin American, 11 times that of a dead Middle Easterner and 12 times that of a dead Asian. Beirman (2006) states that one of the main reasons for the high coverage of the **Bali** terror attack in October 2002 was the fact that the majority of the victims were from Western countries. As inappropriate as this phenomenon is, it still affects the choice of media recovery strategy; for example, if there were no Western casualties in a crisis that has taken place in a third-world country, it is quite likely that the crisis has got very little media attention and the place's image has not been damaged. In that case, the place marketers should ignore the negative event in their ads and PR campaign.

Stage and duration

Crises also differ in their length and have various stages. Time is another important factor for analyzing a crisis: how much time has passed since the crisis started and at what stage is the crisis now? These answers will help us find out if the current negative events are part of an ongoing crisis or a one-off event. The first necessary distinction is between long-term and short-term crises. In the case of the former, where we may expect many negative events, it is more likely that the target audience has heard about the crisis. By contrast, a short-term crisis may well be concluded without news of it reaching the ears of the target audience. In that case, local decision makers might do well to ignore the crisis and act as if it is "business as usual."

As noted earlier, an efficient campaign should ordinarily focus on a single message; at the height of the crisis, in its initial stages, this message should focus on minimizing damage to the place's image, while in the final stages the message should focus on getting back to regular business. Such messages can indicate that the tourism infrastructure is undamaged, attractions are fully open and tourists are back. To conclude, crisis duration and stage have an effect on the choice of media recovery strategy. Every stage in the crisis life cycle renders its unique messages and makes different use of advertising and PR resources to alter the negative image created (Mansfeld, 1999, 2006).

Type of threat and scale of damage

Crises may also differ in their kind, the type of threat they present and the scale of damage they cause. Each of these three factors has an effect over the choice of media recovery strategy.

Types of crisis and types of threat

According to Mansfeld and Pizam (2006), crises may erupt from criminal activity, terror, political unrest, natural disasters and epidemics (for elaboration of types of crisis please see Chapter 5). Each crisis type is perceived differently by the target audience and has different consequences for consumer behavior. For example, it is likely that a crisis threatening the personal safety of tourists will be perceived as more severe than a crisis causing them physical inconvenience resulting from poor infrastructure or extreme climate.

In addition to its direct effect on consumer behavior, the type of crisis may also affect its media coverage, especially in crises that carry emotional overtones. Newspeople seem to have adopted the notion that the more a crisis can trigger viewers' emotions and keep them from switching channels, the more coverage it should get. An emotional element appears in a news story when it involves human drama, tension, romance, adventure, tragedy and victims (Glaesser, 2006). This element, together with others such as physical proximity and cultural proximity, makes up the total news value of the crisis; the higher is this total, the more media coverage the crisis will receive.

Crisis severity and scale of damage caused

Another influential factor in assessing a crisis is the severity of the crisis and the scale of the damage caused. Specifically, it is important to examine whether the tourism infrastructure has been damaged and whether incoming tourists will be able to enjoy the same variety of attractions that the place had to offer before the crisis. Naturally, places that have sustained damage to their tourism infrastructure must employ different recovery strategies than those for places that are not damaged. This conclusion also holds for places that have undergone a crisis and are now trying to attract investors, firms and residents. In this case, the relevant infrastructure includes telecommunication, electrical power and transportation. If these infrastructures have been damaged, it might be better to delay the marketing process and start with infrastructure rehabilitation.

Audience characteristics

Different target audiences are motivated by different needs, have different perceptions of places and are differently affected by the occurrence of a crisis event. Many studies have been conducted on the audience and their important role in the communication process (Caspi, 1993). The target audience has key importance in the marketing process: delivery of messages is useless if the target audience does not accept them. Because of their immense value, we recommend five dimensions for analyzing the target audience: proximity of the audience to the place in crisis, type of audience and their size, knowledge of the crisis and of the place, sources of information and the social–political environment in which the audience live and operate.

Proximity/distance between the target audience and the place in crisis

Different kinds of proximity or distance may exist between the target audience in a certain place and in other places: geographical, social, religious, political–ideological and cultural. The level of proximity or distance affects our knowledge, perceptions and attitudes to other places. It also influences our interest and the relevance of what happened "there" to our life. The most basic kind of proximity is geographical, in that we feel close to places that are physically close to us (in times of peace, of course). By contrast, faraway places are often overlooked by us or our media and are associated with general stereotypes. But it is not just a matter of geographical distance; we feel closer to places which have a similar regime, speak the same language and share the same culture and religion as ours (Avraham, 2003b). This serves for understanding the close relations, say, between **Spain**, **Portugal** and the countries of South America.

Just as this feeling of proximity/distance towards others affects our personal standing, so too does it affect the perceptions of journalists and editors. For example, the **German** media will cover news from **Austria** intensively due to their geographical/cultural proximity and the general belief that the German people are interested in knowing what is happening in that country. On the other hand, media of other countries that have no feeling of proximity to Austria will not cover news from Austria as intensively.

In our case, the level of proximity between two countries will also affect the amount and type of media coverage a crisis will receive. Proximity generates interest, which works on newsroom considerations and routines. For example, it is reasonable to believe that a crisis in Europe, involving world-class tourist attractions and harming European tourists, will receive wide media coverage in the Western media. But a crisis in a third-world country erupting due to local conflicts and affecting the local residents is less likely to gain intensive media coverage in the West.

In addition to its influence on media routines, proximity/distance also affects the way the target audience perceives, accepts and reacts to the news and marketing campaigns of a certain place. In cases of distant places (and not just because of geography), a more extreme media strategy is advised, so as to capture the audience's attention. However, a place that is perceived as close and enjoys proximity to the target audience may use media strategies that highlight the similarity between the residents of the two places, as we shall see later. One such example is a campaign launched by **Israel** aimed at improving its image among Americans. Relying on the motif of proximity, the campaign highlighted that both countries are democracies, were founded by immigrants and are technologically advanced.

Audience type and size

A place that suffers from an image crisis should be marketed differently for different audiences. For example, addressing an audience that goes to a place for religious reasons is different than addressing an audience seeking a quiet holiday, cultural activities and historical monuments. The former will likewise be less concerned about the crisis than the latter. Another important factor to be assessed is the size of the target audience and how many of them know about the crisis. If, for example, the vast majority of the target audience has not heard of the crises, it might be a waste of resources to launch a campaign aimed at overcoming it.

Audience knowledge and place's former image

Images of people, subjects and places evolve over time (Kunczik, 1997). The mind processes new information and adds it to the existing images. If, for example, the media reports the murder of a tourist in a place that was considered safe, it is more likely that part of the audience will preserve the place's former positive image, on the grounds that "That kind of incident can happen anywhere." But another part of the audience that perceives the place differentially will now consider it a "dangerous place" for tourists. Hence the place's former image affects the way new information about the place is accepted and processed. When a place has a history of involvement in conflicts, violence and negative events, one more report on disorder will be received differently from such a report about a place that was never associated to violence and conflict. The result is that when a violent incident occurs in a place known to be risky, it will have a greater influence on that place's image than if it happened at a place free of any existing problematic image. Similarly, a racist incident that occurred in a place that was associated with racism in the past is much more likely to lead the place into crises.

The principle whereby a place's existing image affects its resistance to image crisis is also presented by Elizur (1987). Elizur presents a focus–periphery model (Figure 6.2), with the focus containing the

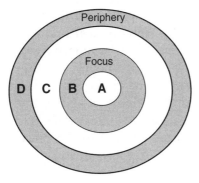

Figure 6.2 Focus–periphery model.
Source: Elizur, 1987

most salient traits in the place's image (the inner circles marked A and B), and less salient traits being located at the periphery (the outer circles marked C and D). Elizur believes that the effects of memory, time and forgetting can be seen on this mapping. "Traits located in the focus of the image are very clear in the mind of the image holder; those located out near the periphery become hazier as distance increases from the focus" (p. 19). We tend to forget the traits of a certain place if we are not given reminders of new traits in the present. Most of these reminders come to us via the mass media when events or crises occur in which places are involved. Cognitive traits are thus able to shift back and forth between focus and periphery. This character of the focus–periphery model turns it into a more dynamic model of image.

An interesting example of the effect of a place's past image on its current image is presented by Krauze (1994, in Kunczik, 1997). In his article, Krauze argued that old stereotypes of **Mexico** affect the present (1994) coverage of this country in the international media. He asserted that the coverage of negative events such as murder, violence and revolt awake the old negative images of Mexico as a "barbarous, violent and unstable country" (p. 7). Another aspect resulting from the place's former image is that the images of places which are well-established brands have a greater durability in crisis events, such as **Club Med, Disneyland** and **Paris**. Since the audience has so many good images associated with these places, these images are much more durable. For places with such a strong and positive image, it is advised to use a more moderate media strategy and sometimes even to ignore the crisis event, letting the passage of time re-establish the place's positive image.

In addition to the need to understand the former image among the audience of the place combating a crisis, it is also important to find out what the audience knows about the crisis event, its causes and its consequences. Answering those questions can assist place marketers in choosing the most appropriate media messages. For example, if the audience has highly stereotypical knowledge about the crisis it might be better to increase their familiarity with the situation so they can break free of their former images. Another central aspect in the audience's knowledge of the crisis is the perceived severity of the crisis. Crises that are perceived as severe and that cause booking cancellations demand an immediate and sharp response. On the other hand, if visitors continue coming to the place despite the negative events, a more moderate response strategy is advised.

Sources and kinds of information

Our source of information can also affect the way we perceive the occurrence of events. In the field of marketing, as noted in Chapter 4, we distinguish between two sources of information: one coming from personal experience and the other coming via a mediator. In the following section, we elaborate on the source of information and its credibility from the perspective of choosing a marketing recovery strategy.

First-hand information is created when we visit a place and see it with our own eyes; a secondary source of information is delivered to us by a mediator, such as a friend or a relative who visited the place, or by the media, which tell us about the place and its characteristics. As noted in Chapter 2, the media are our main source of information about distant places. The information delivered by the media is not perceived as essential for most audiences, so they do not try to reach additional sources about crises in foreign news broadcasts or to obtain first-hand information. In addition, the representation delivered by the media can sometimes be manipulative (Kunczik, 1997), and a check should be made of whether the crisis is represented in a balanced manner, if the causes of the crisis are explained and whether the crisis is being dramatized to increase its news value. In extreme cases, where the media present a distorted image very different from reality, a proper media strategy might include the use of alternative sources in order to deliver contrary messages, as set out in the next chapter.

The source's credibility

Another dimension for estimating an audience's knowledge and perceptions is the source's credibility. Examining this rests on people's tendency to ascribe high credibility to sources such as friends and relatives. It is no use for campaign managers to try and undermine information from those sources or damage their credibility. However, in most cases the main source of information is television or newspapers, which have relatively low credibility in several societies. Once the campaign managers succeed in undermining the media's credibility, the messages and negative images delivered by it will also be perceived as unreliable. Undermining media credibility as a response strategy is not easy to implement, especially in countries where the media are perceived as credible. By contrast, in some Western countries the media and their neutrality are treated with fundamental skepticism, and in those cases this strategy might succeed.

Social–political environment and essential values

Marketing in general and delivering specific messages in particular depend on the social–political environment (Avraham, 2003a). The success of a campaign rests heavily on the setting: some messages can be extremely effective in one society and exert very little influence in another. Accordingly, marketing professionals try to take advantage of local values to promote certain products. For example, if the essential values in a certain society are individualism, modernity and multiculturalism, marketers will utilize them to claim that their product promotes them (Hestroni, 2000).

Marketers also use local myths, stereotypes, celebrities and other common perceptions, aiming to link them to the goods they are selling. For example, First and Avraham (2007) found that real-estate campaigns in **Israel** use many motifs associated with the United States. According to their research, this immense use of the American flag, the English language and American landscapes is founded on the positive image of the United States among Israelis. This example serves as additional proof of the benefits accrued from understanding the target audience's values, especially those they identify with, those they hold in high esteem, what are they afraid of and what their aspirations are. Another interesting example of how marketers use local trends to promote places can be found in research by Avraham (2003a). The study illustrates how advertising firms employ the trend of "getting close to nature" for marketing real-estate projects. Their ads use green as a dominant color, visuals of animals, plants and wild landscapes and projects' names taken from the world of nature.

It is only natural for marketing professionals to analyze the dominant values in a certain society and to use them to promote a place. If the target audience in a certain society appreciates places that are environment-friendly and promote quality of life, these values should be highlighted in the marketing process. Some of those values are stable, others are constantly changing trends. For example, following the 9/11 terror attacks, the marketers of **New York** took advantage of national patriotic feelings to promote the city. This approach was most successful at the time, but it is doubtful that the same messages can be used in other types of crisis. Some response strategies may be limited to certain type of crisis and certain societies.

Place characteristics

Places naturally differ greatly. In the international arena these differences may be expressed by a country's characteristics, such as geographical location, size, international status, type of regime and the economy. Differences between countries are also reflected in the actions that their decision makers can permit themselves. For example, countries with confident leaders can engage a bold response strategy for a crisis that many other countries would never even consider. Likewise successful cities, with high national status and a profusion of resources, can launch expensive campaigns that other cities cannot afford. Even if two countries suffer from the same type of crisis and both aim at the same target audience, they will probably use different recovery strategy due to their characteristics. These differences are especially salient in respect to third-world countries as opposed to first-world countries: in most cases the former have lower status and fewer resources and have to invest far more effort in altering their image.

A place's characteristics should be analyzed in regard to five major concepts: power and status, resources, geographical location, the place's life cycle and the type of regime and leadership. In some cases these concepts may be closely correlated; for example, the location of a country in Western Europe is associated with its status, resources, its life cycle and the type of its regime and leadership. This correlation notwithstanding, we next analyze each factor separately and in depth.

Power and status

As noted, places differ in their national and international power and status. The common factors used to gauge a place's status or power include physical resources such as size, economic stability and natural treasures and abstract resources such as the place's image and cultural centrality. Using these two groups of factors, we distinguish places with salient and accessible power from places with hidden and inaccessible power. A similar distinction, between hard and soft factors, is suggested by Kotler et al. (2002). According to these authors, "The hard factors are those that can be measured in more-or-less objective term (such as economic stability, productivity, costs, local support services and networks, communication infrastructure and strategic location). Soft factors are not so easily measured and represent the more subjective characteristics of a place (quality of life, culture and management style and others)" (p. 68).

Similarly, Wolfsfeld (1991) distinguishes place's general status from its status in the media. General status consists of the place's resources, its physical size and its ability to influence the national decisions makers; in the media, a place's status is measured by its news value and its importance in the minds of journalists and editors. Many studies found a firm link between a place's general power and its power in the media, as the media tend to keep track of the powers that be. Headquarters of news corporations are moreover located in the hubs of political, economical and cultural power, such as **New York**, **London**, **Paris**, **Los Angeles** and **Brussels**, a circumstance that only supports and magnifies their power (Avraham, 2003a). Shoemaker and Reese (1996) argue that the media reflect the "geography of power." Powerful countries in the international arena receive frequent and diverse coverage, whereas weaker countries receive little coverage, usually only in the event of a disaster or crisis. These authors believe that the news reflects society's distribution of power, and that is why media organizations locate their offices close to national sources of power such as financial, bureaucratic, political or cultural institutions. These centers are the sites from which most news stories emanate (Dominick, 1977; Graber, 1989).

Newspeople facilitate access to certain places, providing them with extensive, favorable coverage, thereby winning legitimacy for their status and power. Access to other places is blocked. The groups, classes and places that receive little coverage and are not shown in the media are precisely those that receive little attention in social, economic and cultural life (van Dijk, 1996). People or places that do not belong to the elite or to powerful groups receive media coverage only when they are involved in political activities or are victims of disaster or crime. The result is that a very small number of people or places can influence the construction of reality for a country or a society (Walmsley, 1982). Issues and players on the national news scene are simply a reflection of a country's power and control structure (Jakubowicz et al., 1994). The key concept is *"media access."* Barzel (1976) defines this term as the freedom of a non-media-related person to reach the media: the ease with which any person in society can publicize his/her opinions or actions through the media. Barzel argues that it is reporters who decide who will have this access, and this decision depends on external and internal factors (Avraham, 2003b).

Marginal places' lack of power and low organizational levels cause the media to disregard them or cover them unfavorably. These actions in turn promote the formation of stereotypes and prejudices by the media. van Dijk (1988b) notes that Western media tend to focus on negative events, particularly with regard to non-majority social groups. Negative actions associated with marginal groups or places are of high news value, because they contain deviance, violence and disorder and reinforce the already unfavorable prejudices against marginal groups or places. The result is that violence, crime, disorder and the like continue to be associated with marginal places. As the media do not cover marginal places unless the context is unfavorable, these less-favored groups/places, with few resources at their disposal, resort to acts of protest or even violence in order to receive coverage and deliver their messages of discrimination and injustice. Wolfsfeld (1991) describes this phenomenon as entering the media "through the back door," while the "front door" is reserved for social groups and pivotal places with high media status and abundant resources. Marginal places' entrance through the "back door" has a price: their image is further ruined, and every negative stereotype about them is reinforced still more (Avraham, 2003b).

Resource availability

A place's resources are key elements in choosing a media strategy, as altering a negative image can be very costly in most cases. One reason for the high cost of campaigns is the price of media space, among other things. For example, the campaign to re-attract tourism to **Washington, DC** following 9/11 was estimated at US $3.37 million (Stafford et al., 2006), and the campaign to restore tourism to **Singapore** following the SARS epidemic was estimated at US $33 million (Beirman, 2006). Most places cannot afford such sums, so less costly media strategies are more recommended for them. Other than money, a place may have various resources such as international status and rare attractions.

Allocating resources to event production

Every place needs money to market itself effectively (Avraham, 2003a; Wolfsfeld, 1997). Hiring spokespersons, conducting image surveys, buying media space and producing events can all be very expensive; hence the choice of media strategy is directly affected by the place's resources. For example, if a place chooses to produce sports events, music festivals and other cultural activities to attract visitors and journalists, it requires many resources. Resources can also be used to finance other image-altering initiatives such as providing journalists and opinion shapers with free air tickets, free tours and free entrance to local attractions. This was exactly the case following 9/11, when **New York City** handed out free tickets for Broadway shows to attract tourists. By contrast, places without such resources cannot afford to spend money on producing spotlight events and have to choose modest responses. To conclude, producing mega-events is mainly possible for rich states or cities, a fact that reinforces their image (which is already positive) and facilitates their rapid management of crisis events. Still, it is also possible to rely more on PR than on advertising, to cooperate with local firms and tourist organizations and to create successful events without spending a fortune, as elaborated in Chapter 8.

Type and variety of tourist attractions

Besides financial resources, places differ in the amount, type and variety of tourist attractions they offer and in the demographic characteristics of the visitors they attract. Before elaborating this point, we note that many places still lack a significant amount of attractions of any kind to draw tourists, immigrants or investors. These places will be extremely hard-pressed to improve their images if they cannot attract outside audience and change their negative stereotype as a result. If a place does attract visitors, attention should be paid to the type of attractions it offers and the audience to which they appeal. If, for example, a place that offers sea-and-sun tourism suffers an image crisis, it will be very easy for its audience to find an alternative since the same kind of holiday can be taken at many places. But if a crisis befalls a place that offers unique experiences, such as **Egypt**, **Paris** or **Venice**, it is reasonable to believe that these places will overcome the crisis much faster because the attractions they offer are almost irreplaceable. Similarly, places that offer religious sites usually have high durability for crises. One such place is the city of **Mecca** in Saudi Arabia, which attracts millions of pilgrims every year regardless of tragedies that take place during the pilgrimage, caused by stampedes, fires and hotels collapsing, all of which have happened in recent years. Large numbers of pilgrims likewise travel annually to **Rome**, **Jerusalem** and **Nazareth**, hardly considering the image of those places.

Existence of national/international firms, institutions or celebrities

Another characteristic differentiating places is the presence of local celebrities, firms and institutions that are famous and esteemed on the national level. The importance of having celebrities and prestigious institutions located in a place is their ability to attract positive media attention. Thus, celebrities, firms and institutions can also be considered a resource. In the case of celebrities, the media's tendency to cover them is based on the hypothesis that the public shows keen interest in their lives. Taking advantage of this, many places use celebrities' familiarity, prestige, credibility and status as opinion shapers to alter their image. The utilization of famous musicians, actors and sportspeople is elaborated in Chapter 7. Places can also rely on well-known firms or prestigious institutions in their marketing process. For example, firms such as Coca-Cola, Hershey and Volkswagen and institutions such as MIT, Harvard and the London School of Economics have all been used to promote the places where they are located. Like attractions or historical monuments, institutions and renowned figures are an asset for the status of cities and regions (Packard, in Birnboim-Karmeli, 1994). In her study of the Narcissus Hill neighborhood in **Tel Aviv**, Birnboim-Karmeli (1994) demonstrates how media coverage of institutions located in the area and interviews with celebrity residents raised the status of the neighborhood and identified it with the socio-economic elite. As we have mentioned, due to the media's tendency to cover members of the elite (Barzel, 1976), the more such members are present at a certain event the greater is the likelihood that it will become news (Epstein, 1973; Gans, 1979; Roeh, 1994). Therefore, places with important institutions (hence members of the elite operating in them) will receive more extensive news coverage. Peripheral locations will receive coverage when nationally known figures go there to visit (Barzel, 1976). Brooker-Gross (1983) notes that famous people will be covered by the media regardless of their location, whereas "ordinary" people will be covered only if they are involved in important events in central locations.

Location and closeness to the core of the crisis

According to a popular cliché, the three main factors in choosing a real-estate property are "Location, location and . . . location." Without doubt a good location is an important advantage for any country, city or tourist destination. Imagining for a moment that the people of **Switzerland** had established their country in central Africa, it is very likely that the country's image, economic indicators, type of regime, industry and number of visitors would have been completely different from those in actual Switzerland. For this reason and others, a place's geographical location is another factor used for choosing a proper media strategy. A strategy applied by a country located in Europe or North America and suffering from an image crisis will probably be entirely different from a strategy chosen by a country located in Asia or South America and suffering from a similar crisis. One of the main reasons for this is the proximity and high accessibility of Europeans, who can easily travel to a place that has undergone a crisis and also break the stereotype created by earlier visits. This audience will perceive the place in crisis in a much less stereotypical way and with fewer generalizations than we usually tend to make regarding remote and unfamiliar places that are engaged in crises.

A country's location exerts different kinds of effects on its image. Some geographical regions are associated with conflict, natural disaster or terror, and the occurrence of a single crisis event can easily evoke these associations and cause a full-scale image crisis (Elizur, 1987). For example, a minor terror attack in **Tunisia** may have a severe effect on the country's image due to its location in the Middle East – a region which is perceived as dangerous and unstable. Should the same event occur in a European country, its effect would most probably not be as dramatic because Europe is conceived as safer than the Middle East. Another important factor arising from the place's location is its distance from the core of the crisis. Specifically, it should be assessed whether the place is at this core or on the margins. If the latter is the case, it might be advisable to represent the place as an independent region, as in the cases of **Nova Scotia**, **Sinai** and **Eilat** (for elaboration please see Chapter 8).

A place's life cycle

Like any person or product, places have life cycle. Some places are still at an early stage, battling for recognition and market share, others are developed and well established, and the last kind of places is slowly becoming irrelevant with the passage of time. The marketing of a place is affected by its life-cycle stage; marketing an unfamiliar place is significantly different from marketing one that is well known (Kotler and Armstrong, 1989). Accordingly, crisis-response strategies for places at different stages will differ too; new and unfamiliar places are more likely to choose an extreme and bold strategy, while places which have gained some reputation can achieve the same effect by employing a moderate strategy. Very few sources of knowledge exist about new places, but many people have visited the familiar ones and they counterbalance the stories of the crisis against their own positive experiences. The personal stories of friends and relatives are also perceived as more reliable than the negative media coverage.

What is the type of regime and what is the local leadership quality?

Not surprisingly, local leadership has the power to make a place prosper and, on the other hand, to create place associations of social problems, economic recession and image crises. The field of urban studies is replete with tales of failure or prosperity, all dependent on the actions of the local leadership. The upshot is that places alike in location, population and sources of income have developed differently due to the quality of the local leadership. Raising the discussion to the international level, here too the type of regime can affect countries and their success. Just as the type of regime and the actions of local leaders affect a place's economic prosperity and the way it is managed, they can also affect the choice of media strategy for marketing the place. For example, democracies oblige local leaders to take public opinion into consideration when a decision needs to be made about the place's well being; as a result, those leaders will tend to involve residents in their decision-making and in launching marketing campaigns. By contrast, the role of public opinion in non-democratic regimes is less important than in democracies, and those places are less likely to invite residents to participate in municipal processes. In some of those countries, the government indeed decides where the residents will live, where new factories should be located and what tourist attractions are to be developed. Discussing choice of marketing strategy regarding those places is meaningless; the choice is made solely by the government. In addition, municipalities and local authorities that are run inefficiently will probably do just as poorly when trying to run an advertising and public relations campaign. To conclude, local leadership, the local regime and its functioning exercise a direct effect on the place's image and on the choice of marketing strategy (Avraham, 2003a; Avraham, 2003b).

The campaign's goals and timing

As noted in Chapter 3, every marketing campaign should start with a goal-setting process that outlines the measures to be taken. The goals are set after the decision makers have conducted an in-depth analysis of the place's image and a full preliminary analysis of the crisis, audience and place. Although setting clear goals is an important starting point, the goals can be changed over time and as they are attained. Different places that are undergoing different crises will only naturally set different goals. For example, some places already being consumed will now seek to increase their consumption or to attract other target audiences to a greater degree; places that hardly attract tourism will now wish to increase their appeal and start attracting visitors. Once a place has achieved some of its goals it will often set itself new ones. For example, after a specific place has improved its negative image and managed to attract large numbers of tourists, local decision makers may want to enlarge the audience they appeal to and get them to spend more time and money on that place. In parallel to changing goals, the campaign messages, logo, slogan and visuals should be changed as well.

Analyzing a considerable number of campaigns, we can isolate six major goals for marketing places.

Figure 6.3 illustrates the six major goals in marketing places. Most problematic are places that have suffered from an enduring image crisis and have now decided to alter their image so as to rise on the tourism/investment map. Next come places which have undergone a major crisis that has affected tourism or investments. These places were once consumed and are now looking for a way to be re-consumed, even though the crisis is not yet over (for example, there might still be terror attacks). Then there are places which were once consumed and are now ready to be re-consumed, as the cause of the crisis has faded (for example, a natural disaster). Next are places that are consumed for certain reasons or by certain audiences, and they are now looking to expand their consumption. Next are places that market themselves regularly without any particular image problems. Finally come places that are over-consumed and wish to decrease

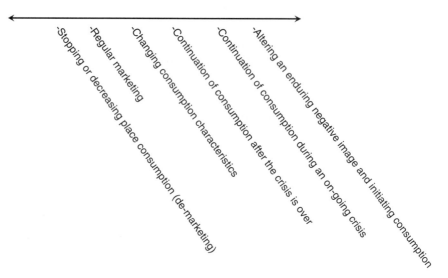

Figure 6.3   Major goals for marketing places

their consumption in order to limit the load of visitors. Below we elaborate each of these six major goals:

1. *Altering an enduring negative image and initiating consumption*: As we know, certain cities and countries are still not attractive to outside audiences. In most cases these places lack tourist attractions, do not attract investors or immigrants and are generally very static. In recent years, a growing number of local decision makers have acted to change their place's image and make it attractive. In most cases, the change starts by running one-day fairs, festivals or sports contests aimed at winning public attention. Next, the place expands these one-day visits to an overnight stay by creating new attractions and a tourism infrastructure.

2. *Continuation of consumption during an ongoing crisis*: This category contains places which are undergoing an image crisis, yet are still interested in attracting tourists, immigrants and investors. The cause of the crisis still exists, but local decision makers struggle for the continuation of consumption in order to maintain the tourism and employment infrastructure. One of the most acute dilemmas for those places is whether to mention the crisis in the marketing campaign or to present a state of "business as usual." In any event, these places are in better condition than those in the first category because they have already made their way into the tourism market. According to tourism professionals, it is important to keep on marketing even in times of crisis in order to remain in consumers' and travel agents' option set. One specific kind of campaign strategy that can be used during a crisis is one that informs tourists which areas are safe and which are unsafe. For example, during an outbreak of a foot and mouth epidemic, the British Tourism Authority published which places in **England** that were safe to visit (Hopper, 2002).

3. *Continuation of consumption after the crisis is over*: In this category are places that are still suffering the effects of a crisis, although its cause has faded. Some crisis situations can threaten the lives of tourists and visitors; in such cases, delaying marketing campaigns is recommended because if tourists arrive and are harmed this might aggravate the image crisis still more. On the other hand, many recommended recovery strategies are available once the crisis is over. Overcoming such a crisis is a complicated task; even when the crisis has passed time will still be needed before tourists throng the streets again. One of the main motifs in a recovery campaign for such places is an explanation that the crisis has ended and that the place is safe again. For example, Beirman (2006) notes that following the SARS crisis a few countries in Asia cooperated

in a joint campaign aimed to reassure travelers that Southeast Asia was free of the epidemic and was welcoming visitors again.

4. *Changing consumption characteristics*: Another possible goal, albeit less common than the previous ones, is to change the consumption characteristics in order to realize the place's potential. For example, this is the case when local decision makers try to convince firms and investors to establish big factories instead of small ones, or to build luxury hotels instead of simple guesthouses. These places are already being consumed, but they wish to expand and diversify their consumption. For example, **Japan** launched a campaign under the slogan "There's more to Japan than business (see Plate 8)."

5. *Regular marketing*: This category is the most popular for places free of any image crisis at the present or for places that have already overcome their crisis. Campaigns of regular place marketing focus on constantly attracting tourists, investors and immigrants. Places undergoing an image crisis will presumably want to be in this category.

6. *Stopping or decreasing place consumption (de-marketing)*: Under this category are places that are over-consumed, especially in the fields of tourism and immigration. This category is not prevalent, but it has become increasingly evident in recent years. Decision makers feel that their place's over-attractiveness over-burdens its infrastructure and harms its inhabitants' quality of life. To protect their uniqueness or their positive image, those places seek to limit their consumption through a process called *de-marketing*. Its goal is the opposite to that of regular marketing. The latter attempts to improve a place's image and present it as attractive; the goal of de-marketing is to deform the image. For example, the mayor of **Venice** distributed unflattering pictures of the city in which it appears dirty and unwelcoming; his purpose was to decrease incoming tourism at the end of the 1990s. Similarly, to lower the number of immigrants to the State of **Oregon**, local decision makers came out with the slogan "You can tell when its summer in Oregon: the rain feels warmer" (Avraham, 2003a).

Summary

This chapter explained how to perform a comprehensive preliminary analysis of crisis situations prior to choosing a response strategy. The preliminary analysis should focus on three types of characteristics: crisis characteristics, audience characteristics and place characteristics (CAP analysis). While a CAP analysis may seem to require too many resources, many place marketers now realize that expending a small amount of resources on effective analysis is more profitable than expending a large amount of resources on an ineffective campaign. Following the introduction of CAP analysis, we outlined the major goals for marketing places, directly resulting from the preliminary analysis, noting that these goals are highly dynamic and should be updated in keeping with changes in the crisis, the target audience or the place. Jointly, CAP analysis and the campaign's goals serve in the choice of a response strategy, as presented in Chapters 7–9.

7 Source strategies

The discussion of media strategies that can serve to improve a place's image can be divided into three major groups: strategies that focus on the source of the message, on the message itself and on the target audience. This chapter reviews the first of these groups, namely the various strategies and techniques used by countries, cities and tourist destinations to improve their public and media images by trying to influence the sources that inform the audience about negative events and the place's unflattering characteristics.

As mentioned in Chapter 2, the literature distinguishes two main sources of information: first-hand experience and secondary sources or mediators such as friends, colleagues and the media (Kunczik, 1997). While one of the most common sources of knowledge of the wider world is the news media (Cohen and Young, 1981; Weimann, 2000), a closer look reveals that these themselves consist of several sub-sources such as journalists, editors and photographers. Each of these groups in turn has its own sources of information (politicians, police, courts, stock exchange, commercial firms, etc.) which they use when writing an article or describing an event.

As noted by a considerable number of researchers (Caspi, 1993; Weimann, 2000), many media consumers relate to messages delivered by the news media as a fact like any other fact, which once given cannot be challenged. For those consumers media messages are a well-established truth, not subject to query or contradiction. However, some local or national decision makers refuse to countenance the negative images delivered by the media and try to interfere with the flow of (negative) information in various ways so as to affect media messages about their place. These efforts exemplify source strategies whereby local decision makers deliberately act against their negative media coverage by attempting to replace or influence the source of the message.

Source strategies can be divided into two main categories: those that seek to replace the source and those that try to influence the source of the unflattering message – the source usually being journalists and editors of the news media (Figure 7.1). Possible sources for

Replacing the source of the message	Affecting the source of the message
1. "Come see for yourself" 2. Using celebrities as an alternative source of message 3. Buying news space	1. Establishing rapport with the news people 2. Exploiting background similarity 3. Blocking media access 4. Applying physical/economic threat

Figure 7.1 Media strategies focusing on the source of the message

delivering negative messages harming the image of an organization, firm or institution could be its competitors, various authorities (the courts, the police, the state comptroller, etc.) and of course the media. In the specific context of countries, for example, sources for delivering negative messages could be international organizations (in fields such as human rights, tourism, environment and ecology), the UN, international courts, travel advisors, other countries and the media. Each of these sources can deliver a message intimating that the country violates its inhabitants' human rights, suffers from high levels of crime or is unsafe and unattractive to visit, invest or live in. Each of these messages can harm the country's image and bring about an image crisis. Considering the media's enormous effect, this chapter will focus on the news media as the main source of information.

Like all other media strategies covered in this book, strategies focusing on the source of the message can be arrayed on a continuum from moderate to extreme measures. Replacing the source of the message is a category containing more moderate media strategies, while interfering in the source's work is a category with media strategies deemed more extreme. A similar arrangement exists within each category, where the first strategies are more moderate than the later. Moderate strategies are those that follow the norms of journalism and communication, "play the game" of advertising and PR and try to affect media image and public opinion in the usual ways. On the other hand, extreme strategies involve attempts by a place's decision makers to force their opinion on the media, doing whatever it takes – from ingratiation to physical force.

Replacing the source of the message

Messages delivered by the media frequently hold different content from what the place's decision makers have in mind. Some decision makers believe that if they could just get the right message through the media, their place's true nature would be revealed and their negative image would disappear. By replacing the source, the marketers of a place aspire to replace the media messages by delivering their alternative and independent voice, which dislodges and challenges the common perceptions delivered by the media. This category is implemented by three major strategies:

1. "Come see for yourself."
2. Using celebrities as an alternative source of information.
3. Buying advertisements and news space.

Come see for yourself

Many places believe that their media image is distorted and unfair and does not present the place as it really is. One strategy used to counter this displeasing situation is to deliver a message inviting the target audience to "Come see for yourself." By means of this strategy, places can deny their mediated image and assert that the reality is different. The marketers believe that if they can get the target audience to the place they will see that the stereotypes and the generalizations (usually spread by the media) about it are false. The marketers' mission with this strategy is to persuade the target audience to come and visit the place; during the visit – the marketers hope – the positive reality in the place will cause a change in how it is perceived.

One place which had a strong feeling that its mediated image was dissimilar to the place's real character is the state of **New Jersey**, often associated with crime, chemical industries and boredom. Trying to reposition it, the state's governor, Richard J. Codey, called the residents of the Garden State to "Take pride in their state" and to suggest a new slogan for it. The state created a website and a telephone hotline and received more than 8000 suggestions in just 3 months. On the website Codey called for the new slogan "to reflect the pride we have in our many parks, open spaces, farmlands, quaint villages, boardwalks and beaches and our exciting cities." Out of the 8000 suggestions, only 5 reached the final round, in which state residents were invited to vote for their favorite by fax, email or telephone. In 2006, the slogan "New Jersey: Come see for yourself" was chosen, implying that the reality in the state was different from the public and mass media image (Curran, 2006; Jones, 2006). By asking people to come and see for themselves, the state marketers undermined the credibility of the sources that spread the unflattering image and invited the audience to come to the state themselves and see how great it is.

A parallel example of use of this slogan was employed by **Israel**, seeking to combat its media image as an unsafe destination. Although the country is often associated with violent conflict and terror attacks, its marketers believed that it had much more to offer. In a campaign launched during the 1990s, Israel used the slogan "Come see for yourself," inviting visitors to see the place with their own eyes. By using this slogan both New Jersey and Israel challenged the mediated image and offered an alternative reality (or image). A similar example of a place that employed the "come see for yourself" strategy to counter its image in the media was the Israeli city of **Netanya**. In the 1970s, Netanya had served as a leading leisure destination in Israel, but its media coverage during the 1990s shifted the focus to themes of crime and violence. Trying to fight its negative image, the Netanya marketers launched a campaign using the slogan "Before you come to criticize, come to visit" (Avraham, 2003a). Through this slogan Netanya asked potential visitors not to judge the place based on its media image but to come and see it with their own eyes.

In sum, places that choose to employ the "come see for yourself" strategy believe that their negative image is rooted mainly in the media and that in reality, there is nothing wrong with the place itself. Once the potential visitors go to see for themselves they will discover that the place is exciting, beautiful and safe, contrary to all the stereotypes created by the media. The essence of this strategy is the effort to replace images created by the media with images created by first-hand experience. One instance that supports this strategy can be found in the case of the **United States**. An international survey conducted in 2005 in 20 countries worldwide found that people who had been to the United States had a much more positive image of the country than those who had not. For example, 52% of the French people who visited the United States had a positive image of the country, in contrast to 17% among the general population; among the Japanese, 46% of the visitors had a positive image of the United States, in contrast to 28% of the general population (*The Marker*, 21 September 2006). The survey shows again that visits to a place usually improve its image.

Using celebrities as an alternative source of information

Another way to dislodge a negative image delivered by the media is replacing the newspeople with other sources. In this strategy, places may use famous persons and celebrities with reputations for being reliable as messengers to deliver an alternative message. The use of this strategy implies that the image projected by the media is distorted, and again, reality is very different, as the celebrity attests. For example, following the 9/11 terror attacks, **New York City** launched several campaigns to restore tourism to the city. One, opened in November 2001, aimed at re-attracting visitors to the city for the Thanksgiving and Christmas holiday season. The campaign consisted of six 30-second television commercials presenting different celebrities associated with New York, including Woody Allen, Henry Kissinger, Robert DeNiro and Billy Crystal. At the end of each commercial New York's mayor Rudolph Giuliani appeared, proclaiming "The New York miracle: Be a part of it" (http://www.cnn.com). In this example, the celebrities in the advertisements served as an alternative source for information, delivering a message that NYC was once again attractive and safe to visit. In addition to delivering an alternative message to the one delivered by the news media – of destruction, death and threat – the familiarity and credibility of the celebrities invested the presented message with an aura of trustworthiness.

A similar use of celebrities as opinion leaders delivering a message that a destination is safe to visit can be found in the case of Israel. On the main page of Israeli tourism's official website (2005) there was a video clip of Madonna's visit to Israel, filmed during a press conference with the world-famous pop star. The headline attached to the clip was the quote "I feel very safe and very welcome." In the clip, Madonna tells the audience that the time she felt the most unsafe during her entire visit was when she encountered outside her hotel some "very naughty paparazzi" (http://www.goisrael.com). In this instance, Israel used Madonna to counteract the common perception of Israel as a place associated with violent conflict. As in the previous case, the use of a reliable celebrity can help get the alternative message across by relying on the celebrity's credibility.

Buying news space

With this strategy, places try to deliver their own message by acting as their own independent source. By buying television/radio airtime or newspaper space, place marketers are free to deliver any message they like, free of the constraints of journalists and editors. Like other "replacing the source of the message" strategies, this one also focuses on delivering an alternative message to that presented in the news media. On the other hand, this strategy enjoys greater independence than the above strategies because the media space is used for regular advertising and it can also publish reports and special advertising features. This high degree of autonomy enables places to deliver almost any kind of message, making this way more extreme than the other two strategies in this group.

In his book, Kunczik (1997) details several cases in which countries bought news space in international newspapers such as *The New York Times*, the *Herald Tribune* and the *Economist*. In so doing, place marketers not only try to transform the place's image, but also aim to challenge the common image of the place as it is portrayed by the media. This challenge is an attempt to replace the source of the message.

Places buy news space to deliverer positive information and explain why the place is worth visiting or investing in (Kotler et al., 1999a). It is important to note that in this analysis buying news space is distinguished from buying space for a regular advertisement campaign. Unlike an advertisement campaign, the message published in a news space is much more informative, more straightforward and frequently written in the form of an article. In addition, the paid advertisement is designed like a newspaper column to give the reader the impression that he/she is reading an objective article rather than consuming a commercial. For example, in the early 2000s **Qatar** and **Dubai**, among other places, bought news space in the leading journals in the world. They filled the spaces with information regarding possible investment, infrastructure, tax reductions and spots and attractions to visit, all designed to look like regular news articles.

One extreme example of a place which took "Buying news space" to a new level is **South Africa** during the apartheid era. In the 1970s, that country suffered an extremely negative image and was portrayed as a "racist regime that eventually will be overthrown by violent revolution" (Kunczik, 1997, p. 212). In addition to buying news space, the South African government made several efforts to actually acquire leading foreign international newspapers and television stations in order to deliver its own messages. In 1974, an attempt was made to purchase the Washington, DC-based daily *The Washington Star*, with funds traced back to the South African government. This effort failed, and the money was used to buy controlling stock in the *Sacramento Union* in the capital of California. The following year South Africa succeeded in purchasing the French magazine *Le Monde Nouvelle*. During those years too, an important West German journal received 1.42 million South African Rand to cultivate the country's image, a procedure that was later replicated with other journals in Europe (Kunczik, 1997).

Case study: Kazakhstan according to Borat

In recent years, the image of **Kazakhstan** has been constantly attacked by the British comedian Sasha Baron Cohen, playing the role of a fictional Kazakh journalist named Borat. In his television comedy show *Da Ali G Show*, "Borat" presented the people of Kazakhstan as primitive, racist and uneducated and whose national drink is horse urine.

In November 2006, following "Borat's" hosting of the MTV Europe Music Awards, the Kazakh Foreign Ministry denounced Mr. Cohen's performance and threatened to take "any legal action to prevent new pranks of this kind." Additionally, the Kazakh government hired Western PR experts to counter "Borat's" presentation of their country and improve its national image. Soon after, Kazakhstan bought a four-page news space in *The New York Times*, which it filled with attestations to the country's democracy, education system and women's rights. Kazakh officials thereby sought to replace the source of the messages (i.e., Cohen's "Borat" character) by publishing their own. In response to the ads, Cohen only re-invigorated his onslaught, which reached new heights in his 2006 movie *Borat: Cultural Learnings of America for Make Benefit Glorious Nation of Kazakhstan*. After the trailer was shown at the Toronto Film Festival in September 2006, Kazakhstan bought another set of advertisements through which it tried to replace the messages delivered by Cohen. In the news space, the Kazakh government emphasized the good relations between the United States and Kazakhstan and the modern lifestyle in "Cosmo-politic Kazakhstan." All this activity was meant to prevent the damage that might be caused by the film, but it ended up supporting the "buzz" and helping to make the film a hit. On its first weekend it took in $26.4 million, on its second $29 million. Cohen went on to win the 2007 Golden Globe award for "Best performance by an actor in a motion picture" for his role in the film.

Such success seemed likely to cause irreparable damage to Kazakhstan; paradoxically matters eventually turned out otherwise. The hubbub surrounding the film sparked great interest in Kazakhstan; its diplomats were invited to speak in the international media, some British tourists decided to visit the country, and demand for the tenge, the Kazakh currency, increased. Kazakh officials stopped seeing the movie as a threat and now regard it as an opportunity to bring their country into international awareness and attract visitors and investors.

Sources: *The New York Times*, 28 September 2006; *Ha'aretz*, 29 September 2006, 13 November 2006, 7 November 2006, 31 October 2006; *NRG*, 7 November 2006.

Influencing the source of the message

Through strategies in the category that influences the source of the
message, place marketers and decision makers try to introduce their
positions into media coverage by newspaper reporters, photographers and editors, radio and television stations and news websites.
This category applies four major strategies, arranged from moderate
to extreme:

1. Establishing rapport with the newspeople;
2. Exploiting ethnic, cultural or religious background similarity to
   gain sympathy;
3. Blocking media access;
4. Applying a physical/economic threat.

Establishing rapport with the newspeople

On the conscious level, reporters who are helped by PR people or
spokespersons who give them exclusive news stories, find informants
and show them around the place, may feel an obligation to return
the favor by providing positive media coverage. On the unconscious
level, mutual friendship and assistance create feelings of empathy
and closeness which affect the way a reporter experiences and covers
the relevant events. Aware of these two levels, many spokespersons
and PR experts try to establish rapport with journalists and editors
to win better media coverage.

As detailed in Chapter 5, newspeople are not always objective
when they set out to cover different events, and often they work, con-
sciously or unconsciously, with an agenda that can promote or shape
a story. For example, a study on the relations between PR experts and
newspeople discovered that good media relations between the two
sides affected the coverage patterns of places in the national media.
In one instance, a journalist received benefits (vouchers for a hotel
and discounts on tickets for attractions) from the local PR office in
charge of creating a positive image for the area. Subsequently it was
found that reporters who got benefits covered the place's positive
aspects more extensively and reduced their coverage of its negative
aspects (Lahav, 2004). Places that established good media relations
were found to receive wider and more positive media coverage than
places that did not create any personal connections with newspeople
(Avraham, 2003b).

A similar example of the way good media relations can affect
media coverage of places can be found in the case of the Jewish West

Bank settlements in **Israel**. Every new editor or reporter assigned to cover the area for the national news would be invited by the PR person to take a private tour of the area. In this "familiarization tour," the newspeople would be taken to see the major settlements, meet local spokespersons and make the acquaintance of some of the settlers' leaders. After any incident journalists would get briefings and updates from the settler information center that assisted them in covering the story. By means of the good media relations they established, the settlers obtained wide media coverage relative to their proportion in the population (Avraham, 2003b).

Good relations with the media are helpful to place marketers during crisis events, but the cases shown here illustrate how they can affect the source of the message and result in better coverage at all times. Forming friendships or other personal relations with reporters, photographers and editors can at times influence their viewpoints and lead to wide and positive media coverage of a place.

Exploiting ethnic, religious or cultural background similarity to gain sympathy

As discussed in Chapter 6, social, cultural and geographical similarity affects a place's media accessibility. The closer the journalist's affinity with the subject covered, the more positive the coverage. This is because ethnic, religious or cultural proximity creates sympathy, affection and understanding, which cause the reporter to identify with the people or place being covered (Shoemaker and Reese, 1996).

Being aware of this, some places try to influence the assigning of journalists, hoping that a reporter with a similar background will give the place better media coverage. A prime example is the case of the kibbutz movement in **Israel**, which worked to have reporters born and raised on a kibbutz assigned to cover kibbutzim in the national newspapers. This, it was believed, would uphold their positive representation in Israeli media (Avraham, 2003b). More explicit use of this strategy can be found in the case of the Jewish West Bank settlements in Israel during the late 1990s. Local decision makers tried to influence their media coverage by dispatching the information they wanted to propagate to a reporter with the same religious affiliation as the settlers in the hope that such a reporter would handle the information far more sympathetically (Avraham, 2003b). In a more recent example, a number of leading Israeli decision makers visited Hollywood in the 2000s, trying to persuade Jewish film producers to shoot their films in Israel. In all these cases, places strove to win better media coverage or representation by utilizing reporters' ethnic, cultural or religious background.

CNN assistance in post-SARS recovery

While some strategies in this chapter perceive the media as the root of all evil, the common dominator of the last two strategies presented is the perception that working together with the media might yield positive results. One instance of the media assisting a place to alter its image is Southeast Asia following the SARS epidemic in 2003. After the epidemic, the CNN network approached the Pacific Asia Travel Association with a proposal for a joint campaign "to help restore confidence in the region, backed by a significant chunk of free airtime and advertising space" (Yates, 2006, p. 267). The offer resulted in an interesting TV campaign called "Welcome Back." Following CNN, other global and regional players took similar initiatives and conducted other SARS recovery campaigns.

Blocking media access

Taking attempts to affect media coverage one step further, some places choose to block any media access to events that might have a negative effect on the place's image. By preventing the presence of newspeople, place decision makers hope that any kind of controversial issue will remain uncovered, and hence will not create a negative image of the place. Places where wars, violent conflict or genocide are common block media access as a matter of course, but here this strategy only refers to places where newspeople were denied access as part of a particularly deliberate and systematic attempt to obstruct negative media coverage. Analysis of media coverage of numerous conflicts reveals that security forces, including those of the **United States**, **Israel** and **Britain**, were often involved in deliberate blocking of media access to conflict areas (Wolfsfeld, 1997).

While the "blocking media access" strategy is well known in case of conflict, it is employed less under other circumstances. One case in which media access was blocked to prevent negative coverage of a natural disaster is the **People's Republic of China**. Following a typhoon in summer 2006 in southeast China, the New China News Agency reported only 17 deaths and 138 people missing. A more careful inspection by the International Red Cross estimated that 2000 local people were killed in the storm. A foreign journalist who tried to visit the devastated area and investigate the disaster was driven off by government officials, who denied access to international as well as local media (*Ha'aretz*, 15 September 2006). By blocking the international media the Chinese authorities took exclusive control of reportage on the event and of the flow of outgoing information. As the only source of information, the Chinese government could minimize the damage wrought to the country's image by the disaster. Similarly, an Al-Jazeera TV network reporter was arrested in January 2007 by the **Egyptian** police for writing and shooting a TV item on torture (*Ha'aretz*, 15 January 2007). As in China, the Egyptian government tried to prevent negative damage to their state's image by preventing media coverage.

Physical/economic threat to newspeople

A strategy applied to take control of the source of the message is an attempt to direct journalists' work. By this very extreme strategy, journalists, photographers and editors are physically/economically threatened or even physically hurt, as a means to prevent them from covering a problematic subject. By threatening the life of journalists, some local decision makers believe they can direct the media and prevent coverage of negative issues that might harm the place's image. In the case of economic threats, some countries have sued foreign journalists for large sums of money in response to their publishing critical material about the place. Countries likewise have pressed charges against journalists and threaten them with cancellation of their visas and exorbitant fines to prevent negative media coverage (Weimann and Nevo, 2001). As an example, the **Egyptian** government sued CNN for $500 million, claiming that the release of a news item on female circumcision damaged the country's image (*Ha'aretz*, 29 December 1997).

One prime example of physical threats being used to influence media content was demonstrated by Nazi **Germany**. During the 1930s the German consul in Los Angeles, George Gyssling, kept close watch on the Hollywood film industry, with the aim of controlling the messages it conveyed regarding his country. Gyssling would send threatening letters to studios and actors, warning them that should they produce anti-German messages, their film, the actors and the studio would be boycotted by Germany. In one case, the threats became an issue of life and death: this concerned the production of *Confessions of a Nazi Spy* in 1938. The German consul threatened Warner Brothers that the release of the film might cause "unpredicted consequences"; he hoped that "the film will never be released." Gyssling further intimated that relatives of the production crew who lived in Germany would be hurt if production of the movie went ahead. Unfortunately, some of those threats materialized when the movie's sales agent in Germany was murdered by Nazi thugs later that year (Kassem, 2006).

Another example of the use of physical threats to prevent media coverage was the well-known case of **Tiananmen Square**. On 4 June 1989, the Chinese government resolved to suppress a series of demonstrations led by students, intellectuals and labor activists which were mounted principally in Tiananmen Square in Beijing. Aiming to protect the way their country would be perceived abroad, Chinese officials tried to control the flow of information and block media access to areas where the demonstrations were taking place. Local and foreign journalists in Beijing at the time were forcibly moved to other parts of the city to stop them observing the suppression of the protests (Mathews, 1998). Photographing or video recording of the demonstrations was also strictly prohibited by the Chinese authorities. Photographers who tried to take pictures of the events or to approach the square were physically removed and arrested, and their lives were threatened (Manheim, 1991).

A more recent example of concealing demonstrations in order to maintain a positive image is taken from the Israeli–Palestinian conflict. The ongoing clashes between Israelis and Palestinians were one of the most covered conflicts in the international media during the 1990s (Wolfsfeld, 1997). In this conflict, the weapons are not just guns and bullets but words and images too. In the battle for media sympathy, both sides used every means they could lay hands on, just as in actual warfare. In recent years, many examples are found of Palestinian officials trying to prevent or disrupt media coverage in various ways. For example, on September 11, 2001, Palestinian security officers threatened the life of an Associated Press television cameraman in **Nablus** after he shot a video of locals celebrating the attack against the United States. Aware of the threat and wishing to minimize danger to their local crew, AP chose not to broadcast the video. A few days later the Palestinian police detained several foreign journalists covering a series of pro-Bin Laden demonstrations in **Gaza**. The police confiscated videotapes, films and some camera equipment to prevent media coverage of the events (McNally, 2002).

Summary

This chapter outlined the use of source strategies by countries, cities and tourist destinations to improve their image. Of the many sources of messages, we focused on the principal one, the mass media. Source strategies fall into two groups: one seeks to influence the source of the message; the other to replace it. By means of the former, local and national decision makers try to reduce negative media coverage and enlarge positive media coverage by affecting the newspeople through various techniques. By means of the latter, places try to displace the messages presented in the news media and deliver their own. The common dominator of the two groups of strategies is the perception that media messages can be influenced, modified or replaced.

While many decision makers believe that their media coverage does not reflect the way the place really is, places that use source strategies decide to take an active role in altering these messages. Influencing the source of the message is just one group of strategies can be applied to alter a place's image. Other groups are message-focused and audience-focused strategies, as presented in the following chapters.

8 *Message-focused strategies*

As noted in the previous chapter, this book proposes three groups of media strategies to improve a place's image: those that focus on the source of negative messages, aiming to replace it or undermine its credibility; those that focus on the message itself; and those that focus on the characteristics of the target audience. This chapter will outline the use of media strategies focused on the message, whose common denominator is their direct handling of the place's negative image.

Message-focused strategies form the largest group of media strategies presented in this book; it sets out 14 such strategies, with dozens of examples and based on hundreds of case studies. For convenience, these strategies are divided into four sub-categories (Figure 8.1):

1. Disregard for/partial acknowledgment of the crisis;
2. Full acknowledgment of the crisis and moderate coping measures;
3. Full acknowledgment of the crisis and extreme coping measures;
4. Disengagement from the place's main characteristics.

The criterion for the classification of a given strategy into one of the four sub-categories is the distance of the strategy's projected new image of the place from the existing one. The more the new image projected in the campaign differs from the previous negative image, the more extreme the strategy is. As in Chapters 7 and 9, the extreme–moderate criterion can also be illustrated with a graphic model in which all the strategies are arrayed along a continuum. At one end are strategies that deny or only partly acknowledge the crisis, such as recognizing the existence of the place's negative image. At the other end are strategies to implement extreme change in the place's image, such as changing its name. These last strategies, involving disengagement from the place's chief characteristics, are the most drastic as the projected new image usually (but not always) has very little to do with the existing one.

(a) Disregard for/partial acknowledgment of the crisis	(b) Full acknowledgment of the crisis and moderate coping measures
1. "Crisis? What crisis?" 2. Acknowledging negative image 3. Reducing the scale of the crisis	1. Tackling the crisis 2. Hosting spotlight events 3. Hosting opinion leaders 4. Using films, TV and books 5. Engaging celebrities
(c) Full acknowledgment of the crisis and extreme coping measures	(d) Disengagement from the place's main characteristics
1. Delivering a counter-message 2. Spinning liabilities into assets 3. Ridiculing the stereotype	1. Branding contrary to the stereotype 2. Geographical isolation 3. Changing the place's name

Figure 8.1 Media strategies focused on the message

Disregard for/partial acknowledgment of the crisis

This sub-category contains three major media strategies, all aimed at reducing or limiting damage to the place's image due to the crisis. These strategies are relatively passive and involve moderate changes both in the place's image and in the physical reality. Accordingly, these strategies are often used in cases where very little is done, or could be done, to change reality and overcome the image crisis. The strategies under this category are (1) "Crisis? What crisis?," (2) acknowledging the negative image, (3) reducing the scale of the crisis.

Crisis? What crisis?

While most strategies presented in this book offer various ways to tackle an image crisis, the "Crisis? What crisis?" strategy is an easy solution whereby place marketers pretend that nothing bad has happened. Some places choose to ignore the damage to their image after negative events as if there never was a crisis, in the hope that new events and the passing of time will erase the crisis from the memory of tourists, investors or new potential residents. This strategy is often employed by places enjoying a generally positive image that undergo a minor crisis event. Local decisions makers believe that using an explicit strategy to resolve the crisis would be "admitting the problem" and might cause added damage. The "Crisis? What crisis?" strategy can apply three techniques: total disregard, limiting the crisis and "business as usual."

Total disregard

The total disregard technique is often used by places that emanate a strong and positive image, endowed with some kind of "crisis resistance," or by places where tackling the issue would be too risky for the management. For example, total disregard was employed by **Spain** following a spate of terrorist attacks in several cities (Efrati, 2002). Tourist advertisements for these cities after the crisis made no mention of the events in any way. The same policy of total disregard was employed by **Turkey** after several terror attacks in the country between 2003 and 2006. During and following the crisis, place ads for both Spain and Turkey continued to focus on sea and sun, attractions and all kind of events, in complete disregard of the acts of terror. Sometimes, it seems, the risk in acknowledging the crisis may be too great and might cause the place image's more harm than good.

Total disregard is also employed in cases of image problems other than security. The city of **Manchester** in northern England, for example, marketed itself during the 1990s as an international business center, ignoring common stereotypes about it (Young and Lever, 1997). Holcomb (1994) cites the example of the American town of **New Milford**, Connecticut, which chose the slogan "A great past, and a greater future," but remained surprisingly silent regarding the present. A comparable example can be found in the Israeli town of **Ramla**, which is commonly associated with poverty, violent crime and drugs. Aware of its problematic image, Ramla now uses the slogan "Discovering the past, looking towards the future" – again, ignoring its challenging present.

Limiting the crisis

Places that cannot ignore the crisis try to portray it as insignificant, irrelevant and marginal. This technique of limiting the crisis is often implemented when the media demand explanations or reactions from decision makers. For example, after a terror attack in Djerbe in **Tunisia** an official said, "There is no terrorism in Tunisia! Why do you always focus on that?" He added that only one synagogue was attacked and that "it is not the end of the world" (http://www.themedialine.org). This was also the case after a suicide bomber attack in Cairo, **Egypt**. Officials tried to convince the media that the terrorist had acted alone and was not part of a new terror network (*Ha'aretz*, 10 April 2005). A similar example of this style of reaction can be found in the words of Egypt's tourism minister, who declared that the terror attack in **Taba (Sinai)**, which left 34 people dead, was only a "minor event that will have an insignificant effect on tourism to the country" (*Ha'aretz*, 22 October 2004). This pattern of response by Egypt was supported by deeds following the terror attacks themselves; in **Sharm-A-Sheikh**, Sinai, a special team was recruited to eliminate any indication of a terror attack that took place in July 2005, killing 83 people and injuring many others. Trying to limit the crisis and save some of the tourist influx into the area, the hotel against which the attack was perpetrated was covered with enormous swathes of cloth aimed at concealing the immense damage. Dozens of employees swiftly removed every sign of the attack such as broken glass, damaged vehicles and bloodstains (*Ha'aretz*, 25 July 2005). All in all, officials in the above four cases were apparently trying to promote the idea that negative events were rare occurrences, intimating that the likelihood of similar events re-occurring was negligible.

Business as usual

Another possible response to a situation in which a crisis cannot be ignored, but the place prefers to downplay it, is the "business as usual" technique. Acting as if nothing untoward has happened, places hope that the crisis will soon be forgotten and flow of tourists will continue unimpeded. For example, following the outbreak of foot and mouth disease, British cabinet ministers spent their holidays in the **United Kingdom** countryside in solidarity with the tourism industry. Their aim was to restore tourism to some of the places by delivering a "business as usual" message (http://bbc.co.uk). Similarly, following the terror attack on **London** on 7 July 2005, the police hurried to announce that at the weekend the city would be open as usual. Tourist attractions, including the National Gallery and other museums, delivered the same message by opening for regular hours the next day (*Ha'aretz*, 18 July 2005).

   Another place that chose to employ "business as usual," together with the technique of limiting the crisis, is **Thailand**, in attempting to recover from the effects of the deadly tsunami. Only 5 weeks after the disaster, in December 2004, Thailand re-launched its marketing campaign as if nothing had happened. At a tourism convention in Israel, the Thai Minister of Tourism presented pictures of hotels and beaches – located in areas hit by the tsunami – that were operating normally. Thailand also tried to reduce the scale of the crisis by delivering a message that 90% of the hotels in **Phuket** island were functioning as usual and that the tourism infrastructure was unharmed (*Ha'aretz*, 31 January 2005).

Acknowledging the negative image

Sometimes acknowledging the negative image directly is the most effective – even if not the most convenient   course of action. This strategy may prove useful during a crisis, or immediately after it has passed, to maintain or regain a trustworthy image (Avraham and Ketter, 2006). In this case, an advertisement may be placed presenting the message that the place, which might have been unsafe, boring or lacking in tourism services before, has been improved and is now attractive again (Burgess, 1982).

"The new era" technique

The strategy of acknowledging the negative image can be applied by several major techniques. One used by many places is "new era" slogans, suggesting that the place has now changed from its problematic past to a promising present or future. The town of **Rehovoth** in Israel uses the slogan "Rehovoth is waking up with a bang." In this example, the campaign planners admit that the city has been virtually comatose for many years, but claim that now it is waking up; the future, it is suggested, will be completely different (Avraham, 2003a). An even more straight-forward approach can be found on the website of **Estonia**, promising that the country is now "positively transforming" (see Plate 9). A similar example is the case of the Israeli town of **Akko (Acre)**. Historically this was a splendid Crusader city, but now it suffers severe neglect and poverty. Applying the "new era" technique, the town launched a campaign in 2005 under the slogan "A thousand years of history come to life." The slogan's subtext admits that the city has been asleep in recent decades, but it also promises a change that is already happening. This technique was similarly adopted in **East Manchester'**s new slogan: "New East Manchester – the new town in the city."

"Fencing off" the crisis

The strategy of acknowledging the negative image can also take the form of "fencing off" the crisis. By this technique destinations acknowledge the existence of a crisis, but restrict it to certain areas only, emphasizing its minor effect on the place. In some cases, destinations even offer tourists candid advice not to visit those areas as an additional means of creating rapport. A prime example of this technique is the approach taken by the London Tourist Board

(LTB) during **England**'s much-publicized outbreak of foot and mouth disease. The LTB persistently emphasized that the problem existed only in rural areas, and that visits to most parts of England were absolutely safe (Frisby, 2002; Hopper, 2002). In the same manner, the **Nepal** Tourism Board proclaimed that much of the violence and riots going on in the country were in remote, rural areas, while top tourist destinations were secure and free of violent incidents. It emphasized, moreover, that tourists had never been targeted by the rebels and that the media had created a misconception (http://www.highlandernepal.com). Similar approaches were taken by **Israel** and the **Philippines**, following a series of local terror attacks (Baral et al., 2004; Beirman, 2002).

Multiple facets

In another technique, places acknowledge their negative facets but try to add new positive ones to their image. **Lichtenstein**, for example, hired a London-based advertising firm to promote its image and to show that the country was not only a place for questionable business deals but a tourism destination as well (*Ha'aretz*, 18 August 2004). The marketers of the American city of **Tulsa**, Oklahoma, similarly used advertisements portraying local sites and residents under the slogan "This should fill in the blank about Tulsa," with the added acknowledgment that "When someone says 'Tulsa' some people draw a blank." While admitting that the city was not well known and had a weak image, the campaign provided the solution: pictures of the city and information about it, in an attempt to enrich its image (Holcomb, 1994). **Turkey** employed this technique, aiming at the Israeli market in a campaign run in the early 2000s. The marketers stressed Turkey's many landscapes, resorts and tourist attractions. According to the advertising office that handled the campaign, it was intended to counter the perception of Turkey as a Muslim country and to decrease the salience of this component in Turkey's image among the Jewish-Israeli target audience (Zimet, 2006).

The humor technique

One last technique to acknowledge a negative image is humor. Places acknowledge their negative characteristics and just laugh about them; the negative components of the place's image turn into a joke. **Houston**, the fourth largest city in the United States, is a place with some image issues, and its residents know it. For many people, the city of Houston, Texas, is associated with heat, humidity, traffic and mosquitoes. In response, two partners in a marketing firm started an unofficial campaign to improve the city's negative image by acknowledging it. The campaign website carries hundreds of comments from people who are aware of the stereotype, but just love the city. For example, no. 496 jokes, "It's an international city: the traffic of LA and the climate of Calcutta." No. 1387 says, "You can wear flip flops for 10 to 11 months a year. What's not to love about it?" And no. 1235 claims that "humidity prevents wrinkles" (http://www.houstonitsworthit.com).

Reducing the scale of the crisis

As noted in Chapter 5, not all crises can be avoided. Accordingly, some places choose to acknowledge the crisis but reduce its scale to minimize damage to their image. This strategy is often applied after a natural disaster, for three main reasons. First, unlike many other events, natural disasters cannot be disregarded or denied; with this strategy the place can maintain its credibility by telling the truth and letting the target audience feel that it has nothing to hide. Second, crises resulting from natural disasters are often perceived as abstract events, especially when they occur in less familiar places. To avoid this "spilling effect," places limit the dimensions and location of the crisis to protect nearby destinations from its negative effect on tourism. Third, by this means the place can deliver the message that business is continuing as usual and that the place's tourist infrastructure is unharmed.

One major natural disaster which led several places to employ the reducing of the crisis strategy was the 2004 tsunami in Southeast Asia. In the **Maldives**, for example, soon after the tidal wave swept the islands' beaches, the republic's Tourist Bureau announced that only 19 resorts had been damaged, and that tourists were welcome at other 55 resorts, which were operating normally (*Ha'aretz*, 7 January 2005). Similarly, in seeking to employ the same strategy for the entire Southeast Asia region, Francesco Frangialli, secretary-general of the World Tourism Organization, urged the media to undertake responsible coverage of the tsunami disaster. In the WTO newsletter, he wrote that "Saturation coverage of the tragedy in the most damaged areas can lead to a certain level of misunderstanding among consumers, especially when around 80% of hotels and resorts in these destinations remain fully operational." As an example, Frangialli gave the case of **Indonesia**, where top tourist destinations such as

Bali and Lombok were not affected at all, but they still faced an image crisis (http://www.hsmai.org) associated with the tsunami.

Another kind of natural disaster which evoked the use of decreasing the crisis strategy is tropical cyclones, also known as hurricanes. The sudden onslaught of Hurricane Katrina on **Louisiana** in September 2005 caused severe damage not only to residents and businesses but also to the country's film industry. The filming of three movies, *Déjà Vu*, *The Guardian* and *The Reaping*, was stopped and the crews were asked to leave the state. In their effort to restore business and avoid damage to the state's image, officials in the local film industry claimed that only 20% of Louisiana had been damaged by the hurricane (*Ha'aretz*, 10 September 2005).

A different kind of natural disaster that can cause an image crisis is the outbreak of a disease. In 1997, the **Dominican Republic** was beset by a tourism crisis resulting from health problems among British visitors. One element of the country's recovery strategy was to reduce the scale of the crisis by demonstrating statistically that less than 1% of the 2 million British tourists in the previous year had fallen ill (World Tourism Organization, 2006). This fact limited the scale of the crisis by emphasizing the hundreds of thousands of people who had traveled safely to the country, rather than the few who had fallen ill.

Full acknowledgment of the crisis and moderate coping measures

This sub-category covers five media strategies involving full acknowledgment of the crisis and using moderate measures to cope with it: (1) tackling the crisis, (2) hosting spotlight events, (3) hosting opinion leaders, (4) using films, TV and books, (5) engaging celebrities. While the previous sub-category was more passive and involved either acknowledging or disregarding the place's existing image, strategies under this sub-category make active PR and advertising efforts to improve the image. The strategies presented here are among the most common in the field of place marketing and can be used successfully by most places in most cases, as the following examples show.

Tackling the crisis

When a place faces an image crisis, sometimes the best way to restore a positive image is to change the reality that caused the crisis. If, for example, a destination is perceived as violent and unsafe, it must combat crime and violence, as was in the case of **New York City**.

In the early 1990s, New York suffered an image crisis resulting from high rates of robbery, assault and violent crimes. Mayor Rudolph Giuliani resolved to tackle the problem by enlarging the local police force, increasing the police presence on every street corner and sub way station, reducing the numbers of homeless people in the city and launching a citywide campaign against perpetrators of crime and violence. As a result of Giuliani's efforts, the city's crime rate dropped and the feeling of safety in the city grew in an unprecedented fashion, bringing the crisis to an end (*Ha'aretz*, 5 June 2005).

One specific case of trying to change a place's reality is action taken after a terror attack. Terrorism has a most dangerous potential for a place's image, and many places seek a real solution to avoid possible crises and prevent future attacks. A terror attack in **Tunisia** in 2002 near a local synagogue exerted a marked adverse effect on tourism from Israel. Perceiving Israelis as an important target market, the Tunisian government formulated new regulations to enhance the sense of security and to make visits by Israeli tourists safer and easier; measures included providing an escort of local police forces for organized groups (*Ha'aretz*, 1 January 2005). Likewise, following a terrorist attack against German tourists, the **Egyptian** government took a hard line against radical Islamic groups and reduced the odds of possible future crises (Efrati, 2002; Wahab, 1996). Both Tunisia and Egypt tried to cope with an image crisis indirectly: instead of dealing directly with the negative image they addressed the problem that caused it.

One prime example of how a change in the reality can transform the place's image is the case of the town of **North Adams** in northwest Massachusetts. In the 1980s, North Adams hit an economic low with nearly 19% unemployment, poverty and social problems. The post-industrial era had overtaken this small industrial town, causing the local economy to collapse. When the last big plant closed it left behind a 700,000 square-foot nineteenth-century industrial complex located in the center of the town. At that point a new initiative by the Massachusetts governor was to change the town's future, making it the home of the largest center for contemporary art in the United States. The Massachusetts Museum of Contemporary Art (MASS MoCA) opened in May 1990, at a total cost of over $30 million. The museum now extends over 13 acres, with 19 galleries, an 850-seat theater, two performance courtyards, workshops and retail space. The museum employs 300 people and has created more than 850 jobs in North Adams, bringing the unemployment rate down to only 5% (http://www.communityarts.net, http://www.massmoca.org).

As an integral part of global competition, tourist destinations worldwide are revitalized through an in-depth change in the local reality. These changes include the construction of conference centers, cultural centers, stadiums, shopping malls, theme-oriented areas, museums, agricultural markets and improved mass transit systems. One example of this renovation can be found in the city of **Syracuse**, NY, which decided to overcome its negative image and embarked on refurbishing the city center through private and public partnerships (Short et al., 1993). To conclude, the cases of North Adams and Syracuse yet again support the claim that real changes in the actual place can cause real change in the place's image.

Miami – a case study in tackling the crisis

In the early 1990s, a growing number of violent crimes against tourists and residents struck the golden beaches of Florida. In **Dade** (now **Miami-Dade**) **County** alone, over 12,000 crimes against tourists occurred in 1992. In 1993, Florida's negative reputation declined still further when 10 foreign visitors, mainly Europeans, were murdered in a short spell of time. The London *Sunday Times* dubbed the Sunshine State the "State of Terror," causing additional damage to Florida's image. As in many other places, the Florida crisis immediately resulted in a significant decrease in the number of visits and revenues from tourism. For example, the number of tourists from Germany to Florida decreased from 608,000 in 1993 to 411,000 in 1994, inflicting heavy economic loss on a state that regarded tourism as one of its most important sources of income.

Overcoming the crisis in Florida required a comprehensive effort, which was undertaken by federal and local decision makers. The state's tourism officials worked to re-attract visitors and restore Florida's positive image; government and law enforcement officials got tough on crime. In an attempt to improve the security for tourists, the local police forces were reinforced and a special tourist police was established. All the efforts to solve the problem and increase personal safety in Florida added up to a great success. Not only did the crime rate fall to the lowest level in a quarter of a century, but tourism too was restored to normal, dispelling the clouds from the skies over the Sunshine State.

Source: Tilson and Stacks (1997); Glaesser (2006).

Hosting spotlight events

The strategy of hosting spotlight events is simple and popular: places host major events to attract visitors and improve their image. One of the most famous examples of using spotlight events (often referred to as "hallmark" or "mega" events) to improve a place's image was the Nazis' use of the 1936 Olympic Games to project a positive image for their regime (Nielsen, 2001). Since 1936 many places have used the Summer and Winter Olympics, the World Expo, the title of Cultural Capital of Europe or the Eurovision Song Contest as great platforms for massive PR-driven image campaigns; in the United States, the Republican and Democratic national conventions likewise fulfill this role (Beriatos and Gospodini, 2004).

Spotlight events focus the media's attention on a particular location for a short, concentrated period, allowing the host place to promote certain chosen images that can be used to improve a negative image, create positive news and shift international media attention from a negative to a positive portrayal of the place. These events entail several significant advantages for the host: (1) the place attracts large numbers of guests and visitors who not would travel there were it not for the event; they can then serve as the place's advocates; (2) spotlight events attract opinion shapers such as journalists, who will later write columns that can improve the place's image; (3) spotlight events encourage local residents to take pride in their place and reinforce their commitment to its image. In addition, those who attend the event consume the services the place offers, and in that way support the local economy in general and businesses such as tourist attractions, restaurants, cafes and hotels in particular.

Hosting the Olympic Games

The most sought-after event a place can host is the Olympic Games, an international multi-sport event held every 4 years. The original Olympic Games were held in Greece from 776 BC until 393 AD. The games were revived in 1896 and took place in Athens, ushering in the modern era of the Olympic Games. The Olympics are one of the most popular sporting events in the world – the **Athens** 2004 Games were watched by 3.9 billion people worldwide (http://www.olympic.org). Since the time of the Berlin 1936 Games, many places have battled to host the contest as a means to draw positive media attention.

One principal example of a place that utilizes the Olympiad to overcome an image crisis is **China**. Following the 1989 Tiananmen Square massacre, in 1990 **Beijing** hosted the Asian Games and made use of the media attention to improve its image and present a more favorable portrait of the country (Hall and O'Sullivan, 1996). Next Beijing is hosting the 2008 Olympic Games. Currently China suffers from some negative images resulting from issues related to human rights and freedom of speech. In the eyes of local decision makers,

"The games will provide a window to the world for China. That window will get bigger and bigger as the games get closer" (Barnet, 2001). To maximize the impact of this opportunity, the equivalent of over $40 billion is being invested in the city in preparation for the Olympic Games (*Ha'aretz*, 29 September 2005).

Being aware of the mass media exposure created by hosting the Olympics, many places are willing to invest enormous amounts of money in their battle to be the home of future Olympiads. In 2005, some of the most popular tourist destinations competed to host the 2012 Olympic Games: **New York**, **Paris**, **London**, **Moscow** and **Madrid**. Although none of these cities was beset by any serious image crisis, each of them believed that hosting the games would contribute a great deal to its future development and its image. At least two of these cities aspired to gain some benefits related to crises they had undergone: New York hoped that hosting the games would help the city recover from the events of 9/11, and Paris hoped to reshape the city by means of the new infrastructures needed for the games. Eventually, the International Olympic Committee chose London, causing the other candidates great disappointment.

Hosting sports events

Other sporting events than the Olympics can also draw journalists, big crowds and international attention. One place which tried to attract a medium-size sports event is the **Republic of Guyana**, a tropical country on the northern coast of South America. According to the president of Guyana's Tourism and Hospitality Association (THA), one of the biggest problems the country faces is lack of foreign awareness: "Most of the international traveling public does not know where Guyana is and what our tourism products are" (http://www.sidenet.org). One way to increase public awareness of the country was to host the 2007 ICC Cricket World Cup, a spotlight sports event that can draw many visitors and increase media attention (http://www.icc-cricket.com, http://www.guyana.org, http://www.guyana-tourism.com).

Another place which decided on using a sports event as a major marketing tool is the city of **Lexington**, Kentucky. Known as the "Horse capital of the world," the city's marketers decided to focus their efforts on its horses. In recent years, horses have been the main attraction of the city, centering on Kentucky Horse Park, the city's racetrack and tours of private stables that are offered. As its spotlight event, Lexington is to host the 2010 World Equestrian Games, which approximately 300,000 visitors are expected to attend (http://www.visitlex.com). Although the event is scheduled for 2010, the city's website started advertising the games in 2005, supporting the city's branding process.

While Lexington's natural resource is the city's horse tradition, the resource used by **Ethiopia** to boost tourism is its people's natural talent for long-distance running. Trying to project a rich and favorable image, Ethiopia now hosts annually "The Great Ethiopian Run." The race, begun in 2001, already attracted over 25,000 participants by its fourth year and has some international sponsors. According to local spokespersons, the event serves as a great opportunity for the Ethiopian people to attract international and positive attention by using their inborn talent (http://www.mediaethiopia.com, http://www.ethiopianrun.org). By hosting "The Great Ethiopian Run," the country can associate itself with positive values linked to running such as health, fitness and lifestyle. In this way, the country can replace negative media images of poverty by positive images of a world-class sports event.

Whereas most places choose to attract sports events, the New York City borough of **Brooklyn** decided to take this technique one step further by establishing its own sports hall. Through a new initiative by the developer, Bruce C. Ratner, a glass-walled basketball arena, the most expensive in the country, will be built in the borough, which is to be the home of the New York Nets. Ratner has offered the Metropolitan Transportation Authority $100 million for the property, in addition to $555 million for building the arena and $3.5 billion for development. The development plan includes 6000 apartments, stores, office space and parks, making this initiative the largest private development in the borough's history. In the new project, named Atlantic Yards, media attention on the basketball arena will be used to promote and create a positive and strong image for the accompanying residential project (*Ha'aretz*, 27 December 2006; Bagli, 2005).

Hosting cultural events

Hosting cultural events can be used to attract visitors or to improve a general image, although some places use such events as a deliberate means to overcome an image crisis. One such place is the city of **Baltimore**, Maryland, which is trying to shed its reputation as a place with a high crime rate. The strategy chosen by Baltimore was the expansion and development of cultural attractions to draw visitors to the city. These include museums, a science center, a zoo and the nationally famous aquarium. Those efforts proved successful when

Frommer's *Travel Guide* crowned Baltimore as one of its top 10 travel destinations for summer 2005 (http://www.baltimore.org).

The city of **Reno**, Nevada, has a hard time competing with its bigger and classier sister, Las Vegas. One way Reno found to attract visitors and to improve the city's image was to brand itself as "Artown." Starting from the summer of 1996, Reno invites tourists, visitors and residents to enjoy "a month-long celebration of cultural diversity and artistic innovation." The Artown project, marketed under the slogan "Thirty-one days – one spectacular event," offers a month-long summer festival with more than 300 events in the fields of visual, performing and human arts. Following a continuous decline in the number of visitors to Reno in the early 1990s, a group of local businesses initiated a plan to "use the arts to improve the city's self-image and give locals a reason to play downtown again." The first festival drew 30,000 people; recent ones have attracted approximately 140,000 spectators, turning this initiative into a success (http://www.renoisartown.com).

As noted earlier, the occurrence of terror attacks might have a fatal impact on a place's image. One way of trying to replace the damaged image with a positive one is by hosting cultural events, demonstrating that the place is safe and friendly. For example, **Egypt** tried to shift international attention from a series of terror attacks by hosting some special international events and promoting visits to its ancient archeological sites (Wahab, 1996). Similarly, **Northern Ireland** tried to overcome its negative image created by violent conflict by promoting local music, dance, literature and theater festivals, (*Ha'aretz*, 30 June 1998; Sonmez et al., 1999). Another place that attempted to replace its damaged image is the city of **Bilbao** in northern Spain. During the 1990s, the city suffered at the hands of Basque terror groups and endured high levels of unemployment. The Guggenheim Museum opened in 1997 as a major attraction, and a set of supporting cultural events turned things around. More than a million tourists visited the city in 2001 (*Ha'aretz*, 12 May 2002).

A further example of a place which used the cultural event technique to overcome an image crisis is the town of **Holon** in Israel. A poll conducted by the town in the early 1990s revealed that although in general it carried a negative image, people who had visited were fond of it. Therefore, as part of the campaign to change the city's image, a decision was made to attract people through special cultural events and performances, which would enrich the image. This strategy was successful and the city's image greatly improved during the late 1990s (Avraham, 2003a; Shir, 2006). Similarly, **Jerusalem** holds frequent cultural events and festivals to attract visitors and thus offset the fear of terrorist activity, which might cause many to avoid the city (Efrati, 2002).

Hosting opinion leaders

Many place decision makers are surprised to discover that while the physical crisis may pass in a short period of time, the resulting stereotypes have a tendency to adhere to the place for a long time. One marketing approach applied to deliver the message that the place is safe and welcoming again is the strategy of hosting opinion leaders. Journalists, stakeholders, tour operators, community and religious leaders and other opinion leaders are invited to the place to see the change with their own eyes. Later, after these opinion leaders return home, they are expected to spread the news and help the place overcome its image crisis.

Many destinations which choose to employ this strategy organize familiarization trips for different opinion leaders in the hope that they will report that the situation in the destination is "business as usual": tourist attractions are open, tourist information booths are operating, cultural events continue and tourist services are available. Leading examples of places that used this strategy are: **Germany** following World War II, hosting many public opinion leaders from all over the world to show them the "new Germany"; **India** during an epidemic in the 1990s; **London** during the foot and mouth outbreak; **Nepal** after the political unrest which threatened to put a halt to the flow of tourists; **Miami** following crime wave against tourists; and **Hong Kong** once China was declared free of SARS (Baral et al., 2004; Beirman, 2002; Frisby, 2002; Hopper, 2002).

Israel, too, during the long conflict with the Palestinians, has hosted yearly at least 2000 public opinion leaders such as academics, clergy, journalists, politicians and community leaders to show them that the country – its sights and people – are very different from those that appear in its media coverage. Support for this strategy can be found in an interview given by a senior executive of the Israeli Hotel Association, hosting an international convention for Microsoft (with Bill Gates present): "International conventions are a great opportunity to promote both the hotel and the State of Israel. Every event of this kind attracts foreign journalists and photographers, who unlike the common belief are more than happy to present a different image of Israel" (*Ha'aretz*, 9 November 2005). The steps taken by Israel are very similar to those taken by the **north of England**, in their quest to overcome negative perceptions held by financial investors and public

opinion leaders concerning cities in the area. Local authorities organized visits for public opinion leaders in the hope that these would
help promote a favorable image that would be passed on to other
people with whom the opinion leaders associated (Burgess, 1982).

An excellent example of the way this strategy is planned and implemented emerges from an interview given by the World Tourism
Organization Secretary General, Francesco Frangialli, advising how
to promote the image of **Iran**. According to Frangialli, "Iran has
mainly depended on regional tourism from neighboring countries.
That's good but in addition it is important to have tourists from
Western Europe." Accordingly, the WTO initiated two projects to
promote Iran's tourism industry: "One is to organize press trips to
Iran to make the international press familiar with Iranian tourism.
The other is a conference which links tourism with handicraft production," said Frangialli. Both projects aimed to draw journalists and
decision makers in the tourism industry and to win some positive
media coverage for the country (Payvand, 2005). Following the same
method suggested by the WTO, the **Caribbean Islands** can serve as
a great evidence of the growing tendency to host opinion leaders
as a strategy to improve the place's image. Shortly after Hurricane
George in 1998, the Caribbean Tourism Organization executed a crisis
management plan to limit the fallout of the crisis. A large number of
journalists and travel agents were invited almost immediately after
the hurricane, indicating the importance attached to opinion leaders
as shapers of public attitudes (http://www.unisdr.org).

Hosting tourism conventions and conferences

One of the most common tactics for attracting opinion leaders is
to hold a tourism conference. This technique has been widely use
in many places, including the Caribbean subsequent to incidents of
crime and Southeast Asia after the tsunami. For example, the positive
image of the Caribbean island of **Aruba** was threatened by a tragic
case of a missing woman tourist. An international tourism security
conference was rapidly arranged in Aruba in June 2006, aimed to
attract tourism professionals to the place (Tarlow, 2005). The conference directly tackled issues concerning the safety of tourists, the
role of tourist police and the effects of crime on a place's image. The
conference organizers thereby achieved two goals: first, the decision
makers who took part at the conference learned of the major efforts
being taken to keep visitors safe and secure; tourism professionals
learned to associate the island of Aruba with tourism safety. Second,
all the professionals and journalists who attended the conference

got the feeling that Aruba was safe, and that they were expected to deliver this message in their home countries.

A similar example can be found in **Indonesia**, which suffered a severe twofold image crisis due to terror attacks against tourists, principally in Bali, and the 2004 tsunami. To restore the country's image, Indonesia held a conference on tourism communications in May 2005. Participating tourism journalists were called upon to provide a "balanced report" on the situation in the country. According to the World Tourism Organization, the event attracted decision makers in international tourism communications and a large group of journalists (http://www.world-tourism.org), all serving as opinion leaders who could bring tourism back to Bali.

Promoting places using films, television series and books

One way of forming an impression of a place, as noted in Chapter 2, is to watch a movie or television series set in that location or reading a book whose plot unfolds at the specific destination. From information propagated by the media, one can get a sense of the place without even leaving one's living room. Many people, for example, have never been to New York City but simply by watching the popular television series *Sex and the City* viewers can form a positive image of the place. The following section outlines the practical effect of films, TV series and books on place image; a more comprehensive discussion of these effects can be found in Chapter 2 of this book.

In recent years, place marketers have found that films, television series and books can serve as powerful PR tools, especially when tourism showed a steep rise following the production of a new film on the place. Conversely, it was found that a television series shot at a particular place and replete with negative images could distort the place's image for many years. The image of destinations created through being portrayed as locations in films, television series and books has several major advantages: the projected image finds its way to a very large, heterogeneous and worldwide market; the image can become an integral part of the popular culture, and it is maintained in every release window: cinema, DVD, pay-per-view television, free television and re-runs (Hudson and Ritchie, 2006).

One growing phenomenon resulting from these productions is film tourism, fueled by the growth of the entertainment industry and of international tourism (Hudson and Ritchie, 2006). Kim and Richardson (2003) found that movies had a statistically significant relationship with a positive empathic, cognitive and affective image of the location and with an interest in visiting it. Another study conducted by the insurance firm Halifax Travel in **Britain** yielded even more impressive data. Places serving as film locations were found to enjoy an increase of over 30% in the number of visitors. Another remarkable finding is that 25% of all British tourists chose their vacation destination on account of a movie, a book or a television series being set there (*Ha'aretz*, 12 August 2005).

To maximize the place's film tourism potential, Hudson and Ritchie (2006) detail three stages of proactive efforts:

1. *Pre-production stage:* Appointment of PR specialists actively to encourage producers and studios to film at the location, involvement in location scouting and offering grants and tax credits to producers.
2. *Production stage:* Evoking media publicity around the film and its location, especially by inviting media to the location and promoting the film's celebrities.
3. *Post-production stage:* Once the film is released, place marketers can employ numerous ways to promote the film's location and leverage its film-tourism potential. Examples are making replicas or keeping the originals of film icons, sites and sets; engaging the film's stars in promoting the destination; hosting events based on the film's theme; creating links to the location on the film's website and offering guided tours, film walks and movie maps.

In this strategy, several kinds of media can be distinguished for promoting places and improving their image. In the following, we discuss in detail the positive and negative effects of motion pictures, television series and works of fiction on places' images, as exemplified in a variety of case studies.

Using films to promote places

A good example of how films and actors are used to promote destinations is the case of **Australia**, as illustrated in the well-known "Shrimp on the Barbie" ("Come and Say G'day") campaign. In 1984, the Australian Tourism Commission launched an international marketing campaign starring Paul Hogan, a local comedian who had his own comedy television program. The campaign got off to a good start, but the release of the film *Crocodile Dundee* (1986) inspired it with new life. The publicity used the lively character of Crocodile Dundee to introduce the people of Australia as friendly, welcoming, easy-going and adventure-loving. The campaign was fashioned out of television and radio ads and was supported by advertising in lifestyle and travel magazines. During the first 3 years of the campaign arrivals to Australia doubled, and over the next 4 years the tourism growth rate exceeded 25% annually (Baker and Bendel, 2006).

Another renowned example of films serving as an effective PR tool concerns **Scotland**, which exploited the success of the movie *Braveheart* to promote tourism. The movie, in which a local historical hero is brought to life in the beautiful Scottish landscapes, had a major positive effect on the country's image. The release of the movie in 1995 increased tourism to certain parts of Scotland by 300% (Hudson and Ritchie, 2006). To increase the film's post-production tourism potential, the Scottish Tourist Board used several techniques, in addition to encouraging private initiatives. One such technique was the distribution of postcard advertisements in cinemas screening *Braveheart*, inviting viewers to send for information on "Braveheart Country." An example of a private initiative is the "Braveheart Bed and Breakfast," offering a "Scottish breakfast, enough for any braveheart" (http://www.braveheartbedandbreakfast.co.uk).

While the success of film tourism in Scotland relies on a historical hero, the small town of **Alnwick** in Norththumberland, England, owes much of its success as a tourist destination to a fictional teenager named Harry Potter. Alnwick was chosen as the location for the filming of the Harry Potter films and is now a popular destination for visitors from all over the world. One way in which the town developed its post-production attractions was by opening a Knight School, offering kids the unique experience of "what it was really like to be a knight" (*Ha'aretz*, 28 December 2004; http://www.alnwickcastle.com).

Being aware of the effect of motion pictures on a place's image, many countries invest money and other resources in promoting local films: **Britain** endeavors to have "Bollywood" movies shot in the United Kingdom in order to increase tourism from Asia in general and India in particular; **Canada**, **Thailand** and the **Bahamas** employ large PR firms to maximize their exposure in film and television; and **Chicago**'s Office of Films and Entertainment has increased the number of films made in the city by employing a product placement specialist (Hudson and Ritchie, 2006).

Another explicit example of the way films are used to improve place image can be found in the **Philippines**. Following a series of violent incidents, the Philippines acquired a somewhat negative image as a country of kidnapping and violence. In response, the Philippines Tourism Secretary, Richard Gordon, took a business trip to California with the aim of banishing the negative image: "I went up to Hollywood and I spoke with some producers there and they were very enthusiastic about coming down to the Philippines." A senior official at the Department of Tourism said in an interview with Reuters: "If Hollywood actors are able to live here and shoot (movies) peacefully, it will bolster our efforts to promote the Philippines internationally" (Madhur, 2002).

In an effort like that of the Philippines, the **Israeli** Minister of Finance visited Hollywood to promote film production in Israel. He offered top producers various grants and incentives to encourage the international film industry to choose Israel as a film location (*Ha'aretz*, 16 November 2006). Israel also tried to use films to improve its image at the 11th Toronto International Film Festival, where the Israeli movie *The Bubble* was shown. The screening was attended by an official Israeli delegation, including representatives of El Al Israel Airlines and the Israeli culture bureau. The Israeli delegates used the movie as a PR tool to improve Israel's international image and attract visitors to Israel (*The Marker*, 25 August 2006).

While many decision makers hope that film production will improve their place's image, some films can backfire, making the place's image even worse. For example, in the mid-1980s, the governor of **Mississippi** approved a request to have the movie *Mississippi Burning* shot in Philadelphia, Mississippi. The movie is based on a true story of the murder of three civil rights activists by the Ku Klux Klan in 1964. Perceiving the new film as an opportunity to demonstrate the major change Mississippi had undergone and its current openness, the governor welcomed the movie's producers. But things turned out otherwise. When the movie was released in 1988 it reinforced the negative image that Mississippi was trying to suppress. Due to the success of the movie, Mississippi was once again associated with racism; this highlighted the great power of motion pictures in public opinion (Kotler et al., 1993).

Using works of fiction to promote places

Some places have attempted to improve their image using works of fiction. **Rosslyn Chapel**, built in 1446 not far from Edinburgh, Scotland, owes much of its popularity to the bestseller *The Da Vinci Code* by Dan Brown. The book lets it be understood that a hidden sign in the chapel holds the key to the location of the legendary Holy Grail. In 2004, following the commercial success of the book, the number of visitors to the Rosslyn Chapel doubled, and the resulting income was used to fund a £4 million reconstruction of the chapel (*Ha'aretz*, 28 July 2004).

The citizens of **Cortona** in Italy used the commercial success of Frances Mayes' book *Under the Tuscan Sun* to promote their small town. The book tells the true story of Mayes, an American citizen, who bought an old house in Tuscany and turned it into a beautiful summer home, with a view of the famous Tuscan landscapes. Cortona, which previously entertained just a handful of passing tourists, is now a highly sought-after destination and host of the "Tuscan Sky Festival." The festival, started at 2003, uses the great success of the book to attract tourists and sustain a high level of interest in the small town (*Ha'aretz*, 19 August 2004).

Engaging celebrities

When launching a campaign, many places choose to focus on their natural resources such as breathtaking landscapes, unique botanical gardens or crystal-clear lagoons. A different kind of resource that can be used in the place marketing process is the place's residents or even better, its celebrity residents. The use of celebrities in advertisements is based on several factors: first, by definition, celebrities are well-known people who can easily attract potential consumers' attention. Engaging celebrities in an ad is a good way to get target consumers to stop for a moment and take a closer look at it. Another factor is that people seek to emulate their favorite celebrities and would like to imitate whatever their favorite celebrities are doing or consuming; visiting the places where they live or vacation is a great way to get one step closer to their role model. A third factor is the social role of celebrities as opinion shapers. Celebrities are usually known for having superb taste and large variety of options to choose from. So once a celebrity chooses a specific destination for a vacation or as a place to live, it acquires a kind of seal of excellence. Being selected by a celebrity also associates the place with the celebrity's image as a well-known brand.

Celebrities as opinion leaders and indicators of excellence

Celebrities can be used in publicity to promote place by means of several techniques. The first is their use as opinion leaders and indicators of excellence, as in the case of **Malta**. This island uses celebrities' visits as testimony to its unique natural beauty. On its website, Malta invites tourists to follow in the footsteps of Russell Crowe, Brad Pitt, Sharon Stone and other celebrities who have visited the island. The website quotes relevant news articles, such as the one in the London *Times*, declaring Malta "the Mediterranean's mini-Hollywood" (http://www.visitmalta.com). Other examples of the use of celebrities as opinion leaders are set forth in Chapter 7 of this book.

Celebrities as brands

The technique of celebrities as brands is applied to stimulate potential visitors to associate themselves with the stars so as to bask in their reflected glory. One case study can be found in the city of **Cleveland**, Ohio. Its official website has a celebrity section presenting pictures from the lives of local heroes such as Marilyn Manson and Drew Carey. On Manson's page, a series of 12 pictures portrays his childhood in Cleveland, including pictures of his home, his high school and the baseball park where he had his first romantic encounter. The great contribution by the comedian Carey, according to the local paper, is that his show, which is set in Cleveland, is "the city's most powerful public relations tool." Cleveland expressed its gratitude when the Mayor presented Carey with the key to the city; he was voted by 400 local business leaders "Cleveland's best spokesman." Although the city's images projected in his show are not always the best, the president of the Greater Cleveland Growth Association was quite clear in his opinion: "Drew is a native Clevelander who is proud of it, and that's something we need as a community" (Henry, 2001). More generally, the use of home-grown or "adopted" celebrities to promote the places where they were born and raised is very popular in the United States; examples include Jimmy Carter with "my **Atlanta**," Kevin Bacon with "my **Philadelphia**," Erykah Badu with "my **Dallas**" and George Lopez with "my **LA**" (Stafford, 2005).

Like Cleveland, **Nigeria** aims to associate itself with local celebrities as well. For years Nigeria carried a negative image, being associated with corruption, armed robbery and ethnic and religious violence. According to Chief Chukwuemeka Chikelu, Minister of Information and National Orientation, the poor national image of Nigeria was responsible for economic damage and for the paltry amount of foreign investment in the country (http://www.iht.com). In response, in July 2004 the Nigeria Image Project launched a national marketing campaign using the slogan "Nigeria – the heart of Africa." In an interview, Chikelu said that as a major part of the campaign "outstanding Nigerians that have made the country proud in various fields of endeavor would be given recognition and promoted as role models" (http://www.nigeriafirst.org).

Poland likewise, in the 2005 version of its official tourism website (http://www.polandtour.org), had a section dedicated to "Famous Poles." There one could find pictures of Roman Polanski, Krzysof Kicslowski, Chopin and other Polish celebrities. As in the previous cases, Poland wishes to associate itself with famous musicians and film directors as a mean of improving the country's national image. The marketers of Poland are aware that those celebrities have many fans and they hope that if these people knew that their favorite celebrity was connected to Poland it would improve the country's image in their eyes.

One specific class of celebrities used to promote places is fashion models. In 2006 campaigns, **Israel** used the model Bar Refaeli and **Germany** used the Dusseldorf-born supermodel Claudia Schiffer. In the case of Germany, Schiffer appeared in a campaign to promote investments to the country. The advertisements showed the apparently naked Schiffer wrapped in the German flag under the teasing slogans "Size does matter," "Come on over to my place," "Interested in a serious relationship?" and "Invest in Germany, boys" (http://www.german-embassy.org.uk).

While some places use celebrities as brands, other places associate themselves with positive and familiar celebrities (as noted in Chapter 8), organizations and widely known firms in order to bask in their reflected glory. For example, in the marketing of **Atlanta**, Georgia, the marketers highlighted international firms such as CNN and Coca-Cola whose head offices are located in the city. Similarly, the city of **Memphis**, Tennessee, emphasized the location of Federal Express headquarters in the city (Short and Kim, 1993). On the international level, **Korea**, the **United States**, **Japan** and **Scotland** have all made use of global brands that are headquartered in those countries, but market their products worldwide, to promote their national image (Anholt, 2005).

Celebrities as a means to attract public attention

The last technique noted here of using celebrities is as a means to attract public attention. For example, the legendary Hollywood star Tony Curtis starred in a television campaign to promote tourism to **Hungary**. Curtis volunteered to take part in the commercial in honor of his parents, Hungarian Jews who immigrated to the United States many years before. According to a press release issued by the Hungarian Tourism Office in 2003, "One of the most important target groups in North America is the 55+ age group. We were glad to take the opportunity of addressing them through Tony Curtis by using his celebrity status in the US as a hook for potential American visitors" (http://www.gotohungary.com; http://travelvideo.tv).

Full acknowledgment of the crisis and extreme coping measures

The three media strategies constituting this sub-category are based on the accumulated experience of dozens of places that suffered acute image crises. They are (1) delivering a counter-message, (2) spinning liabilities into assets and (3) ridiculing the stereotype. For most places that used these strategies, changing their local or national image was not merely an act of repositioning to improve their competitive edge but an actual battle for the place's future. The following examples include stark, audacious and sometimes even rude media messages from places that have much to gain and very little to lose.

Delivering a counter-message

Many places that undergo an image crisis often prefer the opposite image to their current one. Places perceived as dangerous would like to be perceived as safe; places perceived boring – interesting; and so on. With this simple reasoning, the strategy of delivering counter-messages aims to do battle with places' negative perceptions. For example, places considered boring can market a series of events, festivals and attractions aimed at dispelling their negative image.

Battling images of crime and terror

One common cause of an image crisis arises from issues of safety and security. Many places have learned that even a single event of violent crime against tourists, a small-scale terror attack or social–racial riots can result in a prolonged image crisis. In striving to suppress such negative images, many places opt to deliver a counter-message, highlighting how safe and welcoming the place really is. For example, following a spate of violent incidents against tourists, as mentioned, the **Miami** Convention Bureau embarked on an advertising campaign addressing tourist safety and portraying the city as a safe place (Tilson and Stacks, 1997).

Tunisia responded similarly to a terrorist attack in 2002 in which 18 people were killed, most of them from Germany. Soon after the incident Tunisia's tourism office adopted an advertising campaign aiming to instill visitors with feelings of "Peace and tranquility" (http://www.themedialine.org). Tunisia's official website contained newspaper articles describing the country's contribution to the "Preservation of world peace" and its "Unique relationship of mutual respect" with the United States (http://www.tunisiaonline.com). Tunisia did not use this strategy very long, but many other countries such as **Syria**, **Israel**, northern **Ireland** and others have also tried to promote the perception that they are safe for tourists.

Another country that constantly delivers anti-terror messages is **Saudi Arabia**, which spent millions of dollars to improve its national image after 9/11, trying to create the perception of a peaceful country. Later in 2001, only a few weeks after the 9/11 terror attacks, a campaign was launched presenting King Fahd as a "Man of peace." In 2002, two television advertisements were devised with the assistance of a Washington DC PR firm. Both advertisements featured quotes by American officials and showed how they had been misunderstood by the media and used spuriously against Saudi Arabia. The commercials got controversial responses, with at least nine national broadcasting networks refusing to show them. In another broadcast campaign launched in 2003 on American television, Saudi Arabia is presented as a modern and peaceful country, an ally and a close friend of the United States (*Ha'aretz*, 26 November 2001; 9 May 2002; 22 May 2002; 2 July 2003; 27 July 2003).

Battling images of illness and epidemics

Another possible cause of image crises is plagues and epidemics, which could have a rapid and deadly effect on tourism and foreign investments. In 2006, only 10 months after **Hong Kong** was officially declared "SARS-free," a new campaign was launched to deliver the news. Using the slogan "Live it. Love it," the city tried to create the impression that it was alive again. The new slogan was designed to contradict two negative perceptions: that Hong Kong was not alive, because of the deadly SARS epidemic; the other was that tourists no longer visited Hong Kong, and the city was not "alive" in the sense of being vibrant, dynamic and vital. Printed brochures that were also part of the campaign referred directly to the SARS epidemic, asserting that it had actually brought about a positive change in Hong Kong, creating an atmosphere of friendliness and hospitality among the local citizenry. A similar marketing initiative was taken by **Singapore**, which also suffered from the SARS crisis during 2003. Using the slogan "Singapore OK", the country informed the travel industry and potential consumers in key markets that it was safe again and free of SARS (Beirman, 2006).

While Hong Kong and Singapore were associated "only" with the SARS epidemic, **India** faced even greater challenges. Although perceived as magical and fascinating, India had only a small number of American tourists each year. For most Americans, India was associated with epidemics, floods and poverty. In spring 2001, the Indian Tourist Bureau launched a campaign aimed at delivering a counter-message. In it India was presented as a peaceful, beautiful and spiritual place, in an effort to portray the image of a safe and stress-free country (*Ha'aretz*, 29 June 2001).

Battling images of boredom

Being perceived as boring and lacking "things to do" might cause places enormous economic damage, especially when their economy is based on tourism. One such attempt to combat an image of boredom was undertaken by the **Negev Desert**, an arid region of southern Israel. The "Negev Action" campaign, launched in the late 1990s, challenged the perception of the region as boring, remote, uneventful and monotonous. The campaign offered trips, extreme-sports events and family-oriented activities, trying to contradict the common perceptions and to prove that the area was "filled with action." The visuals of the campaign focused on active recreation photographs such as hot-air balloons and dune buggies (Avraham, 2003a).

Battling one-track images

Another common problem for place marketers concerns places that have a poor image and are perceived as one-track. The target audience's image of the place often consists of one dominant trait. To make the image richer and more attractive, some places deliver a message contrary to the one-track stereotype. For example, in 1986 **Portugal** launched a counter-campaign, published in *Conde Nast Traveller*, to show it had much more to offer than just a "sea and sun" vacation. One of the campaign's advertisements showed the usual picture of a golden sunny beach under the headline "One view of Portugal." But below it was a picture of a wide green field, set upside-down, with the headline "Another view of Portugal." The text following the pictures contained a lengthy description of other aspects of Portugal, contrasting the well-known image. The text emphasized elements such as the varied landscapes across the country, the abundant night life, spas, a variety of arts and so on – all in order to enrich the country's image.

Likewise, **Malta** endeavored to elevate itself above the conventional "sea and sun" image. According to the island's tourism minister, to compete successfully with other tourist destinations in the area Malta had to develop a unique brand. In its new image, Malta appeared not just as a great place for sunbathing but as a fascinating country, rich in history, culture, architecture and archeological sites. To project this new image, two great castles on the island were reconstructed, and every second Sunday people encased in knights' armor fired cannonballs into the sea (*Ha'aretz*, 23 June 1997). In the new campaign, Malta marketed itself as "The heart of the Mediterranean," trying to position itself as a center for both culture and leisure (http://www.visitmalta.com).

While the marketers of both Portugal and Malta had a positive image they wanted to enrich, the **Republic of Mozambique** was beset by a more intricate problem. In a recent initiative, the marketers of the southeast African country launched a new campaign to fight the nation's one-track image as a traditional African country. The slogan chosen for the campaign is "Land of contrasts," most likely aimed at creating the impression that there is much more to Mozambique than the stereotype of an underdeveloped African country. The word "contrasts" in the slogan implies that aside from the one-dimensional knowledge of the place, there is a whole other side waiting to be discovered.

Spinning liabilities into assets

The strategy of spinning liabilities into assets takes the key point of a previous strategy – acknowledging the negative image – a step further, by recognizing a negative factor responsible for the image and spinning it into a positive trait (Avraham and Ketter, 2006). This strategy is based on the positive perception that in every bad thing there is also something good. Places that have employed this strategy tried to overcome negative perceptions related to extreme climate, controversial heritage, ethnicity and ethnic diversity, underdevelopment and natural and environmental disasters; they attempt to highlight a positive aspect instead. Now they put a fresh twist on the characteristics deemed responsible for the place's negative image, so as to turn them into assets.

Spinning extreme climate into an asset

An important factor in a place's image, especially when it is consumed for vacation, is its climate. Many visitors prefer warm and pleasant weather for their vacations, so places with an extreme cold or hot climate are hard-pressed to attract tourists. This makes sense, as no one wants to go sightseeing, visit an attraction or even take a short walk when it is scorching hot or freezing cold. To handle these cases of extreme climate, some places choose the strategy of spinning a liability into an asset: in this case the problematic climate is being presented as an advantage.

Lapland, a province in the northern part of Scandinavia, has made successful use of this strategy. For long, Lapland was known only for its extreme cold, a fact that damaged the destination's image and kept visitors away. Today, however, these cold winters are marketed as unique and have become a top tourist attraction, with various winter cultural events and festivals under the slogan "Vitality from nature" (http://www.laplandfinland.com). **Minnesota** tried to handle its extremely cold winters similarly. For many years, the state's winter kept visitors away and damaged its image. But nowadays these winters are marketed as unique and have become a tourist attraction with various cultural events, ice fishing activities and festivals catering to many (Kotler et al., 1993).

Another place with an extremely cold climate is **Harbin**, a city in northeast China. The temperature there drops to 40° below zero and remains below freezing for nearly half the year. Given the extreme climate, one of the only options left was spinning a liability into an asset: celebrating winter instead of freezing in the cold. Although ice sculpturing in Harbin dates back many years, the first annual Snow and Ice Festival started in 1985 and has grown into a massive event since. Presently the festival brings many tourists to the city from all over the world every winter. Most of the sculptures at the snow festival are the work of competing teams, coming from Russia, Japan, Canada, France and even South Africa. The ice festival, a few miles away from the snow festival, is anything but dull and colorless. Bright neon lights shine everywhere, deep within huge blocks of ice forming structures as many as 100 feet high. The ice structures in recent years have included a replica of the Great Wall of China, an entire ship with passengers and a Thai temple complete with hallways and rooms. All the ice used in the festival comes from a nearby river, which provides a limitless supply for the builders (King, 2005).

The opposite problem of heat besets some places. The **Negev Desert** in southern Israel is well known for its hot, dry climate and for its typical desert landscapes. For many years local decision makers tried to create a counter-image by delivering messages that the Negev Desert was green and blooming; however, a recent campaign endeavored to go with the existing stereotype. In the new campaign, the message being delivered is one of local pride: the Negev is proud of what it is and is beautiful in its brown desert colors. The slogan for the new campaign calls the visitors "To get excited by different colors," meaning that the yellow and the brown are just as exciting as any other landscape. According to a local spokesman, "The Negev Desert doesn't need to hide beneath images of blooming flowers or extreme sports. Everyone around us sells images of green grass and waterfalls; the desert is unique, it has its own character, it is magical, exciting and peaceful. The Negev is beautiful just the way it is and we should be proud of that."

Spinning a controversial heritage into an asset

Some places have a long and glorious heritage, others a controversial one bearing a variety of problematic images. Using the technique of spinning controversial heritage into an asset, those places take pride in their local traditions, presenting them in a new, exciting and positive light. For example, **Haiti** has a long-standing negative image, associated with poverty, voodoo and black magic. In an effort to transform these liabilities into assets, Haiti launched a tourism campaign using the slogan "Haiti, it's spellbinding." With this slogan, Haiti tried to turn the negative image of voodoo witchcraft into a positive, mysterious and mystical image (Kotler et al., 1993).

Similarly, **Romania** has struggled with a problematic image concerned with its mythical traditions. Known as the homeland of the legendary vampire Count Dracula, Romania has been associated with horror stories, blood and darkness. In 1995, the Romanian Tourism Office launched the first International Dracula Congress, trying to turn a frightening mythical vampire into a glamorous top-selling attraction (Kotler et al., 1999). Another such place is **Verkosta**, a Russian town which was the site of a *gulag*, part of the Soviet system of forced labor camps build under the Stalinist regime in the 1930s. Worse still, Verkosta lies 1200 miles northeast of Moscow, in the middle of the frozen Arctic tundra. In an extremely bold marketing act, Verkosta's mayor suggested reconstructing the gulag as a center for extreme tourism. In his boundless imagination, the mayor envisaged American tourists coming to the gulag, working in the coal mines, eating turnip soup and sleeping on the original bunks. After experiencing prison camp life, the tourists would manage to escape and then try to survive in the frozen wilderness by hunting and fishing, while hiding from the Russian guards chasing them (*Ha'aretz*, 12 June 2005).

Spinning ethnicity and ethnic conflicts into assets

For some people ethnic diversity is associated with violent conflict, poverty and primitive traditions; for others it is a wonderful asset, displaying a mixture of cultures, tastes and colors. Being an area of many interracial conflicts, **Indonesia** sustained a negative image for many years. Knowing that they could not ignore the existing perceptions of their country, the marketers of Indonesia decided to turn its multicultural diversity into an asset. A recent campaign now highlights the positive aspects of the country's ethnic diversity, using the slogans "Indonesia – Endless Beauty of Diversity" and "Indonesia – The Ultimate in Diversity" (http://www.my-indonesia.info).

Another place which tried to turn its ethnic mixture to an asset was **Bradford**, a city in the county of Yorkshire in England. For years Bradford carried a negative image due to the many foreign immigrants who had settled there and the ethnic and racial clashes that ensued. During the 1990s, the city tried to turn this characteristic into an advantage by marketing itself as a multicultural oasis, where different social groups and races coexist in harmony and in a spirit of cooperation. To deliver this new positive spirit, the city launched a marketing campaign under the slogan "Flavors of Asia" (Bramwell and Rawding, 1996). Through this slogan Bradford's image as a melting pot for immigrants from Asia is presented as an advantage, promising an exciting mixture of cultures, tastes and colors.

In the eyes of the Western culture, Eastern cultures can be seen not only as backward and primitive, but also as friendly, open and welcoming. **Be'er Sheva**, a city in southern Israel, also known as the capital of the Negev Desert, is commonly considered to be very old-fashioned and primitive (Avraham, 2003b). Several researchers (Fenster et al., 1994), aware of this negative image, suggested to local authorities in a refreshing marketing initiative that they should market the city as a modern and unique – for Israel – embodiment of an exotic oriental desert city. This suggestion made use of the positive perceptions linked to the desert and its habitats and associating them with the city. The researchers suggested the use of Eastern architecture (e.g., a unique oriental shopping center and a Bedouin market) and other activities that would promote its image as the "modern desert city." According to the new vision, the "Eastern" character suggested refers to perceptions of the East as innocent, unspoiled, hospitable, spirited and lively. In this manner, Be'er Sheva would still be the "capital of the desert," but this time the negative traits of the desert would be turned into positive ones (Avraham, 2003a).

Spinning stereotypes of under-development into assets

As illustrated in the foregoing techniques, many stereotypes are associated with both positive and negative traits. With the present technique too, places perceived as suffering from under-development can spin this liability into an asset by focusing on their innocent, natural and authentic environment. A good example is the state of **Georgia** in the United States, wishing to overcome its negative image as an undeveloped region that attracted very few visitors. In a campaign launched in the 1970s, Georgia tried to turn this stereotype into a wild and exotic one, using the slogan "Georgia, the Unspoiled." A similar example is **South Korea**, which had little tourism and a feeble image for many years. In a campaign in the early 2000s, the marketers of South Korea tried to spin this liability into an asset by referring to itself as "South Korea – Asia's best kept secret." Here being a less popular destination than nearby places such as Japan or Thailand is presented as an advantage, implying that the country has kept its pure and innocent nature. Another illustration emerges from the Eastern European countries, which since the 1990s have been in constant competition for tourists and visitors, in contrast to the past. **Bratislava**, capital of the **Slovak Republic**, employs a very interesting strategy to enlarge the number of its visitors. Through clever use of its weak image and its associations as an under-developed city, it chose to market itself as "Bratislava – the small big city" and as "Bratislava, Europe's hidden treasure" (http://www.bratislava.sk).

Spinning natural and historical disasters into assets

Spinning liabilities into assets can also be done in cases of natural and historical disasters.

In 1988, a severe wildfire raged in **Yellowstone** and **Glacier National Parks**, destroying more than a third of the famous natural reserves. Large parts of the parks' camping grounds, cabins and other infrastructure were burnt to ashes. As a direct result of this wide-scale natural disaster, visits to the parks decreased dramatically, threatening their position as two of the most popular parks in North America. Restoring the parks to their original state was impossible, so the park managers resolved to change public opinion about wildfires. In a brilliant strategic move, wildfires were no longer presented as an unpredictable enemy of plants, animals and humans, but as a natural, necessary ecological process. Glacier National Park set up a new educational program for its visitors, which included detailed displays showing the role of fire in the forest's ecosystem, roadside exhibits in places damaged by the fire and evening talks at camping ground amphitheaters. Local park rangers offered visitors special trips to burnt areas to create personal experience with the aftermath of a fire. The new educational program not only increased tourism to the burnt areas, but also led to a wider acceptance of wildfire as a natural process. When additional heavy fires broke out in 2000 there was no significant decline in the number of visits to the parks (Glaesser, 2006).

While Yellowstone and Glacier National parks succeeded in turning a natural disaster into an asset, **Southampton,** a port city on the southern coast of England, succeeded in becoming a tourist destination through a historical disaster. On the night between Sunday and Monday, 14 April 1912, RMS *Titanic* struck an iceberg and sank, taking the lives of approximately 1,500 passengers and crew. More than 500 of those who perished in the terrible accident were residents of Southampton, the *Titanic*'s port of departure. Soon after the event several memorials were built to immortalize the special link between Southampton and the doomed vessel. In recent years, capitalizing on the blockbuster movie, local initiators decided to spin the potential of the past tragedy into a successful way of attracting tourists. The Southampton City Council designed a self-guided walk through the city, leading visitors past key landmarks in the epic of the *Titanic*. In addition to the memorials, tourists can visit a first-class hotel where some of the ship's passengers spent their last night, and other related attractions (Glaesser, 2006).

Spinning geographical location into an asset

The destination's physical location is one of its most important assets. Being close to main roads, airports, population centers or to other tourist destinations can make the place more accessible to its potential customers; at the same time, being located out in the country can decrease the place's potential sharply (Avraham, 2003a). This is the unfortunate condition of **Azuz,** a small desert settlement in Israel, on the border with Egypt, and far from main roads, attractions and other towns. In September 2006, Azuz launched the Exodus Festival, aimed at using its rural location as a means to attract visitors.

The festival connects Israel and Africa by focusing on the relations between Israeli and African music, the culture of Israeli Jews who immigrated – or whose parents immigrated – from Ethiopia and other Israelis and modern Israelis with the history of the Israelites in ancient Egypt (http://www.africanegev.com). By creating the festival, the marketers of Azuz turned their liability, a remote location on the border with Egypt, into an asset, a unique link between Israeli and the African culture.

Ridicule the stereotype

Sometimes stereotypes of a place can be exaggerated, prejudiced or simply out of all proportion. To combat such perceptions effectively a strategy of ridiculing the stereotype has been applied. A place's negative stereotype is taken to the extreme and then dispelled by showing how absurd it actually is (Avraham and Ketter, 2006). An excellent example can be found in the case of **Poland**, trying to overcome negative stereotypes of Poles. Eastern European countries joining the European Union sparked fears of cheap labor flooding Western Europe. In France, a few local politicians opposed to the EU constitution expressed their fears stating that the "Polish plumber" will come to work in France and will take the place of local labor. In response, the Polish tourist bureau launched a campaign to improve the country's national image and attract French tourists. The campaign advertisement shows a picture of a young, sexy and handsome Polish plumber, wearing simple overalls and holding plumbing tools, with views of Poland in the background. The caption in French reads "I'm staying in Poland – come." In the next ad in the campaign, a beautiful young nurse is featured with the caption "Poland: I'm waiting for you" (*Ha'aretz*, 1 July 2005; 18 July 2005). In the campaign, the stereotype attributed to Poles is pushed to the extreme, in order to dispel it. Both advertisements are part of Poland's long ongoing campaign to transform its gloomy, communist, grim, poor and cold image into a more positive one.

Israel found another use for this strategy. Concerned with its negative image as an unsafe place, an Israeli NGO handed out condoms to American students who were considering coming to Israel for a visit. The condom wrappers were in the blue and white colors of the Israeli flag and carried the catchphrase "Israel – It's still safe to come." Similarly, in a campaign created by a private consultancy partnership in Israel, the same strategy was used to illustrate how ridiculous Israel's stereotype was. In the commercial, a young female tourist is walking along the seashore in Israel, when she suddenly spots a handsome man sitting on the sand. Continuing walking, the young woman keeps looking at the attractive guy and bumps into a pole. At that point the narrator announces "Indeed, Israel can be a dangerous place." The potential customer thereby realizes that the stereotype of Israel is overdone and the potential hazards one might face would be no more than colliding with a wooden post on one of Israel's sunny beaches.

Disengagement from the place's main characteristics

The sub-category of media strategies involving disengagement from the place's main characteristics is the most extreme group. It contains three major media strategies, all aimed at elimination of the place's problematic image and replacing it with a new one: (1) branding contrary to the stereotype; (2) geographical isolation; (3) changing the place's name. As with the previous group of strategies, most places that have implemented the strategies assembled in this sub-category had long struggled with an acute image crisis that required drastic action, as can be seen in the following examples.

Branding contrary to the stereotype

Numerous cities, countries and tourism destinations are associated with negative stereotypes that they would be happy to shed. Many of those stereotypes took shape in the aftermath of a war, a terror attack, the industrial era or other past events, all long gone. Whatever the cause of the negative stereotype, past experience indicates that changing it is a long and complex task (Avraham and Ketter, 2006). One possible way is branding contrary to the stereotype, a strategy that fights the stereotype by constructing an opposite image. This takes the previously mentioned strategy of delivering a counter-message one step further by adopting an all-embracing approach. The place tries to change its image (and usually its reality) dramatically and to acquire a new image that is the opposite of the existing one.

Branding contrary to war stereotypes

The first of several possible techniques of the counter-branding strategy operates in the case of place stereotypes created as a result of war. The long and bloody war between Serbs and Croats resulted in **Croatia** suffering a severe image crisis, causing a sharp decline in tourism. This decline continued even in Croatia's long post-crisis period, from 1996 to 2002. To restore its favorable image as a tourist destination and to expunge the association with violent conflict, Croatia resolved to adopt a new national image. In its new campaign, Croatia appears as a peaceful Mediterranean country, a land of culture and beaches. The current image carries the appropriate slogan "The Mediterranean as it once was," trying to create a fresh and peaceful impression, the opposite of its old bloody image (http://www.sourcewatch.org; http://www.croatia.hr).

Another place that has labored under a post-war image crisis is the German city of **Nuremberg**, one of the principal symbols of the Nazi regime, the name of which is linked to the post-war trials of Nazi leaders. To counter its old image, Nuremberg steadily positioned itself in recent decades as a center of "Peace and human rights." The positioning succeeded, as Nuremberg won international recognition by UNESCO. The chosen position was the direct opposite of the negative image imposed on the city by its Nazi past: instead of war, racism, destruction and nationalism, Nuremberg now stands for justice, freedom, peace and equality. This change in the positioning was accomplished by the creation and promotion of museums, monuments, art exhibits, cultural events and conferences dedicated to human rights and social justice (*Ha'aretz*, 5 December 2003).

Branding contrary to industrial stereotypes

Heavy industry, polluting factories and smog are another cause of image crises. In the 1960s, the city of **Kita-Kyushu** in Japan was stigmatized as a "deadly" city due to the high levels of air and sea pollution caused by its petrochemical and other heavy industries. In response, citizens, businesses and the government united in a comprehensive program against pollution. After a series of long and well-planned efforts, in 1975 Kita-Kyushu was proclaimed to have overcome its pollution problems. To impart to its image the same makeover that the city experienced, Kita-Kyusha transformed its image from "dark city" to "green city." But the city did not stop there. In 1986, it began industrial environment programs, where knowledge of technology and the environment was conveyed to professionals in developing countries (Global Development Research Center, 2005). In this way, Kita-Kyushu transformed its polluted past into an environment-friendly present, ensuring itself and other cities around the world a brighter future.

A similar example is the city of **Hamilton**, Ontario, formerly nicknamed "Steel Town." In an official publication, Hamilton's transition from the old stereotype to the new city vision is made clear: "It's time to bury old perceptions and celebrate new realities. It is time to re-brand Hamilton with a new logo, a new theme, and a new promise for the future." Its new slogan, "Reach, dream, rise and shine," was devised to communicate the message of Hamilton as "A wonderful place to live, work and grow," in contrast to its negative industrial image (http://www.tourismhamilton.com, http://www.city.hamilton.on.ca; http://www.joelkotkin.com).

Branding contrary to economic recession stereotypes

While many places opt for the counter-branding strategy in the fields of hospitality and tourism, some have used it to re-attract immigrants and businesses, combating stereotypes of economic recession. Like the public sector, the business sector is also greatly influenced by images and the range of possible investments; commerce or the establishment of new businesses could be greatly affected by the place's image (Avraham, 2003a).

One example for the use of this strategy to promote economic interests is offered by **South Africa**, displaying itself as a business destination. The new campaign, launched in summer 2005, was a 90-second television commercial telling the story of global investors who had done well in business in South Africa and illustrating the advantages of the country as a gateway to the rest of Africa. The new slogan chosen for the campaign was "Alive with possibility" (see Plate 3); this ran counter to South Africa's negative image during the apartheid regime and for several years after it, as a place that was unsafe and unstable, and where doing business was almost impossible (http://www.imc.org.az).

Geographical isolation

As noted earlier in this chapter, geographical location is one of the place's most important characteristics. In addition to physical characteristics such as climate, landscapes and proximity to other places, geographical location is linked to a range of characteristics such as culture, language, history and heritage. Geographical location also exerts a major effect on the place's image: for example, places in the northeast of the **United States** will have a different image from places in the Midwest. Taking this example to an extreme, the very continent itself has an effect on a place's image, as different mental notions exist for places in Africa, Central Asia, Western Europe and so on. For some places, the image crisis is caused not by the place's characteristics but by their association with certain geographical areas that carry a negative image. In that case, a good strategy might be *geographical isolation*. Distancing itself from the problematic region with which it is identified can help a country to reverse its negative image and produce a positive one (Avraham and Ketter, 2006). This strategy is particularly effective in respect of safety and security issues, which create a "spillover effect": visitors' tendency to associate a security incident with an entire region (Santana, 2003). This strategy, which has also been called "destination-specific" (Pizam and Mansfeld, 1996) or "isolation" (Beirman, 2002), is recommended for promoting destinations near problematic regions or in countries enduring ongoing image crises.

Africa, provides an extreme example of the spillover effect. Its division into over 50 different countries does not prevent the continent frequently being perceived as a single whole in terms of negative stereotypes. This perception is especially common among Europeans, who tend to prefer any destination to Africa. In general, Africa is associated with hunger, poverty, contagious diseases – especially AIDS – drought, civil war and political instability. Ignorance of the different countries in Africa prevents people from identifying the unique characteristics of each place and promotes the spillover effect. As a result, a conflict occurring in one location in Africa can affect tourism in other African countries, thousands of miles away (Glaesser, 2006).

As in Africa, the violent conflicts in the **Middle East** are also perceived as "a general state of war," hindering the ability to distinguish between the different places. As a result, several tourist destinations in the Middle East employ the *geographical isolation strategy* to differentiate themselves from conflict zones. To disconnect itself from the problematic image of Israel, the marketers of the Israeli resort of **Eilat** "re-located" it, presenting it as "Eilat on the Red Sea" in disregard of the city's formal location (Avraham, 2006). In a 2005 campaign aimed at the European market, Eilat was shown at the hub of an illustrated map. Yellow sunrays depicted on the map gave distances between Eilat and various European capitals, but no lines radiated to nearby places perceived unsafe such as Jerusalem and Cairo.

Israel also illustrates explicit awareness of the harmful potential of the spillover effect. In response to a series of negative events that occurred in the summer of 2005, including terror attacks in London and Sinai and the disengagement between Israel and the Palestinian Authority, executives of the Israeli Hotels Association called for more effort in the marketing of Israel. According to these executives, a marketing plan was needed to prevent the spillover effect of the recent adverse events on tourism to Israel (*Ha'aretz*, 28 July 2005).

South of Eilat, between the Gulf of Eilat (Gulf of Aqaba) and the Gulf of Suez, is the **Sinai Peninsula**, along whose coasts are some of the world's most famous scuba diving resorts. Following the same strategy used by Eilat, various resorts there market themselves as the "Red Sea Riviera." Being located between Israel and Egypt, the Sinai marketers labor under the same difficulties as their Eilat counterparts, having no wish to associate their destination with either country. Instead, they prefer to be perceived as an independent entity: the Riviera on the Red Sea. Similarly, following another outbreak of violent conflict between Israel and the Palestinians at the end of 2000, **Jordan** launched a campaign aimed "To differentiate destination Jordan from destination Israel" (Beirman, 2002, p. 174). This strategy can also be found the island of **Bali**, which is traditionally promoted as a destination with little reference to Indonesia (Beirman, 2006).

While these places try to isolate themselves from images of war and terror, others try to differentiate themselves from more general stereotypes, such as being cold and distant. A survey of the US travel market in 1985 found that most of the Americans surveyed had no intention of visiting Canada. In response, the province of **Nova Scotia** launched a creative campaign, presenting itself as a freestanding entity. The result of this surprising move was a 90% increase in US visitors to Nova Scotia, supporting the efficiency of this strategy (Kotler et al., 1993).

Geographical association

The reverse of isolation strategy is the geographical association, a strategy to link the marketed destination to a place with a favorable image so as to bask in its reflected glory. One such place is **Kansas City**, suffering from the weak image of a Midwestern city. To associate itself with leading metropolises such as **New York**, **Los Angeles** and **Washington, DC**, Kansas City now markets itself as KC. According to the Think-one-KC website, "By making 'KC' the recognized moniker for our region, we are putting ourselves in the same league as these world-class metros, showing a confidence and self-awareness that Kansas City is not traditionally known for." A graphic representation of this statement can be found in one of KC's logos, carrying the following names arrayed as a column: "NY, LA, DC, KC" (see Plate 11) (http://www.thinkonekc.com). A similar example can be found in a marketing campaign by **Barbados**. In an ad in the summer 2006, the tropical island used the text "After surveying NY, LA, San Francisco and Washington DC restaurants, Zagat (restaurant rating guide) discovered the perfect place for vacation."

Estonia too adopted the association strategy. In its search for new identity after the collapse of the Soviet Union and the possibility of joining the EU, Estonian politicians exercised some effort to have their country identified as Nordic (Scandinavian) rather than Baltic (like Latvia and Lithuania). They did so by suggesting changing the country's flag into a tricolor Scandinavian-style cross-design banner and renaming it Estland, akin to Iceland and Greenland (http://www.norden.org).

San Fernando Valley is traditionally known as the less-successful sister of Hollywood and was dubbed "Smogadena, Unknown Actorville, and Pornadelphia" by Jay Leno (Stephens, 2001). In response to its hardly glorious and sometime negative images, local decision makers decided to brand San Fernando Valley as "Valley of the Stars," associating it with nearby Hollywood. To bolster the new image, ethnic and arts festivals are now held annually to create the feel of a dynamic, diverse and family-oriented community. The campaign is aimed at investors, businesses and residents, trying to increase the awareness of the valley as an ideal place to live, work and play (http://www.valleyofthestars.net).

Changing the place's name

A place's name is one of the most fundamental components of its image. Usually it is the first element that comes to mind, followed by a row of associations to create the place's image. Aware of this, some place marketers believe that in order to create a profound change in a place's image a name change is required. Such a strategy is very extreme and used only in rare circumstances. First is the existence of an extremely potent negative image; for such places, changing the name represents the hope of elimination of the negative image along with the deletion of the old associated name and the onset of a new era for the place. Second is places with a weak image, hardly known to the public, that try to associate themselves with familiar places by changing their name accordingly. Unlike places that change their name because of the image it carries, some places have names so singular that their sound alone can attract or repel visitors, such as the towns of *Chicken* in **Alaska**; *Why* in **Arizona**; *Hooker* in **California**; *Chicken Head* and *Two Eggs* in **Florida**; *Hot Coffee* in **Mississippi**; *Toast* in **North Carolina**; *Boring* in **Oregon**; and more (*Ambassador*, August 1998).

One of the earliest known cases of changing a place's name to improve its image concerns **Greenland** in 982 CE. According to a local tradition, Erik the Red was exiled from Iceland, and along with his family and slaves he settled in Greenland. He named the island Greenland to create a positive image for the place and attract more people to settle (http://www.wikipedia.org). Another historical milestone in the use of the name-changing strategy is the case of the city of **Lexington**, Nebraska, which was established in 1872 as Plum Creek. In 1888, the community leaders were concerned about the similarity of the name Plum Creek to Elm Creek, just 19 miles east of the town. The city fathers also believed that "Plum Creek is not the proper name for a progressive city with plans to grow and prosper." In 1889, the new name "Lexington" was chosen, probably to capitalize on the renown of Lexington, Massachusetts, the famous site of one of the earliest battles in the American Revolution; it has served as the city's name ever since and as a pioneer step in the field of place marketing (http://www.lexingtonneced.com).

Name-changing as a dissociation technique

As indicated earlier, the name-changing strategy applies two techniques, differentiated by the purpose of the change. The first aims at dissociation from a powerful negative image, the second (discussed in the next section) at association with a strong positive image.

A case exemplifying the first technique is **North Dakota**. This state has begun taking steps to be known simply as "Dakota," since the qualifier "North" engenders perceptions of the state as cold, snowy and unattractive (Singer, 2002). A similar case of a place seeking to dissociate itself from a geographical location is the **Azata region** in Israel. This terrain lies near the Gaza Strip (in Hebrew "Aza"), hence its name. Following years of violent incidents, the Gaza Strip came to acquire a strong negative image, which projected over all the surrounding area. In 2002, the Azata regional council decided to change its name to Sdot Negev (Negev Fields), aiming to disassociate itself from the Gaza Strip (http://www.sdotnegev.org.il). Local decision makers hoped thereby to shed the negative image of Gaza and to assume a more natural one, like that of the Negev region.

Johannesburg wants to disconnect from its past

One specific reason for changing a place's name is a strong association with racism and discrimination. During the 1990s **Johannesburg** in South Africa was beset by an image crisis, being associated with apartheid, crime and poverty. In 2001, the city decided to brand itself afresh, to re-attract visitors, investors and businesses. The goal of the new branding process was to present Johannesburg as a world-class city, an international center serving as the gate to Africa. According to Amos Masondo, executive mayor of Johannesburg, "the current identity of the city is outdated and conservative. It is not in keeping with the modern, world-class city we are building." Masondo described the new brand as "a world-class African city – young, ambitious and successful." Surveys and focus groups showed that Johannesburg was linked to a variety of negative images, with violent crime, prostitution and drugs being the most common. To start anew, the city eventually resolved to formally adopt the nickname **Joburg** – until then used only informally – which was found to be associated with close familiarity and affection for the city. The noun "city" was also dropped, as the new name stands for the union of the City of Johannesburg Metropolitan Municipality, representing 11 municipal regions of which less than 10% would be considered as urban. That way, the new name imparted a better representation of the unique conglomerate the city consists of.

Joburg's branding process was accompanied by a change in the city logo as well, as a way to express a more dynamic and youthful Johannesburg. In the new logo, the "b" of Joburg is designed as an exclamation mark, the vertical stroke depicting the Hillbrow Tower and the dot below it golden. Hillbrow Tower is a famous landmark on the city's landscape and the gold dot represents the city's past as a gold-mining town, linking past and future.

(http://www.iol.co.za; http://www.joburg.org.za; http://www.brand channel.com; http://www.eprop.co.za; http://www.suntimes.co.za).

Another example of a place seeking to detach itself from racist associations is **White Settlement**, Texas. In the mid-nineteenth century settlers from southern Texas moved north and founded a new settlement. Because the area was inhabited by white settlers only, it was decided to name the new place White Settlement. The innocuous intentions at the time notwithstanding, the name White Settlement might be a disadvantage today, associating the place with racial discrimination and discouraging investors. Accordingly, the mayor and the chamber of commerce decided to ask the town's residents to approve a name change. In November 2005, they were requested to vote on whether the town should keep its original name or change it to a less offensive one such as West Settlement or simply Settlement. A resident who supported the change said, "Today our name keeps us from having a meaningful discussion with potential partners. It doesn't mean there's any racial strife here, but something like West Settlement would go down a lot easier." In fact, the new initiative did not prosper, mustering a paltry support ratio of just about one in nine (Romero, 2005). A closer look at this case illustrates how challenging is the task of changing a place's name. As obviously necessary as a name change might seem, for many residents it does not look that way at all. The name is an essential part of a place's identity, and thus of its residents' identity. Many inhabitants feel a strong bond of affection with the name of their city, town or place and will not give it up that easily. In the case of White Settlement, the place's residents apparently are attached to their town's name too much even to consider a change.

Another common reason for changing a place's name is its association with wars or other violent incidents. Wanting to discard its negative image as a place associated with the Vietnam War, the city of **Saigon** also embarked on a process of change. To make it more attractive to investors, the government changed the city's name and it is now known as **Ho Chi Minh City** (*Ha'aretz*, 19 April 1997). A similar example is the **Vichy** in France. By a bold initiative, a member of the French parliament tabled a motion meant to ban the use of the term "Vichy government." According to the initiator, that phrase exerted a harmful effect on the development of the city of Vichy. Formerly a center of health tourism, Vichy was also the seat of the Nazi-collaborating World War II "Vichy government" in France, a term that has survived ever since. Despite the passage of time the city's name is still problematic, and tourists, conference organizers and visitors refrain from going there (*Ha'aretz*, 23 November 1999).

Name-changing as an association technique

Contrary to the above, the second technique in the name-changing strategy focuses on associating the place with a strong positive image. For example, for many people the image of California was always associated with the Pacific Ocean and the suntanned surfers on its golden beaches. For two cities in the state, **Santa Cruise** and **Huntington Beach**, this image is extremely important, as each wants to market itself as the "surfers' city." They now constantly compete over this title, each claiming to be the "real" surfers' city of the United States. The dispute started early in 2005, when Huntington Beach launched its new website (http://www.surfercityusa.com) and applied to register "Surfers' City" as its trademark. In response, Santa Cruise filed a competing application for the identical trademark. According to local tradition, in 1885 two Hawaiian princes visited Santa Cruise, bringing the new pastime to the United States and making Santa Cruise the first place where people surfed outside of Hawaii. An initiative was raised calling for ending the dispute in the most proper way: a surfing competition (*Ha'aretz*, 28 July 2005).

For most people, the small north Colombian town of **Aracataca** is nothing but an unfamiliar destination. For a few, Aracataca holds a far higher value, being the birthplace in 1928 of the Nobel laureate Gabriel Garcia Marques and the inspiration for his famous book *One Hundred Years of Solitude*. The plot of the bestselling book unfolds in a small imaginary village named Macondo, which according to many is modeled on Aracataca. Marques lived there with his grandparents until he was nine. Through a recent initiative by the town's mayor, an attempt has been made to change its name from Aracataca to Macondo. According to local decision makers, the aim is to attract visitors and to bathe in Marques' reflected glory. At present about 2000 visitors travel to town annually on account of the famous novel, and those who support the initiative hope to increase this number dramatically once the change is made (*Ha'aretz*, 13 January 2006).

Summary

This chapter outlined 14 media strategies, divided into four categories: disregard for/partial acknowledgment of the crisis, full acknowledgment of the crisis and moderate coping measures, full acknowledgment of the crisis and extreme coping measures and disengagement from the place's main characteristics. As is clear from these titles, the media strategies were distributed among the different categories according to the degree of transformation of the place's former image into the projected one.

The dozens of case studies described in this chapter are the core of this book. This chapter has provided examples from every corner of the globe, from Singapore in Asia and Mozambique in Africa to Portugal in Europe and Aracataca in South America and to Sinai in the Middle East and Nova Scotia in North America. The immense variety of case studies surveyed here enables almost every place marketer and local decision maker to find a relevant solution for their place. Whether the problem is post-industrial images, extreme climate, natural disasters, terror attacks or epidemics, this chapter holds a range of response strategies suitable for every crisis.

9 Media strategies focused on the target audience

Following the discussion of media strategies that focus on the source of the message and those that focus on the message itself, this chapter considers media strategies that focus on the target audience. The common denominator of the strategies in this category is the awareness and intensive use of the feelings and values of the target audience as a means to improve the place's negative image. The main perspective here is not that of the marketer but of the target audience itself. The use of messages which focus on the target audience can be divided into three major strategies (Figure 9.1):

1. Similarity of the place's residences to the target audience;
2. Patriotism and nationalism;
3. Changing target audience.

As in previous chapters, these three media strategies can also be set on a moderate–extreme continuum, with similarity to the target audience being the most moderate and changing the target audience being the most extreme strategy. The reasoning behind this distribution is the amount of change/modification the communication process undergoes. The strategies of similarity to the target audience and patriotism or nationalism involve only a minor change in the communication process: it remains the same, and only the message changes. On the other hand, the strategy of changing the target audience requires wide-scale modification of the communication process because it necessitates changing the campaign messages, the channels for delivering the message and so forth.

Figure 9.1   Media strategies focused on the target audience

Similarity to the target audience

While some visitors are looking for an exotic or spiritual experience, many tourists prefer to feel at their chosen destination as if they were still in the comfort of their homes. To create this feeling of comfort and familiarity, many destinations offer accommodation, food and other services specifically geared to the demands of their target market. Although many commercial enterprises try to create feelings of sympathy to the product or service among the target audience, the strategy of similarity to the target audience takes this attempt one step further. Behind this strategy lies the marketers' attempts to show that significant proximity and similarity exist between the marketed place and the target audience. When a campaign message tries to persuade us that "we are similar, we have the same values, perceptions and beliefs," it is actually saying, "there is no reason for you not to identify with us, love us and change your negative image of us, because we are alike." Marketers who use this strategy believe that once the audience discerns this similarity, feelings of affection, sympathy and understanding will arise. All these will improve the image of a place suffering an image crisis.

Many countries which are in ongoing conflict situations try to create sympathy among the American audience, in the belief that this audience can affect American decision makers and their international policy (Bard, 2005; Manheim and Albritton, 1984). For example, in the early 1990s the *America-Israel Friendship League* launched a campaign aimed at reminding Americans of the values common to both nations and the special bond between them. The campaign highlighted such joint values as democracy, freedom of speech, cultural heritage, scientific and technological research and immigration absorption. Following the same strategy, the slogan presented on the AIFL website is "Building friendship based on common values" (http://www.aifl.org). Similarly, East European countries that were candidates for joining the European Economic Community launched campaigns aimed at emphasizing their similarity to Western European countries (Szondi, 2007).

Another example of use of this strategy is demonstrated by **Israel**, which found a most original way to attract tourists from

Japan: arranging a traditional Sumo wrestling match in Caesarea, a leading tourist destination in Israel. In an interview, Isaac Herzog, the former Israeli Minster of Tourism, said, "The visit of Sumo wrestlers to Israel is a strategic marketing move, serving to increase incoming tourism from Japan." The tour, for 15 Sumo wrestlers, included visits to the Old City of Jerusalem, Sumo training on a Mediterranean beach, handing out gifts in hospitals and of course, floating in the Dead Sea (*Israeli*, 14 May 2006). One of the visit's aims was to draw Japanese media attention to Israel by hosting the Sumo wrestlers, considered mega celebrities in Japanese culture. A more important aim was to give the Japanese people the feeling that their traditional culture was being embraced by Israel and that the Israeli and the Japanese people shared similar interests, ideas and values. In this way, Israel was delivering the massage that Japanese people were welcome and would feel very comfortable visiting Israel.

A similar case in which this strategy was used to attract tourists from Japan was in 1993, when the British Tourism Authority (BTA) decided to launch a campaign aimed at Japanese women, who accounted for 80% of the Japanese holidaymakers to **Britain**. According to one BTA member, the image held by the Japanese during the early 1990s was of the United Kingdom as a heroic place of masculine castles which might not be of interest to many women. In the new campaign, "Tea and Roses," the marketers of Britain tried to create a softer and more feminine image, aimed at the new target audience. The new campaign emphasized afternoon tea as its main motif, since it had grown very fashionable among Japanese women and it could portray Britain in a more feminine light (Seaton and Bennett, 1996).

Patriotism and nationalism

In times of major crisis caused by grave economic depression, war or a large-scale terror attack, many citizens are suddenly flooded with feelings of patriotism, nationalism and local pride. According to *Webster's Dictionary*, patriotism is "devotion to the welfare of one's country; the passion which inspires one to serve one's country." Through the use of patriotic feelings as a marketing strategy, the product turns to an abstract symbol of common beliefs, perceptions, social values and local identity (Vatikay, 2000). Accordingly, the consuming process is a means for customers to identify and express their support for those values. The strategy of patriotism and nationalism can be divided into three main techniques: explicit use of patriotic feelings, association with national motifs and enhancing local pride.

Explicit use of patriotic feelings

The most fundamental and straightforward way to use patriotic feelings is to address residents directly and ask them to demonstrate those feelings. With this technique the marketing message is clear and explicit, and in consuming the product the customers support the campaign's message. A prime case study for explicit use of patriotic feelings as a marketing strategy can be found in the **United States** following the 9/11 terror attacks in 2001. Feeling that their country was in a state of war and united in their grief and sorrow, Americans around the country were flooded with feelings of patriotism. Shortly after the terrible event, American flags were hoisted outside homes, offices and factories, expressing the support of the country's inhabitants. Responding to this national patriotic spirit, the city of **New York** together with the New York State government launched several campaigns to re-attract visitors and tourists to the city. In one of the advertisements, the city calls the American people to "Come show your love for New York State." In another, New York City invites visitors to "Paint the town red, white and blue" in a show of patriotism. Similarly, the New York Sports Club launched a "Keep America Strong" campaign, based on the same post 9/11 national spirit (http://www.ynet.co.il).

A similar example of the use of patriotic feelings in the post-9/11 era can be found in the case of **Washington, DC**, the American capital. In the weeks following the terror attack Washington, DC, was often referred to as a "capital under siege" or "at the heart of an international crisis." During that time period, people were afraid to fly, to travel away from home and specifically to visit Washington, DC, as it was perceived as a prime target for any additional terrorist activity. In addition to this natural concern, the city's tourism infrastructure was also interrupted: Reagan National Airport was closed, the number of flights to the city was reduced and famous tourist attractions such as the Capitol Building and the White House were closed to visitors. As a result hotel occupancy fell by more than half, and a similar decrease was indicated in the hotels' revenues. Trying to overcome this crisis, the Washington, DC Convention & Tourism Corporation (WCTC) launched the "City of Inspiration" marketing campaign in October 2001, only 5 weeks after the attack. The theme chosen for the local market campaign was "Be inspired in your own hometown," and "Washington, DC is the city of inspiration. Home of the American Experience" (see Plate 6) for the national campaign. The campaign called on people to come and demonstrate their patriotism and support for their home city on the one hand and be inspired by the strong atmosphere of courage and national pride on the other. Advertising for the campaign was also supported by some of America's most recognized political leaders, including the mayor of Washington, DC and the First Lady, Laura Bush (Stafford et al., 2006).

Another case in which there was explicit use of patriotic feelings concerns the British Tourist Authority, when it marked the 50th anniversary of D-Day. In a high-cost campaign launched for the American market, the members of the BTA wanted to remind the Americans of the comradeship created in June 1944 so as to increase tourism in the summer of 1994. The campaign was built round the theme "Celebrating an alliance forged in war and dedicated to peace" and was run in American newspapers, magazines, radio broadcasts and video news releases that reached 12 million viewers. According to BTA data, approximately 100,000 Americans may have been influenced by the campaign to come and visit Britain (Seaton and Bennett, 1996).

Association with national motifs

National motifs are symbols or themes which are considered to be widely known or of national importance. By using these motifs, places can capture feelings of patriotism and nationalism and associate them with the place. An example of this can be found in the marketing of **Canberra**, capital of Australia. Competing against successful tourist destinations such as Sydney and Melbourne, Canberra is forced to find new and creative ways to improve its competitive edge. In its latest campaign, Canberra uses national motifs as a means to attract tourists and visitors. According to the Australian Capital Territory Tourism Minister, "Canberra is the national capital, a unique place where the city life meets the beauty of the Australian bush. Canberra reflects who we are as Australians, where we are from, what we are proud of and the things we love." The chosen slogan for the new campaign is "See yourself in Canberra," and the new logo of a star is taken from the Australian flag (http://www.business.act.gov.au). By using the Australian federation star, Canberra positions itself as a symbol of the nation, using patriotic feelings as a means of place marketing.

In the United States, the American spirit is a strong and positive national symbol, standing for values such as freedom, hard work and endless opportunities. Throughout the history of the United States many places and products have tried to capture the American spirit and use it as a marketing motif. A recent example is the case of **Cleveland**, Ohio. Trying to refresh its image and to be associated with those strong and positive values, the city of Cleveland now markets itself as "The new American city" (http://www.cleveland.oh.us). One possible factor behind this slogan is the growing competition among big cities in the northeastern United States, forcing places to use abstract symbols and values as a means to overcome their resemblance in the physical aspects. Similarly, following the vast destruction caused by Hurricane Katrina in 2005, the state of **Louisiana** used the slogan "Louisiana Rebirth: Restoring the soul of America" to gain sympathy and support and bring back the tourists (see Plate 5).

Another place associating itself with a national motif is the city of **Tiberias** in Israel, located on the shore of Lake Kinneret. The Kinneret, also known as the Sea of Galilee, is the main source of fresh water in Israel. For a country under constant threat of drought, a satisfactory water level of the Kinneret is considered a major asset and has almost become a national obsession. Recently Tiberias decided to make this national symbol its own: a 15-foot high sculpture of Lake Kinneret now stands in the city, showing real-time data of its water level. According to one of the city's marketing councilors, "The level of the Kinneret is a consensus. It is often said that the level of the Kinneret can influence the level of optimism of the nation. From now on, based on this national symbol, Tiberias will serve as the national gauge of the state of Israel" (*Ha'aretz*, 11 April 2006).

Enhancing local pride

As noted earlier, we believe that the best way to succeed in marketing a place is to adopt the strategic approach to public relations. By this approach, promoting places is a holistic process based on much more than the place's image (Avraham, 2003a). For example, for the new image to "stick" it has to be accompanied by a profound change in the place's physical features and in the way its residents feel about it. The residents, as mentioned, are considered the place's best ambassadors, and their opinion can greatly influence the success of the new campaign (for further reading on local pride and the role of the place's residents please see Chapter 1). Following this approach, many places start their branding process with internal campaigns aimed at increasing residents' local pride. A precondition for using this technique is an overall positive atmosphere among the place's residents. In the right context, this technique can dramatically enhance local pride and project the positive image onto the surrounding areas. On the other hand, used in a place with a generally negative atmosphere, the campaign will be ridiculed and might actually harm the place's image.

One city that is well aware of the importance of the city's residents in the marketing process is **Oklahoma City**. This city had a rough time improving its negative image after several economic crises during the 1980s and 1990s and the bombing of the Federal Building in 1995 in which 168 people lost their lives. As a result, local decision makers decided to turn to the patriotic feelings of the city's residents and the external audience, launching a double campaign at a total cost of $650 000. The theme for the locals was "I believe in Oklahoma," and for out-of-staters it was "Oklahoma: Believing in the American dream" (Brown, 2002). Another city which based its advertisements on the "belief" motif was **Baltimore**. As part of a wider campaign to improve Baltimore's image, a smaller campaign kicked off in April 2002 using the slogan "Baltimore Believe." This campaign was aimed at improving the city's image from within, by increasing local patriotism and feelings of local pride (http://www.jhnewsletter.com).

Another common theme for enhancing local pride is the use of the personal pronouns "I" and "we." One city that has used them, and placed great emphasis on the role of its residents in the marketing process, is **Syracuse**, New York. As part of its branding plan, stickers declaring "I have a part in Syracuse" and "We grow together" were handed out, and local residents were invited to participate in campaign decisions, such as choosing the city's new logo (Short et al., 1993). A similar use for these pronouns can be found in the city of **Dunedin**, New Zealand, which distributed "I am Dunedin" stickers as part of its local pride campaign (http://www.cityofdunedin.com).

Changing the target audience

A place's image is not an objective entity but is formed subjectively through the eyes of different target audiences. As a result, a feature of a place that might be negative for one target audience could be considered positive by a different audience. Exploiting this relativity, some destinations learned that by changing the target audience, features serving as major disadvantages could suddenly go unnoticed or even be considered advantages by different public. In **Israel**, for example, as a result of the damage caused to general tourism by the ongoing conflicts, advertising campaigns began to concentrate on religious tourists in the United States and Europe, assuming that this type of tourism would be less sensitive to security issues. In the new campaign, Jews and Evangelical Christians became the prime target audience, while internal tourism was also encouraged at different levels. The new advertisements attempt to use the potential tourists' religious identity to persuade them to visit Israel, using the slogan

"Don't let your soul wait any longer. Come visit Israel" (*Ha'aretz*, 5 June 2003; http://www.themedialine.org).

A similar case of a shift in the target audience as a result of security issues can be found in **North Carolina**. In a recent initiative, the marketers of North Carolina decided to take an interesting approach to marketing itself, turning a recent crisis in the tourism industry into an asset. North Carolina tourism websites try to convince the state's residents to stay within the country: "From the tragic event of September 11th, 2001, through the wars in Afghanistan and Iraq, travel can be dangerous and airport security measures are tight. Gas prices have risen, and it is becoming more expensive to travel far from home." The campaign has been reported to pay off, yielding an increase in domestic tourism and convincing residents to follow the new slogan and "Discover the state you're in" (http://www.ncpress.com).

Another country which suffered greatly from the global tourism crisis following the terrorist events of September 11 is **Syria**. The crisis impelled Syria to begin a campaign based on the slogan "Syria, Land of Civilizations" in order to attract tourists across the Arab world who no longer felt comfortable traveling to the West (*Ha'aretz*, 30 July 2002). **Jordan** took a similar approach and began concentrating on regional tourism, attracting visitors from the Gulf states and neighboring countries (http://www.themedialine.org). The **Philippines** too, after its image was tarnished by the terror attacks and the SARS epidemic, used the same strategy. In the 2003 campaign, this country targeted the 8 million Filipino nationals living aboard and encouraged them to visit their homeland (Beirman, 2006).

Summary

As noted in earlier chapters, the campaign's target audience is one of the key factors in designing the campaign. The three media strategies presented in this chapter take the target audience's importance one step further and place it at the forefront. In the first and second strategies, place marketers attempt to utilize the target audience's feelings: in the first strategy they deliver the message "I can gain sympathy by convincing you we are similar"; in the second strategy the concept is "I can gain sympathy by using your patriotic feelings." In the third strategy, the place marketers understand that persuading other audiences to visit can be more beneficial than courting the existing one.

Whatever the case, media strategies that focus on the target audience are usually undertaken when the target audience has distinct characteristics or special needs, such as a strong preference for national motifs or the stimulation of national patriotic feelings following a national disaster. Using this third and last set of audience media strategies for marketing places is an important complement to the marketing tools outlined in previous chapters – source and message strategies – and it can be used effectively to improve a place's image and attract tourists, investors and immigrants.

10 The multi-step model for altering place image

Following the introduction of the CAP (crisis, audience, place) analysis and the SAM (source, audience, message) strategies, it is now time to introduce a holistic model for altering a place's image. This model, simulating the decision-making process of place marketers, is based on theoretical and practical knowledge in the field and on the analysis of dozens of case studies, as demonstrated in the second part of this book.

According to the multi-step model for altering a place's image (Figure 10.1), the first step for handling an image crisis is a preliminary analysis of the CAP characteristics. By this measure place marketers examine the crisis, the place where the crisis occurred and single out the target audience for whom the place tries to alter its image. That done, place marketers define their goals and the timing of the launch of the campaign. Next is the stage of choosing the most suitable marketing strategy, or a mix of several strategies, as indicated by the preliminary analysis and the campaign objectives and timing. The choice can be among three groups of media strategies – those which focus on the source of the message, those which focus on the message itself and those which focus on the target audience: a total of 24 media strategies in all. A media strategy having been chosen, several techniques (PR, advertising, direct marketing and sales promotion) and channels (television, newspapers and magazines, Internet, radio and billboards) are available for delivering the campaign. Afterwards it is advisable to evaluate whether the target audience has received and internalized the campaign messages. This evaluation carries major significance as feedback about the campaign effectiveness; if the campaign has not proved effective, the strategy, the channel or the technique should be replaced.

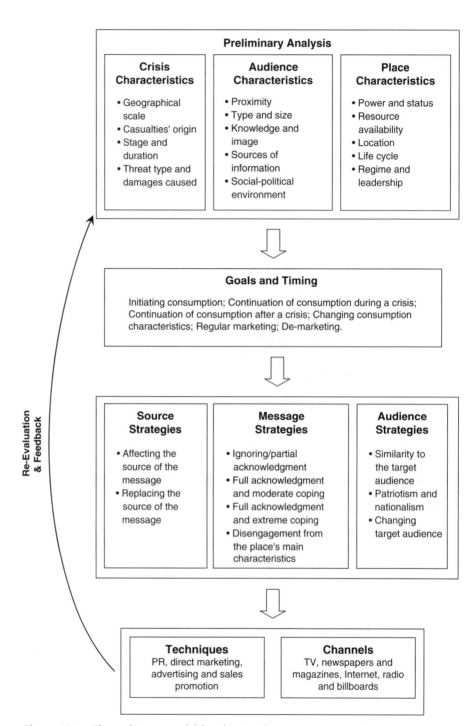

Figure 10.1 The multi-step model for altering place image

Innovation in the multi-step model for altering place image

The multi-step model for altering place image is not the first model for choosing a response or recovery strategy. The field of crisis communication and PR is composed of several existing models that provide suggestions on how firms and organizations can handle an image crisis. For example (and as noted in Chapter 5), Stocker (1997) states that the basic response strategy includes three or four steps: expression of regret that the situation has happened, action to resolve the situation, ensuring the situation will not occur again and if necessary the offer of restitution to the injured parties. A more elaborate model is offered by Benoit (1995, 1997), who lists five communication strategies that can be used in response to a crisis: denial, evasion of responsibility, reducing offensiveness of events, corrective action and mortification. Similarly, Coombs (1999) identifies seven communication strategies: attacking the accuser, denial, excuse, justification, ingratiation, corrective action and full apology.

At first sight, the communication strategies offered by these models seem usable by any place undergoing an image crisis. Viewed more closely, the suggested solutions appear much more relevant for firms and organizations, but not the ideal answer for places suffering from an image crisis. Earlier models were designed for firms and organizations that follow the rules of commercial marketing, while places are sold by means of social-public marketing (Gold and Ward, 1994). The rules of commercial marketing and of social-public marketing differ greatly in general, and in reaction to a crisis in particular. For example, one specifically important characteristic of social-public marketing is that places, unlike firms, cannot promise the public that they will change overnight so that the crisis will not recur (for elaboration on social-public marketing, see Chapter 1). Contrary to the earlier models, the model proposed here was exclusively designed and created for marketing cities, countries and tourist destinations. It is based upon hundreds of case studies in the field of place marketing and offers 24 media strategies that can all be adopted by places.

One presumption of the earlier models is the existence of a misstep of some type in the organization's actions that caused the crisis. Accordingly, the organization is advised to accept responsibility for the crisis and to apologize so as to bring the crisis to an end. Such strategies may be highly beneficial for firms and organizations, but such a course of action is irrelevant for most places. Many crises, such as natural disasters, plagues, war and terror attacks, are beyond the place's control. Place managers can hardly be blamed for them or for the damage they cause, so the option of their taking responsibility is clearly not available to them. The same applies to the many crises conceptualized as "acts of God": place leaders are unlikely to promise that this kind of negative event will not recur, blame someone else for it, justify it, apologize for it or express regret, as suggested by the earlier models.

Arguments regarding lack of place leaders' control over negative events and their inability to take responsibility are even stronger in long and ongoing crises. Very rarely is a mayor seen apologizing for his/her share in the city's image crisis or its economic and social difficulties. In such cases, however, mayors are far more likely to blame the central government or the previous mayor for those problems. Furthermore, place leaders who have initiated a marketing process will not apologize but will be proud to be those who make the change. To conclude, the response strategies in earlier models seem not always relevant for handling places' image crises, and the proposed model is much more apt for this task.

The multi-step model for altering a place's image is preferable to the earlier models also because of its inclusiveness: the proposed model offers a detailed preliminary analysis, a variety of media strategies and other factors such as goals, timing, channels and techniques. The many media strategies detailed in the model furnish a wide range of solutions for almost every possible crisis. An additional advantage is the preliminary analysis, detailed in Chapter 6. Previous models paid scant attention to this, instead giving general advice: for example, "If there is evidence the organization is at fault, the organization should accept responsibility." This kind of counsel may prove extremely helpful for organizations, but again, places undergoing image crises are better served by conducting a deeper analysis. Throughout this book we have observed that the success of the response strategy is greatly affected by the characteristics of the crisis, the audience and the place, as exclusively described in the proposed model.

Another innovative element in the proposed model is the role of the campaign goals and timing and the decision-making process. The variety of goals (initiating consumption; continuation of consumption during an ongoing crisis; continuation of consumption after the crisis is over; changing consumption characteristics; regular marketing; de-marketing) suggested by the model is innovative and is much more elaborate than foregoing goals such as "altering a negative image" or "overcoming an image crisis." Like the preliminary analysis, the campaign goals and timing affect the choice of the most appropriate response strategy.

Choosing the most appropriate strategy

One of the motifs repeated through the entire book is that overcoming an image crisis is a long and complicated process, requiring much more than a change of logo and slogans. Choosing the most appropriate response strategy is a difficult decision that might affect the place for years. Careful analysis of different strategies used by various places to alter their image indicates the absence of any fixed patterns of action in an image crisis. The immense variety impedes any recommendation of the "right" or "appropriate" response strategy in a given crisis or statements such as "Employ strategy F in case of a single terror attack." The proposed model is not a magic potion that once taken will improve the place's image immediately, as if no crisis had ever occurred.

Because altering a place's image involves many factors, every recommendation set out in this chapter should be examined in the context of a particular place, audience and crisis. Moreover, exceptions always exist, reminding us that every crisis has its unique and distinctive characteristics. As stated above, no instant recipes are available, such as "Employ strategy C in case of B-type crisis." Also, using a single strategy is often insufficient, and the use of several strategies and techniques is advised instead. For example, **Egypt**, **New York City**, **Miami** and **Singapore** have all used a mix of several strategies to alter their image, including tackling the physical crisis, improving tourism infrastructure, hosting opinion leaders and lowering price levels. In these cases, it is very difficult to asses which individual strategies and techniques were the most efficient or what was the main strategy behind the place's success in overcoming the crisis.

Despite the complexity of devising "ready-made recipes," here we list a set of guidelines for choosing the most appropriate response strategy. Based on the dozens of case studies in this book, and many others, we have been able to deduce a set of links between CAP characteristics and choice of SAM strategy. Properly integrated in the model, these guidelines can serve every place marketer or place leader in making a quick and easy choice of an effective response strategy.

Due to the inclusiveness of the multi-step model for altering a place's image, a discussion of the link of each of the 24 media strategies to each of the 14 characteristics in the preliminary analysis will miss our point of designing an easy-to-use and user-friendly model. To keep it simple, each group of media strategies is arrayed along a moderate–extreme continuum, and the following guidelines link a moderate crisis (as indicated by the CAP analysis) to a moderate response strategy and vice versa. Again, extreme strategies involve a fundamental change in the place's characteristics, such as its name or its target audience. But moderate strategies involve a minor change, if any, in a place's characteristics, such as establishing rapport with newspeople, reducing the scale of the crisis and highlighting similarity to the target audience. As noted in previous chapters, extreme strategies are usually employed by places that know that it will take much more than a facelift to improve their image or feel that only an extreme strategy will bring their image crisis to an end. In contrast, moderate strategies are usually employed by places which have or had a positive image and just need a boost to get back in business. Whatever the case, below we offer a wide range of easy-to-use guidelines linking CAP characteristics to the choice of an appropriate response strategy.

Crisis characteristics

- *Geographical scale*: The crisis level is linked to the strategy that a place should choose in response. Places with small-scale crises (or which are located at the rim of the crisis) should use moderate strategies such as lowering the scale of the crisis or ignoring it.
- *Casualties*: The casualties' national origin affects the place's reaction to the crisis. If the casualties are Western tourists, resolving the crisis is more likely to require the use of more extreme strategies.
- *Stage and duration*: The duration and stage of the crisis need to be considered. Prolonged crises or those that have swelled into full-scale events require more extreme strategies than short ones and vice versa.
- *Threat and damages*: The existence of a threat affects marketing strategy. If the threat still continues and the tourism infrastructure has been severely damaged, it is advisable to start with rehabilitation before marketing the place. But if the threat is persistent but of very low level, intensive marketing should be put into action.

Audience characteristics

- *Proximity to the place in crisis*: The proximity or distance between the target audience and the place affects the kind of strategy places should choose to overcome the crisis. In cases of high proximity, moderate strategies should be used (such as similarity to the target audience) and vice versa.

- *Type and size*: The kind of tourism and the audience characteristics affect the way the crisis is perceived. For example, a religious audience is less likely to be affected by the crisis than sea-and-sun tourists and therefore requires the use of moderate strategies.
- *Knowledge and image*: The audience's knowledge of the place and its former image affect crisis perception. The more the target audience is familiar with the place (and has a positive image about it) the better are the chances of a speedy resolution of the image crisis. Accordingly, in the case of a knowledgeable audience and a former positive image, moderate strategies should be employed.
- *Sources of information*: The source of information whereby an audience experiences a place affects crisis perception. Audience who rely on the mass media as their main source of information require more extreme media strategies than audience that have first-hand experience of the place.
- *Values*: If the place residents and the target audience share the same values, it is advisable to use strategies such as similarity to the target audience or to appeal to patriotic/nationalistic feelings.

Place characteristics

- *Power and status*: Place status affects the recovery stage. Countries which enjoy higher international or national status are less likely to be affected by the crisis, and their recovery period will be shorter than countries with lower status.
- *Resources*: The more resources a place has, the easier it is to overcome an image crisis. Places with multiple resources can use expensive but effective strategies such as hosting spotlight events and opinion leaders, attracting film productions or tackling the crisis in a comprehensive manner.
- *Location*: Place location affects the kind of media strategy local decisions makers adopt. The image of places in Europe or North America is less likely to be affected by one negative event. On the other hand, places in Africa or the Middle East might be more sensitive and should use more extreme strategies to combat image crisis.
- *Life cycle*: Degree of familiarity with a place affects its pace of recovery. Closely familiar places that are recognized brands will overcome the crisis faster than a new place that has just started marketing itself. Places that have just taken their first steps in the international tourism arena should use more extreme strategies than highly familiar places.

- *Regime and leaders*: Leadership quality exerts an effect on crisis management and handling the image crisis. Places with efficient and well-established leaders can use bolder and more extreme strategies than other places. Dictatorial regimes are more likely to try and force certain messages onto journalists by using extreme strategies such as blocking media access and physical/economic threats.

In addition to drawing conclusions from the CAP characteristics as to the choice of SAM strategies, the reverse can be done as well – deducing the CAP characteristics from the strategies employed by places.

Source strategies

- *Blocking or threatening newspeople*: Non-democratic countries are more likely to apply an extreme strategy regarding the media since freedom of press is a central value in most democracies. We emphasize that we strongly censure these strategies and do not recommend their use under any circumstance.
- *Establishing a rapport with newspeople*: Creating a rapport with journalists and editors is strongly recommended for every place, regardless of its image (for elaboration on the importance of media relations, see Chapter 5). Specifically, when the audience's main source of knowledge of the place is the news media additional efforts should be invested in those relations.
- *Buying news space*: Buying advertisements and news space is mainly done by countries which have many resources.
- *Come and see for yourself*: This strategy has often been employed by places that suffer from powerful and established stereotypes which they feel to be false and unfair.

Audience strategies

- *Similarity to the target audience*: As its title suggests, this strategy can be used only when there is some kind of proximity between the target audience and the place's residents.
- *Patriotism and nationalism*: Although very effective, the use of patriotic feelings is restricted to specific times and audiences. This strategy has mostly been used immediately following a crisis and for the country's own residents.

- *Changing target audience*: When a place endures a long-term crisis, aiming at other target audiences that are less affected by the causes of the crisis is highly recommended.

Message strategies

- *Ignoring the crisis*: While many places choose to employ the strategy of ignoring the crisis, it has been proven effective only in specific circumstances. Pretending that nothing has happened should only be done by places that are a well-established brand with distinctive and unique attractions, such as **London**, **New York City** and **Washington, DC**. Moreover, this strategy should be supported by other strategies, such as hosting opinion leaders and a massive investment in PR.
- *Moderate changes in the place's image*: If the target audience has very little knowledge of the crisis and it has been covered by local media only, it is advisable to choose a moderate response strategy to prevent negative media attention.
- *Hosting spotlight events*: The creation of mega-events is mainly restricted to places with many resources.
- *Hosting opinion leaders*: While this strategy is usually highly beneficial, it can also backfire if the place has not fully overcome the crisis and tourism infrastructures have not been rehabilitated.
- *Elaborating place's image*: This strategy should be employed by places that are perceived stereotypically and whose image consists of one or two major components.
- *Extreme changes in the place's image*: Places that are undergoing a long-term crisis, that have a persistently negative image among the public and newspeople and that feel they have nothing to lose are more likely to employ extreme response strategies.

Following the introduction of the links between the CAP characteristics and the SAM strategies, we may now draw more general conclusions. A place will have a greater tendency to apply moderate strategies under the following circumstances: it is more familiar; it is better known as an established brand; the sources of knowledge about it are more varied (including personal experience); it has unique attractions, celebrities, firms and organizations; it is located near international centers; it enjoys high status; its residents are similar to the target audience; and the crisis it has undergone was minor. The moderate strategies might be to ignore the crisis (with message strategy), to highlight similarity to the target audience (with audience strategy) or to establish rapport with newspeople (with source strategy). By contrast, a place will tend to employ extreme strategies under these circumstances: it is more peripheral, unfamiliar and new in the international tourism arena; it holds replicable attractions (e.g., sea-and-sun tourism); it lacks well-known celebrities, firms and organizations; it is located in a third-world country; it has low international status and a persistently negative image; and it has endured a major crisis with many casualties from Western countries. The extreme strategies could be counter-stereotype branding (with message strategy), changing the target audience (with audience strategy) or blocking media access (with source strategy).

Case studies illustrating the multi-step model for altering place image

To clarify the multi-step model as much as possible, we will now analyze several case studies in which the different stages of the model are evident. This analysis is meant to simulate the place marketers' decision-making process when they choose an appropriate media strategy to alter the place's image. The case studies presented here illustrate three types of crises: a sudden crisis caused by terror attack, a cumulative crisis caused by ongoing conflict and a cumulative crisis caused by increasing crime rates. For each crisis, we shall examine and evaluate the preliminary analysis, the goals and timing, the choice of SAM strategy, the technique and channel that were used and the overall coping with the crisis.

Madrid

The crisis: A series of coordinated bombings in Madrid's train system on 11 March 2004 killed approximately 190 people and injured more than 2,000 (*Ha'aretz*, 12 March 2004). The terror attack attracted major international attention and constituted an immediate threat to the country's tourism industry.

CAP analysis: In order to simulate the decision-making of Madrid's marketers, we should start with a preliminary analysis of the place, audience and crisis characteristics. Examining the *place characteristics* indicates that Madrid is a strong and well-known international brand, a tourist destination of long standing, enjoys high international status, is located in Western Europe and has many resources and a large variety of successful attractions for different purposes (business, historical and cultural and urban tourism). The *crisis characteristics* attest that the crisis was limited to one set of events and to a certain geographical area, and most of the casualties were local. The tourism infrastructure was not damaged and this kind of event was unlikely to recur. The *audience characteristics* indicate that target audience in Western Europe and North America has physical/cultural proximity to the place, a positive previous image, and many members of that audience have sources of information about the place other than the media, such as friends and colleagues who were in Madrid. Furthermore, since Madrid has a former positive image and since terror attacks in the post-9/11 era are perceived as something that can happen anywhere, it is less likely that such an attack will come to be seen as a salient characteristic of the place. On the other hand, the attack was widely covered and it is very likely that the target audience has heard about it.

Goals and timing: In keeping with the list of goals in Chapter 6, it can be inferred that Madrid's goal was the continuation of consumption after the crisis was over.

SAM strategies: The main strategy employed by the city marketers was to ignore the crisis. Following the CAP analysis, Madrid marketers realized that the terror attack gave rise to a passing and limited crisis, with a minor effect on the city's image. Madrid is a well-known brand with a strong and positive image, and highlighting the crisis might prove more harmful than helpful. To conclude, Madrid classified the crisis as very moderate and as a result employed the most moderate strategy: ignoring the crisis and going about business as usual.

Evaluation: Madrid successfully coped with the image crisis resulting from the terror attack. The key to Madrid's success was a careful preliminary analysis and specifically the public's affection for Madrid as a tourist destination and its ability to react in a balanced way to terror attacks following 9/11. The passage of time, together with the message of "business as usual," caused the public to forget the one-off crisis and continue to visit and enjoy the city of Madrid.

Israel

The crisis: Violent conflict has always been a part of the Israeli reality, making the task of marketing Israel extremely complicated. On the other hand, Israel's unique characteristics and its centrality to Judaism, Christianity and Islam, together with its constant and ongoing efforts to market itself, make Israel one of the most interesting examples in the field of marketing places during image crises.

CAP analysis: The *place characteristics* show that Israel is positioned at an important strategic location and enjoys relatively high international status. The country offers several world-class tourist attractions, mainly religious and historical, and its tourism infrastructure is on a high level. On the other hand, Israel is in the Middle East, an area associated with bloody conflict. Additionally, resources allocated to marketing Israel are low compared with other Mediterranean countries. The *crisis characteristics* indicate that most of the casualties are local people, the tourism infrastructure has not been damaged during the long crisis and most of the violent events take place in certain regions at the margins of the country (although terror attacks have occurred in Tel Aviv, Jerusalem and Bethlehem). The *audience characteristics* attest that many audiences worldwide are familiar with the crisis in Israel because of its massive coverage in international media. As Israel has been associated with violent conflict since its establishment in 1948, one of the country's most dominant traits is the perception of lack of personal safety. According to the focus–periphery model (Chapter 6), such a dominant trait turns every minor incident into a major threat to the country's image. In contrast, the attractiveness of Israel to Jewish and Christian pilgrims has remained more or less the same over the years, with a stable demand for religious tourism.

Goals and timing: As Israel is still engaged in persistent conflict with some of its neighbors, its marketing should be classified as continuation of consumption during an ongoing crisis. The conflict is not over, but marketers can still convince tourists that now is a relatively safe time to come.

SAM strategy: The intensive coverage of the Israeli–Palestinian conflict in the international media deprives Israel of the option of ignoring the crisis, as was done by Madrid. Israel's marketing strategy has experienced several changes over the years, and we shall now focus on some of the major strategies employed by the country. As with other places enduring ongoing crises, Israel's marketers had to decide on important issues, such as how to address the continuing conflict, the risks of visiting Israel, its image in the news media and the perceptions of Israel among the target markets. Over the years Israel has employed several *source strategies*, such as seeking to prevent media coverage of violent conflicts (as in the Lebanon war in 1982 and the first *intifada* in 1987), trying to recruit Jewish film makers and persuade them to shoot films in Israel (exploiting background similarity), using Madonna to star in a campaign stating that Israel is safe to visit and criticizing the unbalanced coverage of the news by the BBC and CNN.

Israel has also employed several *message strategies*, such as ridiculing and trying to eliminate the stereotype of non-safety and hosting hundreds of opinion leaders annually. Several video-commercials, made mainly during the 2000s, aimed to soften the image of Israel, which was mainly associated with issues of war and terror, by focusing on its sunny beaches and models in bikinis. Other efforts included the strategy of spinning liabilities into assets, in which special action tours offered a ride in an army vehicle in the West Bank and sightseeing at places where Iraqi missiles struck in the first Gulf War. The most extreme strategy was employed by Eilat, a city at the southernmost point of Israel. It used the strategy of geographical isolation, marketing itself as "Eilat on the Red Sea." Israel also provides some prime examples of use of *audience strategies*, such as focusing on Evangelists and Jews and launching a campaign to highlight the similarity between Israelis and Americans.

Channel and technique: The extensive use of so many strategies has caused Israel's marketers to use every possible means, but dominantly the techniques of PR and advertising.

Evaluation: Because of the severity of the crisis, it has been only natural for Israel to try different strategies, including extreme ones. The Israeli case strongly supports the CAP analysis, illustrating the way changes in the crisis or in the audience can directly affect the choice of media strategy. The use of extreme strategies should have resulted in a positive change in Israel's image. However, the country has not succeeded in superseding the crisis. This is chiefly because the crisis reaches new peaks every several years, preventing image recovery and fuelling the negative images (Mansfeld, 1999).

In addition to the ongoing nature of the Israeli–Palestinian conflict, analysis of Israel's marketing policy indicates that several mistakes were made:

1. Over the years several attempts have been made to brand Israel as a sea-and-sun destination, contrary to the country's image. The choice of sea-and-sun branding is inappropriate for countries constantly in crisis, as this branding offers strong competition with much safer destinations. This fruitless branding also resulted in the loss of many resources allocated to it.
2. In the absence of a single unified marketing authority, Israel's marketing has been conducted by different government agencies, NGOs, travel agents, airlines and private entrepreneurs in commerce, tourism and agriculture. This situation, where a place is marketed through different agents who deliver different messages, is problematic and prevents successful marketing (Wolfsfeld, 1991).
3. Israel's overall marketing budget has been very low and spread over too many target audiences. As a result, many campaigns have been launched with insufficient budgets, preventing them from becoming effective.

Other factors too have indirectly affected Israel's status in the international tourism arena: high costs of flights and tourism services, the country's location far from other (major) tourist destinations and the lack of medium-level accommodations. In other words, the Israeli case is also a clear reminder that there are other factors affecting the image recovery besides those related to the media. In such cases, it is important to take these factors into account when choosing a response strategy.

To summarize, the various initiatives for marketing Israel appear to have been episodic and lacking an overall long-term strategy. Instead of being consistent, the slogans, visuals and media messages were replaced every few years. In 2006, Israel hired the services of Ernst and Young to assess the country's tourism potential and to formulate a marketing strategy. According to their findings, they recommended branding Israel as a center of cultural–historical–religious tourism, rather than a sea-and-sun destination. Ernst and Young also advised enlarging Israel's marketing budget and focusing on specific target audiences, as a means to improve its marketing effectiveness (*Ha'aretz*, 22 November 2006).

Miami

The crisis: In the early 1990s, the crime rate in the city of Miami rose steeply. A number of foreign tourists were murdered in the city, attracting wide negative attention in the international media. Public surveys showed that Miami was perceived as the most unsafe city in the United States. For these reasons and more, the city's hotel occupancy dropped by 50%, threatening an industry of approximately 700,000 employees.

CAP analysis: The *place characteristics* indicate that Miami is a major and important city in the United States, with high national and international standing and many resources. The city is a well-known tourist destination and attracts audience of diverse orientations, such as business, urban, nightlife and sea–and sun. On the other hand, Miami was located at the heart of the crisis, which directly involved the city. The *crisis characteristics* show that it significantly threatened potential visitors and was perceived to be present everywhere in the city. Additionally, those hurt by the crisis were foreign tourists, mainly from Europe, which drew even more attention to the crisis. In contrast, Miami's tourism infrastructure was not damaged and all of the city's attractions operated regularly. The *audience characteristics* show that most of the audience was aware of the city's high crime rate, and those negative images were consistent with the image created of the city by the television series *Miami Vice*, in the mid- and late 1980s. As for the social–political environment, crime is a highly problematic issue in the United States, and places suffering from high crime rates are soon labeled with negative stereotypes.

Goals and timing: Local decision makers seem to have defined the campaign objectives as continuation of consumption after the crisis was over. The reason for declaring the crisis over was the major efforts invested in battling local crime, using local police and FBI forces.

SAM strategy: In parallel to employing media strategies, assorted actions were taken to tackle the crisis. They included the establishment of tourist police, allocation of policemen to every tourist attraction in the city and installation of emergency buttons in rented vehicles. According to Tilson and Stacks (1997), several strategies were employed to alter Miami's image. As for *source strategies*, major efforts were taken both to use the media to deliver positive messages and to bypass the media as a source of information. For example, representatives of Miami's tourism industry were sent to Europe and Latin America to update local media on the measures applied by the city to reduce crime and increase tourism safety. At the same time, residents, PR experts, lawyers, city council members, business people and tourism professionals were recruited and they received assignments in resolving the crisis. Some of those volunteers were sent abroad, where they met local leaders, gave interviews in the local news and spoke to tourism marketers and travel agents, thus bypassing the media as information sources. Efforts were likewise invested in attracting producers of popular American talk shows to come down and shoot in Miami-based locations. As regards *audience strategies*, none of these strategies were found to be relevant in this case, so none were applied.

For *message strategies*, a PR firm was hired at a cost of $500,000 to attract international events to Miami. The events attracted national and international journalists, tour agents and international opinion leaders. Those leaders were invited on free tours of the city, cultural events and other benefits, all sponsored by the city of Miami. Local tour operators were invited to attend workshops on improving customer services and handling customers' stereotypes of the city. To spread the word about all these positive changes, advertising campaigns were launched in Canada, the northeast United States and Europe (the European campaign was estimated to cost $6.5 million) (Tilson and Stacks, 1997).

Channel and technique: During the crisis, almost every possible channel and technique was used.

Evaluation: The Miami case study is a prime example of crisis management in place marketing. The story is an inspiring illustration of the way holistic and comprehensive treatment can alter a negative image and overcome a crisis situation. Nevertheless, it was only in 1995 that the number of visitors began to rise again, highlighting the destructive nature of crises and the importance of long-term planning.

A careful analysis of the media strategies chosen by Miami indicates that most of them were of the moderate kind. In addition to the proper use of SAM strategies, taking the strategic approach to PR (see Chapter 1) for managing the crisis was a key factor in overcoming it. It is important to note that all the work done by Miami was directed through one single committee, which was responsible for all aspects of the crisis.

One of the most significant factors in Miami's success was the practical steps taken to eliminate the crisis: cooperating with local police on reducing crime and increasing visitor's safety, using residents and local business people as partners and ambassadors in the process, allocating many resources for the problem, full cooperation between the private and public sectors and using a large variety of media strategies.

Summary

This chapter introduced the multi-step model for altering place image and highlighted its inventiveness and high usability compared with earlier models. Summarizing the links between the different parts of the model yields more overall conclusions: A place will have a greater tendency to apply moderate strategies under the following circumstances: it is more familiar; it is as an established brand; the sources of knowledge about it are more varied (including personal experience); it has unique attractions and invites celebrities, firms and organizations; it is located near international centers; it enjoys high status; its residents are similar to the target audience; and the crisis it has undergone was minor. By contrast, extreme strategies are often used by peripheral places, places that are unfamiliar, lack attractions and have low international standing.

This chapter also presented several case studies and the decision-making process at each place, based on the multi-step model for altering a place's image. The case of **Madrid** represents the effort by a strong international brand to overcome a sudden and unexpected crisis, using the strategy of ignoring it. The case of **Israel** represents the attempt to attract tourism undertaken by a country under constant threat of an ongoing crisis. The problematic nature of this situation causes places such as Israel to tend to extreme strategies to alter their image. As anticipated, Israel's marketers made a number of attempts to use extreme SAM strategies. Unfortunately, these were inadequate, and absence of strategic planning, consistency in delivering messages and resources prevented Israel from fully overcoming the crisis. Last was the successful case of Miami, demonstrating how a preplanned, patient and flexible use of moderate strategies can alter a place's image and re-attract visitors, investors and residents.

Final observations and lessons

This book answers a question asked by many local and national decision makers all around the world: "Which marketing and PR strategies should be employed to alter the image of a place undergoing an image crisis?" To answer this question we have developed a unique model, meant to assist decision makers in improving their places' images and re-attracting tourists, visitors, investors and residents. The multi-step model for altering place image is based on dozens of case studies and a vast literature in the fields of place marketing, mass communication, image management, crisis management, strategic management and PR. The model set out here has five stages: preliminary analysis of the crisis, audience and place (CAP analysis); setting goals and timing; choosing a source/audience/message response strategy (SAM strategies); choosing channels and techniques for delivering the message; and receiving constant feedback. Of these five stages, CAP analysis, as detailed in Chapter 6, is an innovation in the field of place marketing and is crucial for choosing an appropriate response strategy. CAP analysis, moreover, illustrates why some strategies are ineffective for certain crises, places and target audiences, and very effective in other cases. Another innovation of the multi-step model is the wide variety of media strategies. For the first time, a total of 24 media strategies are assembled, all designed for marketing places with a negative image.

Milestones for success

Throughout the book we offer many suggestions for altering a place's image. In this summary, we would like to highlight some of them, serving as milestones for success.

Leadership

Local leaders differ in the way they manage not only a place, but also the place's image. Local leaders who fail to overcome the difficulties their place faces will probably fail to overcome crises in its image (Avraham, 2003b). Such a connection between place management and image management was also found by Beirman (2006). This author found evidence of amateurism and superficiality in managing a recovery campaign following a terror attack in a country of Southeast Asia. In this case, the pre-existing amateurism in place management, for example, lack of readiness for an emergency situation, was replicated in the recovery campaign management, with actions such as not following the advice of international marketing professionals and not compensating the victims; all these behavior patterns, Beirman argued, resulted in very slow recovery by that tourist destination.

Here we wish to emphasis again and again that local leadership is a key factor in altering place image. Only successful leaders with a clear vision can initiate a change, allocate resources and lead the long recovery process. Leaders of this kind are no longer few and far between; more and more local decision makers understand that their place's public image is essential for its future and that a negative image injures its ability to compete for resources and national/international status. In 2006, it was noted that in more than 12 000 cities and towns worldwide, local decisions makers were striving to change their place's image and to promote various kinds of branding processes (*Globes*, 10 August 2006).

When a crisis erupts, local decision makers are hard at work resolving the immediate problems caused by the crisis; they have no time to think about the recovery plan or building the place's vision. In certain cases, the local leaders are engrossed in the acute circumstances, rather than working on solutions to settle the prolonged crisis. By contrast, some places use the crisis as a stimulus for change, perceiving it as a window of opportunity. For example, the process of altering **Manchester**'s image started after a bomb exploded in the downtown area in 1996. The city's local decision makers utilized that terrible event as an instrument to change its actual reality and image. Today Manchester is without doubt one of the success stories among cities that employ a strategic plan to change their image.

Effective marketing takes resources

Altering a place's image is a resource-consuming process. This constitutes a major problem for places that lack resources but must alter their image to improve their socio-economic situation; usually these places cannot afford to create events or implement most of the strate-gies we offer in the book (Anholt, 2005). At the same time, since initiating events and implementing expensive campaigns are mostly possible for places rich in resources they are able to recover from a crisis faster.

Awareness of the importance of changing a place's public image after a crisis may be increasing, but it is easier said than done. Manifold resources and time are needed, as well as cooperation with many different factors; and possible resistance by the opposition has to be taken into account. Local opposition tends to object to such changes, claiming that the mayor is "spending the public's money on personal PR" or asking "Why not build a bridge or a much needed road instead of spending money on expensive ads and billboards?" Local decision makers must be ready for an array of objections to their plan to change the place's image and to convince people that their efforts, in the end, will cause their city or town to prosper.

Be ready for future crises

The best way to handle an image crisis, obviously, is to be ready for it. Decision makers in every country, city and tourist destination should try and foresee the kinds of crisis they might have to face and to envisage the preparations that should be made to handle them. The international and national media exert a major effect on a place's image in a time of crisis, and being familiar with crisis communication techniques would be advantageous. Being prepared to withstand a crisis can significantly reduce its negative and long-term effects on the place's image and help it maintain its existing image. Chapter 5, elaborating the link between crisis management and crisis communication management, may prove extremely helpful in preparing for future crises and in understanding the role of the media in the life cycle of the crisis.

Employ a strategic approach

We strongly recommend that every place, in crisis or not, employ the strategic approach. This approach highlights the comprehensiveness of the marketing process and attaches the marketed image to the actual physical place. Handling an image crisis is a multi-dimensional task, involving much more than delivering a counter-message. With this kind of mission, changing slogans and logos is insufficient; a long-term plan is needed that will cover all the different aspects of a crisis, including, in the case of marketing countries, cooperation with ministries of foreign affairs, tourism and international trade, airlines and hotels. Similarly, when marketing a city, cooperation is needed with local residents, local and national government, the tourism industry, academic research, advertisers and newspeople, as discussed in Chapters 1 and 3. Many places that adopted this strategic approach managed to overcome their crises quickly and effectively: examples are **Singapore** (Beirman, 2006), **Miami** (Tilson and Stacks, 1997), **Glasgow** (Paddison, 1993), **Holon** (Shir, 2006) and **London** (Frisby, 2002; Hopper, 2002).

Back up your campaign with a real change

Despite the importance of a place's image, we emphasize throughout the book that a meaningful change in the reality itself is far more important than launching a campaign. So if a country is perceived as unsafe for tourists due to a high rate of crime, the best way to proceed is to reduce the crime rate significantly. In recent years, many places have used a variety of slogans aimed at altering their image; yet paradoxically, these slogans seem only to have lengthened the odds against serious discussion about the link between the campaign and the actual place (Avraham, 2003a). It is clear by now that cosmetic changes such as slogans and logos are insufficient, and in-depth changes in the place are required for a new image to "catch on." For example, in **Syracuse**, New York, the city marketing campaign was backed by reconstruction of the city and the building of a convention center, sports stadium, malls, museums, a market and an improved transportation system (Short et al., 1993). Once they see that the campaign is accompanied by real significant change, visitors and residents will confirm and support the campaign messages, serving as ambassadors of the place.

In contrast to Syracuse, many campaigns have failed because decision makers focused on the marketing aspects and neglected the actual physical elements of the place such as improving infrastructure and services. Paddison (1993) notes that successful marketing of a new image must be accompanied by physical changes, matching the image and the place. This author further argues that launching a campaign for a place still suffering from a problematic reality is pointless. In other words, campaigns alone cannot erase the link between certain places and their negative traits, especially those of terror and violence. Still, some researchers believe that even during the crisis, campaigns carrying positive information should be delivered in order to contradict the negative news (Beirman, 2002).

Enhance local pride and work with the residents

In parallel to launching a campaign, it is essential to enhance local pride and enthusiasm regarding the change process. For example, stickers with the slogan "Baltimore Believe" were handed out to the residents of **Baltimore**, and stickers with the slogan "I am Dunedin" were handed out as part of a campaign to improve the image of **Dunedin**, New Zealand. Distributing stickers is a good start, but it takes much more than that to turn the place's residents into full partners in the changing process. To encourage residents to join the campaign's work, factors such as residents' satisfaction with the place, their needs, the way they consume local services and their demand for other services that are not available should be assessed.

Analysis of the factors involved in place marketing reveals that in many places the process of change does not begin with local decision makers but with the residents themselves. Residents believed that the place's existing image was false and that its actual reality was much better than the common perception. The proud residents of a city can serve as ambassadors of good will, spreading the good news more effectively than most campaign messages. Such was the case in **Miami**, when residents assumed an important role in altering the city's image and assisting in the recovery of the local tourism industry (Tilson and Stacks, 1997).

Marketing campaign is not enough

In addition to marketing campaigns, local leaders should contact investors and firms, make sure the place is represented at tourism fairs and use social networks to promote it. Public relations and advertising campaigns are very important but are no substitute for personal meetings with entrepreneurs, travel agents and tour operators, at which economic benefits, incentives and assistance in recruiting human resources or in relocating – a business or a firm – should be offered. In addition to the different stages of the campaign, as noted in Chapter 3, the use of varied techniques such as PR, sales promotion and direct marketing is highly recommended. However, when using more than one technique, it is important to stick to one unified message for each target audience. For example, Morgan and Pritchard (2001) found that the wide variety of messages used in marketing **Morocco** actually damaged the country's marketing efforts.

In addition, local leaders who are interested in re-attracting visitors following a crisis should be ready for actions such as reducing prices, subsidizing cheap flights, reimbursing or compensating airlines for empty seats and financing travel insurance for visitors (Beirman, 2002). An example of one such action can be found in the case of **Iran**, which offered tour operators $20 for every Western tourist they sent to the country (*Yediot Acharonot*, 1 November 2006). In any event, we note yet again that managing a crisis is a holistic act. This is well borne out by a comment by Mansfeld (2006): "Effective management of a given tourism crisis is dependent on many factors such as the availability of reliable contingency plans, the availability of contingency funds, the level and the type of public and private sector cooperation, and concerted efforts to change the situation by all tourism stakeholders" (p. 274).

Take a deep breath

Because the process of change calls for extensive strategic planning, many physical changes and cooperation with different partners, a long time must elapse before the image change is felt. According to Fenster et al. (1994), a real and in-depth change in a place's image can take 6–8 years. Such a change is not a miracle happening overnight (Stafford, 2005) but a multi-stage process in which the order of the stages must be maintained. At each stage the place's marketers should examine whether their messages have been accepted by the target audience and the way the place's residents and the audience react to these messages. Following this examination, it can be assessed whether the messages are appropriate or whether they should be replaced. Another important test concerns the audience's social environment, needs, knowledge of the place and behavior, as described in Chapters 4 and 6. There is nothing wrong in adjusting the campaign messages according to these examinations. For example, the city of **Salford** in the United Kingdom focused its marketing messages around LS Lowry, a famous artist born in the city. As part of the strategy, the city built the Lowry Art & Entertainment Centre, the Lowry Museum and the Lowry outlet mall. Following the success of the first stage, the marketers of Salford decided to expand the city's image using the slogan: "There's more to Salford than its world renowned favorite son." The city marketers moved from the strategy of "association with a familiar brand" to an attempt to expand the place's image. This example shows us that to manage the place's image well the marketing strategy must be constantly adjusted.

Heed the advice of professionals

Local decision makers should recognize that professionalism is the key to success. Every step in the marketing process should be taken comprehensively, without skipping any. One of the most important stages, which some places do tend to omit, is conducting a preliminary survey to assess the place's image among the target audience. Instead, some local leaders prefer to act on their intuition and as a result launch ineffective campaigns for irrelevant audiences. Moreover, regarding a city, changing an image cannot be done by the mayor or spokesperson alone; it is a process in which every city employee should take part. Every one of them needs to know the city's vision, the new branding and how his/her job can promote the city's new image (Avraham, 2003a).

Future research

This book offers an entire set of response strategies for altering the image of a country, a city or a tourist destination. The 24 media strategies presented here are a preliminary attempt to analyze, assess and group the response strategies that have been adopted by a wide variety of places and for a wide variety of audiences. While this book is all-embracing, future research may well be advised to concentrate on a set of places that are similar in their characteristics (similar former image, similar geographical location), which have undergone the same kind of crisis (such as a natural disaster or terror attack) and which are targeting the same audience. That way it will be easier to determine which of the media strategies presented are more effective than the others. In other words, holding the CAP constructs as fixed will afford us better understanding of the use of SAM strategies. This kind of study should be based on reliable data and on clear indicators of crisis resolution, such as comparing the numbers of visitors or investments before, during and after the crisis. In addition, we strongly believe that the multi-step model for altering place image can be helpful in diverse kinds of image restoration: after crises have befallen politicians, executives, celebrities, organizations, firms or institutions. Another aspect for future research is the role of the Internet in place marketing. In recent years, a growing number of places have acquired websites and use the Internet as a promotion tool. We expect this phenomenon to become even more popular, and we advise future researchers and marketers to study and take advantage of this technology and others, in this rapidly changing and exciting world of place marketing.

References

Adams, W. C. (1986). Whose lives count? TV coverage of natural disasters. *Journal of Communication*, 35 (2), 113–122.

Adoni, H. and Mane, S. (1984). Media and the social construction of reality: toward and integration of theory and research. *Communication Research*, 11 (3), 323–340.

Ambassador (1998). Unusual town names. 24–26 August.

Anderson, R. (1988). Visions of instability: U.S. television's law and order news of El Salvador. *Media, Culture and Society*, 10 (2), 236–264.

Anholt, S. (2005). *Brand new justice: how branding places and products can help the developing world*. Oxford: Elsevier.

Ashworth, G. and Goodal, B. (eds) (1995). *Marketing tourism places*. New York: Routledge. Ritchie & Zins, 1978.

Ashworth, G. J. (2006). *Can we, do we, should we, brand places? (Or are we doing what we think and say we are doing?)*. Paper presented at CIRM, Manchester Metropolitan University, 6–7 September.

Ashworth, G. J. and Voogd, H. (1990). *Selling the city*. West Sussex: Wiley.

Avraham, E. (2003a). *Campaigns for promoting and marketing cities in Israel*. Jerusalem: The Floersheimer Institute for Policy Studies. (In Hebrew).

Avraham, E. (2003b). *Behind media marginality: coverage of social groups and places in the Israeli press*. Lanham, MD: Lexington Books.

Avraham, E. (2004). Media strategies for improving an unfavorable city image. *Cities*, 21 (6), 471–479.

Avraham, E. (2006). Public relations and advertising strategies for managing tourist destination image crises. In: Y. Mansfeld and A. Pizam (eds) *Tourism and security: a case approach*, pp. 233–249. London: Butterworth Heinemann.

Avraham, E. and Ketter, E. (2006). Media strategies for improving national images during tourism crisis. In: M. Kozak and L. Andreu (eds) *Progress in tourism marketing*, pp. 115–125. Oxford: Elsevier.

Bagli, C. V. (2005). *"Offer is doubled by developer to build arena in Brooklyn"*. Retrieved on 7 September from http://www.nytimes.com.

Baker, B. and Bendel, P. (2006). *"Come and say G'Day!"* Retrieved on 1 September from http://www.atme.org/pubs/archives/77_1898_11926.cfm.

Baral, A., Baral, S. and Morgan, N. (2004). Marketing Nepal in an uncertain climate: confronting perceptions of risk and insecurity. *Journal of Vacation Marketing*, 10 (2), 186–192.

Bard, M. (2005). *"Does the media's anti-Israel bias matter?"* Retrieved on 8 April from http://www.israelinsider.com.

Barnet, K. (2001). *"Beijing stretches its image to fit through the Olympic rings"*. Retrieved on 13 August from http://www.brandchannel.com.

Barzel, A. (1976). *Who has the right to speak? Freedom of access to the media*. Jerusalem: Israel Broadcasting Authority, Training Center. (In Hebrew).

Beirman, D. (2002). Marketing of tourism destinations during a prolonged crisis: Israel and Middle East. *Journal of Vacation Marketing*, 8, 167–176.

Beirman, D. (2006). A comparative assessment of three Southeast Asian tourism recovery campaigns: Singapore roars: post SARS 2003; Bali post the October 12, 2002 bombing; and WOW Philippines 2003. In: Y. Mansfeld and A. Pizam (eds) *Tourism, security and safety; from theory to practice*. Burlington, MA: Butterworth-Heinemann.

Benoit, W. L. (1995). *Accounts, excuses, and apologies: a theory of image restoration strategies*. Albany, NY: State University of New York Press.

Benoit, W. L. (1997). Image repair discourse and crisis communication. *Public Relations Review*, 23 (2), 177–187.

Beriatos, E. and Gospodini, A. (2004). "Glocalising" urban landscapes: Athens and the 2004 Olympics. *Cities*, 21, 187–202.

Birnboim-Karmeli, D. (1994). *A good place in the center: place of residence as a means to modeling of layered identity*. Unpublished doctoral dissertation, Hebrew University in Jerusalem. (In Hebrew).

Bjornlund, L. (1996). *Media relations for local government: communication for results*. Washington, DC: ICMA.

Bornstein, E. (1995). Modi'in: the Israeli dream on television commercials. *Otot*, 180, 8–12. (In Hebrew).

Bradley, A., Hall, T. and Harrison, M. (2002). Selling cities: promoting new images for meetings tourism. *Cities*, 19 (1), 61–70.

Bramwell, B. and Rawding, L. (1996). Tourism marketing images of industrial cities. *Annals of Tourism Research*, 23, 201–221.

Brkic, N. and Mulabegovic, E. (2006). *The image of Bosnia and Herzegovina as a tourism destination.* Paper presented at CIRM, Manchester Metropolitan University, 6–7 September.

Brooker-Gross, S. (1983). Spatial aspects of newsworthiness. *Geografiska Annaler,* 65B (1), 1–9.

Brown, J. L. (2002). *"Oklahoma: a 'cow town' spends a billion on image makeover".* Retrieved on 15 November from http://www.phillyburbs.com.

Burgess, J. and Gold, J. R. (eds) (1985). *Geography, the media and popular culture.* New York, NY: St. Martin's Press.

Burgess, J. and Wood, P. (1988). Decoding Docklands: place advertising and decision-making strategies of small firms. In: J. Eyles and D. M. Smith (eds) *Qualitative methods in human geography.* Cambridge, MA: Polity Press.

Burgess, J. A. (1982). Selling places: environmental images for the executive. *Regional Studies,* 16 (1), 1–17.

Byrom, J. (2006). *Place management from an Australian perspective.* Paper presented at CIRM, Manchester Metropolitan University, 6–7 September.

Caspi, D. (1993). *Mass communication.* Tel Aviv: The Open University of Israel. (In Hebrew).

Coca-Stefaniak, A., Parker, C., Quin, S. and Rinaldi, R. (2006). *Evolution of town centre and place management models: a European perspective.* Paper presented at CIRM, Manchester Metropolitan University, 6–7 September.

Codato, G. and Franco, E. (2006). *Branding Turin: the 2006 winter Olympics' legacy for downtown regeneration.* Paper presented at CIRM, Manchester Metropolitan University, 6–7 September.

Cohen, S. and Young, J. (eds) (1981). *The manufacture of news: deviance, social problems and the mass media* (2nd rev. edition). London: Constable/Sage.

Coombs, W. T. (1999). *Ongoing crisis communication: planning, managing and responding.* California: Sage.

Crane, D. (1994). Introduction: the challenge of the sociology of culture to sociology as a discipline. In: D. Crane (ed.) *The sociology of culture,* pp. 45–62. Cambridge, MA: Blackwell.

Curran, J. (2006). *"Get a load of this: New Jersey looks for a new slogan".* Retrieved on 15 November from http://www.usatoday.com.

Dahlgren, P. and Chakrapani, S. (1982). The third world on T.V. news: western way of seeing the "other." In: W. Adams (ed.) *Television coverage of international affairs,* pp. 45–62. Norwood, NJ: Ablex.

Davis, D. K. (1990). News and politics. In: D. Nimmo and D. L. Swanson (eds) *New directions in political communication,* pp. 147–184. New York, NY: Sage.

Deuschl, D. E. (2006). *Travel and tourism public relations*. Burlington, MA: Butterworth-Heinemann.

Dominick, G. (1977). Geographic bias in national TV news. *Journal of Communication*, 27, 94–99.

Dougherty, D. (1992). *Crisis communication*. New York, NY: Walker and Company.

Dunn, K. M., McQuirk, P. M. and Winchester, H. P. (1995). Place making: the social construction of Newcastle. *Australian Geographical Studies*, 33, 149–166.

Efrati, B. (2002). Not welcoming. *Kol Ha'ir*, 6 September. (In Hebrew).

Elizur, J. (1987). *National images*. Jerusalem: Hebrew University.

Elizur, J. (1994). *Israel and the U.S.: images of flawed paradise*. Paper presented at the American–Israeli Relations and the "New World Order" Conference, The Davis Institute of the Hebrew University of Jerusalem, Jerusalem, 6 June.

Epstein, E. J. (1973). *News from nowhere*. New York, NY: Random House.

Fair, J. E. (1993). War, famine and poverty: race in the construction of Africa's media image. *Journal of Communication Inquiry*, 17 (2), 5–22.

Fallon, P. and Schofield, P. (2006). *University alumni as a short break market: the case of Greater Manchester*. Paper presented at CIRM, Manchester Metropolitan University, 6–7 September.

Fearn-Banks, K. (1996). *Crisis communication: a casebook approach*. Mahwah, NJ: LEA.

Felsenstein, D. (1994). *The enterprising city: promoting economic development at the local level*. Jerusalem: Floersheimer Institute for Policy Studies. (In Hebrew).

Felsenstein, D. (1995). *Planning or marketing? On the status of local economic development in Israel*. Jerusalem: The Floersheimer Institute for Policy Studies. (In Hebrew).

Fenster, T., Herman, D. and Levinson, E. (1994). *Selling the city: physical, social and administrative aspects of a marketing plan for Beer Sheva*. Beer Sheva: Ben-Gurion University of the Negev. (In Hebrew).

First, A. and Avraham, E. (2004). *Media representation of the Arab population in the Hebrew media: comparison between the coverage of the First Land Day (1976) and the Al-Akza Intifada (2000)*. Tel Aviv: Tel Aviv University, Tami Steinmetz Center for Peace Research. (In Hebrew).

First, A. and Avraham, E. (2007). When the "holy land" turns into real estate: national identity, globalization/Americanization, and representation of the land in Israeli advertising. *Popular Communication*, 5 (4), 1–17.

Fishman, M. (1980). *Manufacturing the news*. Austin, TX: University of Texas Press.

Frisby, E. (2002). Communication in a crisis: the British Tourist Authority's responses to the foot-and-mouth outbreak and 11th September, 2001. *Journal of Vacation Marketing*, 9, 89–100.

Gabor, K. (2006). *Place marketing.* Debrecen.

Galician, M. L. and Vestra, N. D. (1987). Effects of "good news" and "bad news" on newscast image and community image. *Journalism Quarterly*, 64, 399–405.

Galtung, J. and Ruge, M. H. (1965). The structure of foreign news. *Journal of Peace Research*, 2, 64–90.

Gamson, W. A. and Wolfsfeld, G. (1993). Movements and media as interacting system. *Annals of American Academy of Political and Social Science*, 528, 114–125.

Gans, H. J. (1979). *Deciding what's news.* New York, NY: Pantheon Books.

Glaesser, D. (2006). *Crisis management in the tourism industry.* Burlington, MA: Butterworth-Heinemann.

Global Development Research Center (2005). *"Kita-Kyushu: international cooperation to solve environmental problems"*. Retrieved on 13 October from http://www.gdrc.org/uem/japan/kitakyushu.html.

Globes. Various dates.

Gold, J. R. (1980). *An introduction to behavioral geography.* Oxford: Oxford University Press.

Gold, J. R. (1994). Locating the message: place promotion as image communication. In: J. R. Gold and S. V. Ward (eds) *Place promotion: the use of publicity and marketing to sell towns and regions*, pp. 19–37. Chichester: Wiley & Sons.

Gold, J. R. and Ward, S. V. (eds) (1994). *Place promotion: the use of publicity and marketing to sell towns and regions.* Chichester: Wiley.

Gonen, A. (1995). *Between city and suburb.* Hants, England: Avebury.

Gonzalez-Herrero, A. and Pratt, C. B. (1996). An integrated symmetrical model for crisis-communication management. *Journal of Public Relation Research*, 8 (2), 79–105.

Gould, P. and White, R. (1986). *Mental maps.* Boston, MA: Allen and Unwin.

Graber, D. A. (1989). Flashlight coverage: state news on national broadcasts. *American Politics Quarterly*, 17 (3), 277–290.

Ha'aretz. Various dates.

Hackett, R. A. (1984). Decline of the paradigm? Bias and objectivity in news media studies. *Critical Studies in Mass Communication*, 1 (3), 229–259.

Hall, C. M. and O'Sullivan, V. (1996). Tourism, political stability and violence. In: A. Pizam and Y. Mansfield (eds) *Tourism, crime and international security issues*, pp. 105–121. Chichester: Wiley.

Hall, S. (1977). Culture, the media and the "ideological effect". In: J. Curran, M. Gurevitch and J. Woollacott (eds) *Mass communications and society*. London: Edward Arnold.

Ha'reuveny, A. (2002). Jerusalem's decided to stop its campaign to promote local tourism. *Kol Ha'ear*, 12 April.

Harel-Dor, G. (2005). Sex appeal and the city. *Globes Brand Index*, pp. 144–149.

Harrison, S. (1995). *Public relations: an introduction.* London: Routledge.

Hason, S. (1996). *The new urban order: urban coalitions in Israel.* Jerusalem: The Floersheimer Institute for Policy Studies. (In Hebrew).

Henderson, N. and Turnbull, A. (2006). *Destination branding: promoting Shetland.* Paper presented at CIRM 2006, Manchester Metropolitan University, 6–7 September.

Henry, F. (2001). "*Drew Carey's Cleveland*". Retrieved on 9 July 9 from http://www.cleveland.com/homegrown/index.ssf?/tv/more/drew/herodrew.html.

Herstein, R. (2000). *Brand management: developing brand image strategies.* Tel Aviv: Cherrykover. (In Hebrew).

Herzog, H. and Shamir, R. (1994). Media discourse on Jewish/Arab relations. *Israel Social Science Research*, 9 (1/2), 55–88.

Hestroni, A. (2000). The relationship between values and appeals in Israeli advertising: a smallest space analysis. *Journal of Advertising*, 29 (3), 55–68.

Hoare, A. G. (1991). Making the news, spatial and non-spatial biases in British parliamentary reports of the Rowntree-Mackiontosh takeover. *Geografiska Annaler*, 73B (2), 95–109.

Holcomb, B. (1994). City make-over: marketing the post-industrial city. In: J. R. Gold and S. V. Ward (eds) *Place promotion: the use of publicity and marketing to sell towns and regions*, pp. 115–131. Chichester: Wiley.

Hopper, P. (2002). Marketing London in a difficult climate. *Journal of Vacation Marketing*, 9 (1), 81–88.

http://rentonwa.gov/; accessed on 5 June 2006.

http://travelvideo.tv; accessed on 2 October 2005.

http://www.africanegev.com; accessed on 12 November 2006.

http://www.aifl.org; accessed on 28 January 2007.

http://www.alnwickcastle.com; accessed on 28 December 2004.

http://www.baltimore.org; accessed on 22 September 2005.

http://www.biobelt.org; accessed on 23 June 2006.

http://www.brandchannel.com; accessed on 7 August 2005; 13 August 2001; 14 July 2003.

http://www.bratislava.sk; accessed on 17 October 2006.

http://www.braveheartbedandbreakfast.co.uk; accessed on 11 May 2006.

http://www.business.act.gov.au; accessed on 19 November 2005.

http://www.city.hamilton.on.ca; accessed on 7 August 2006.

http://www.city.toronto.on.ca; accessed on 3 August 2005.

http://www.cityofdunedin.com; accessed on 16 August 2005.

http://www.cleveland.oh.us; accessed on 16 August 2005.

http://www.cnn.com; accessed on 17 December 2001.

http://www.communityarts.net; accessed on 8 October 2005.

http://www.croatia.hr; accessed on 24 September 2005.

http://www.eprop.co.za; accessed on 28 August 2005.

http://www.ethiopianrun.org; accessed on 12 September 2006.

http://www.german-embassy.org.uk; accessed on 20 April 2007.

http://www.goisrael.com; accessed on 4 June 2005.

http://www.gotohungary.com; accessed on 2 October 2005.

http://www.guyana.org; accessed on 15 November 2006.

http://www.guyana-tourism.com; accessed on 15 November 2006.

http://www.highlandernepal.com; accessed on 22 June 2005.

http://www.houstonitsworthit.com; accessed on 12 December 2004.

http://www.hsmai.org; accessed on 18 August 2006.

http://www.icc-cricket.com; accessed on 15 November 2006.

http://www.iht.com; accessed on 25 March 2006.

http://www.imc.org.az; accessed on 1 November 2005.

http://www.iol.co.za; accessed on 28 August 2005.

http://www.jhnewsletter.com; accessed on 7 April 2002.

http://www.joburg.org.za; accessed on 28 August 2005.

http://www.joelkotkin.com; accessed on 7 August 2006.

http://www.laplandfinland.com; accessed on 4 August 2005.

http://www.lexingtonneced.com; accessed on 16 May 2006.

http://www.massmoca.org; accessed on 21 November 2005.

http://www.mediaethiopia.com; accessed on 12 September 2006.

http://www.metrotimes.com; accessed on 7 August 2005.

http://www.my-indonesia.info; accessed on 18 September 2005.

http://www.ncpress.com; accessed on 2 October 2005.

http://www.nigeriafirst.org; accessed on 30 July 2004.

http://www.norden.org; accessed on 18 August 2006.

http://www.nrg.co.il; accessed on 7 November 2006.

http://www.pcc.govt.nz; accessed on 24 July 2005.

http://www.polandtour.org; accessed on 21 December 2004.

http://www.renoisartown.com; accessed on 14 October 2004.

http://www.satte.org; accessed on 8 February 2006.

http://www.sdotnegev.org.il; accessed on 24 July 2005.

http://www.sidenet.org; accessed on 15 November 2006.

http://www.sourcewatch.org; accessed on 24 September 2005.

http://www.suntimes.co.za; accessed on 28 August 2005.

http://www.surfercityusa.com; accessed on 28 July 2005.

http://www.tel-aviv.gov.il; accessed on 18 August 2006.

http://www.themedialine.org; accessed on 29 April 2002.

http://www.thinkonekc.com; accessed on 18 August 2006.

http://www.torontounlimited.ca; accessed on 3 August 2005.

http://www.tourism.australia.com; accessed on 8 February 2006.

http://www.tourismhamilton.com; accessed on 7 August 2006.

http://www.tunisiaonline.com; accessed on 20 April 2002.

http://www.unisdr.org; accessed on 24 July 2005.

http://www.valleyofthestars.net; accessed on 19 September 2005.

http://www.vision2020.hamilton-went.on.ca; accessed on 4 March 2005.

http://www.visitlex.com; accessed on 8 August 2005.

http://www.visitmalta.com; accessed on 27 June 2005.

http://www.wikipedia.org; accessed on 24 July 2005.

http://www.world-tourism.org; accessed on 19 June 2005.

http://www.wroclaw.pl; accessed on 18 August 2006.

http://www.ynet.co.il; accessed on 17 December 2001.

Huang, Y. H. (2006). Crisis situations, communication strategies, and media coverage. *Communication Research*, 33 (3), 180–205.

Hudson, S. and Ritchie, J. R. B. (2006). Promoting destinations via film tourism: an empirical identification of supporting marketing initiatives. *Journal of Travel Research*, 44 (4), 387–396.

Israeli (2006). Japanese Sumo wrestlers will promote tourism to Israel. 14 May.

Jakubowicz, A., Goodall, H., Marin, J., Mitchell, T., Randall, L. and Seneviratne, K. (1994). *Racism, ethnicity and the media*. St. Leonards, Australia: Allen and Unwin.

Jerin, R. A. and Field, C. B. (1994). Murder and mayhem in the USA today: a quantitative analysis of national reporting of states' news. In: G. Barak (ed.) *Media, process, and social construction of crime*. New York, NY: Galand Publishing.

Johnson, M. A. (1997). Predicting news flow from Mexico. *Journalism and Mass Communication Quarterly*, 74, 315–330.

Jones, R. L. (2006). *"New Jersey picks a slogan"*. Retrieved on 13 January from http://www.wirednewyork.com.

Kaniss, P. (1991). *Making local news*. Chicago, IL: University of Chicago Press.

Kariel, H. G. and Rosenvall, L. A. (1978). Circulation of newspaper news within Canada. *Canadian Geographer*, 22 (2), 85–111.

Kariel, H. G. and Rosenvall, L. A. (1981). Analyzing news origin profiles of Canadian daily newspapers. *Journalism Quarterly* (summer), 58, 254–259.

Kassem, H. (2006). *Reconstructing the representations of Germany in Hollywood in view of the goals of American foreign policy: 1939–1966.* Thesis work submitted at the University of Haifa.

Kent, P. (1995). People, places, and priorities: opportunity sets and consumer's holyday choice. In: G. Ashworth and B. Goodal (eds) *Marketing tourism places.* New York, NY: Routledge.

Kim, H. and Richardson, S. L. (2003). Motion picture impacts on destination images. *Annals of Tourism Research,* 30 (1), 216–237.

Kim, K. and Barnett, G. A. (1996). The determinants of international news flow: a network. *Communication Research,* 23, 323–352.

King, R. T. (2005). *"Harbin snow and ice festival".* Retrieved on 13 October from http://www.rtoddking.com/chinawin2003_hb_if.htm.

Kirby, A. (1993). *Power/resistance: local politics and chaotic state.* Indianapolis, IN: Indiana University Press.

Kotler, P. and Armstrong, G. (1989). *Principles of marketing* (4th edition). New Jersey: Prentice-Hall.

Kotler, P., Haider, D. H. and Rein, I. (1993). *Marketing places.* New York: Free Press.

Kotler, P., Asplund, C., Rein, I. and Haider, D. H. (1999a). *Marketing places Europe.* Edinburgh: Financial Times, Prentice-Hall.

Kotler, P., Bowen, J. and Makens, J. (1999b). *Marketing for hospitality and tourism.* New Jersey: Prentice-Hall.

Kolter, P., Hamlin, M.A., Rein, I., Haider, D. H. (2002). *Marketing Asian places: attracting investment, industry and tourism to cities, states and nations.* Singapore: John Wiley & Sons.

Kunczik, M. (1997). *Images of nations and international public relations.* Mahwah, NJ: LEA.

Lahav, T. (2004). *The correlation between the operation of an alignment of public relations and the coverage patterns of places: the case study of the Upper Galilee Moshavot.* Thesis work submitted at the University of Haifa.

Larson, J. F. (1984). *Television's window on the world: international affairs coverage on the U.S. networks.* Norwood, NJ: Ablex.

Lee, M. A. and Solomon, N. (1990) *Unreliable sources.* New York: Carol Publishing Group.

Liss, D. (2002). *"Putting out the fire: managing through crisis".* Retrieved on 23 September from http://www.brandchannel.com.

Madhur, G. (2002). *"Philippines go to Hollywood to repair tattered image".* Retrieved on 7 July from http://groups.google.com.

Manheim, J. B. (1991). *All of the people, all of the time.* New York, NY: M. E. Sharpe.

Manheim, J. R. and Albritton, R. B. (1984). Changing national images: international public relation and media agenda setting. *American Political Science Review,* 78, 641–657.

Mansfeld, Y. (1999). Cycles of war, terror and peace: determinants and management of crisis and recovery of the Israeli tourism industry. *Journal of Travel Research*, 38 (1), 30–36.

Mansfeld, Y. (2006). The role of security information in tourism crisis management: the missing link. In: Y. Mansfeld and A. Pizam (eds) *Tourism, security and safety; from theory to practice*, pp. 271–290. Burlington, MA: Butterworth-Heinemann.

Mansfeld, Y. and Pizam, A. (eds) (2006) *Tourism, security and safety; from theory to practice*. Burlington, MA: Butterworth-Heinemann.

Manufacturers Association of Israel (2002). *Cities attractiveness for industry and investment*.

Mathews, J. (1998). Reporting the myth of Tiananmen and the price of passive press. *Columbia Journalism Review*, September/October. Available at: http://backissus.cjrarchives.org/year/98/5/tiananmen.asp

McNally, S. (2002). Caught in the middle. *Columbia Journalism Review*, January/February. Available at: http://cjrarchives.org/issues/2002/1/letter-mcnally.asp

Meyrowitz, J. (1985). *No sense of place*. New York, NY: Oxford University Press.

Mitroff, I. I. and Pearson, C. M. (1993). *Crisis management*. San Francisco, CA: Jossey-Bass Publishers.

Morgan, N. and Pritchard, A. (1998). *Tourism promotion and power: creating images, creating identities*. Chichester: Wiley.

Morgan, N. and Pritchard, A. (2001). *Advertising in Tourism & Leisure*. Woburn: Butterworth-Heinemann.

Morgan, N., Pritchard, A. and Pride, R. (2002). Introduction. In: N. Morgan, A. Pritchard and R. Pride (eds) *Destination branding: creating the unique destination proposition*. Woburn: Butterworth-Heinemann.

Nielsen, C. (2001). *Tourism and the media*. Melbourne: Hospitality press.

Nir, A. and Rahav, A. (1993). *Television advertising: the medium, the message, the money*. Tel Aviv: Matar. (In Hebrew).

Olins, W. (2001). *Viewpoints: Poland and national identity*. Available at http://www.wallyolins.com/includes/poland.pdf.

Olsson, K. and Bergland E. (2006). *Challenges using culture as a resource in city marketing practice*. Paper presented at CIRM, Manchester Metropolitan University, 6–7 September.

Pacific Asia Travel Association (2003). *Crisis management manual*. Bangkok: Pacific Asia Travel Association.

Paddison, R. (1993). City marketing, image reconstruction and urban regeneration. *Urban Studies*, 30 (2), 339–350.

Payvand (2005). *"Iran needs to attract more European tourists"*. Retrieved on 3 December from http://www.payvand.com/news/05/mar/1105.html.

Perry, D. (1987). The image gap: How international news affect perceptions of nations. *Journalism Quartely.* Summer-autumn, 416–433.

Pike, B. (1981). *The image of the city in modern literature.* Princeton, NJ: Princeton University Press.

Pizam, A. and Mansfeld, Y. (eds) (1996) *Tourism, crime and International Security Issues.* Chichester: John wiley & Sons.

Pocock, D. and Hudson, R. (1978). *Images of the urban environment.* London: Womack Macmillian Press.

Popesku, J. (2006). *The image of Serbia as a tourist destination.* Paper presented at CIRM, Manchester Metropolitan University, 6–7 September.

Relph, E. (1976). *Place and placelessness.* London: Pion.

Ries, A. and Ries, L. (2004). *The fall of advertising and the rise of PR.* New York, NY: Harper Collins Publishers.

Ritchie, B., Dorrell, H., Miller, D. and Miller, G. (2003). Crisis communication and recovery for the tourism industry: Lessons from the 2001 foot and mouth disease outbreak in the UK. *Journal of Travel and Tourism Marketing*, 15, 199–216.

Roeh, I. (1994). *Communications, differently.* Even Yehuda: Reches. (In Hebrew).

Romero, S. (2005). A town with a provocative name says no to change. *White Settlement Journal*, 13 November.

Rosen, A. (2000). *A dialogue with the public.* Tel Aviv: Pecker Publishing. (In Hebrew).

Santana, G. (2003). Crisis management and tourism: beyond the rhetoric. *Journal of Travel and Tourism*, 15, 299–321.

Seaton, A. V. and Bennett, M. M. (1996). *Marketing tourism products: concepts, issues, cases.* London: Thompson Business Press.

Shaw, G. and Williams, A. M. (2002). *Critical issues in tourism – a geographical perspective.* Oxford: Blackwell.

Shields, R. (1992). *Places on the margin.* London: Routledge.

Shir, I. (2006). *Place branding in Israel: the case of Holon.* Paper presented at CIRM, Manchester Metropolitan University, 6–7 September.

Shoemaker, P. J. (1991). Gatekeeping. *Communication concepts 3.* Newbury Park, CA: Sage.

Shoemaker, P. J. and Reese, S. D. (1996). *Mediating the message: theories of influences on mass media content* (2nd edition). New York, NY: Longman.

Short, J. R. and Kim, Y. H. (1993). Urban representations: selling the city in difficult times. In: T. Hall and P. Hubbard (eds) *The entrepreneurial city: geographies of politics, regime and representation*, pp. 55–75. Chichester: Wiley.

Short, J. R. Benton, L. M., Luce, W. B. and Walton, J. (1993). Reconstructing the image of the industrial city. *Annals of Association of American Geographers*, 83 (2), 207–224.

Short, J. R., Breitbach, S., Buckman, S. and Essex, J. (2000). From world cities to gateway cities. *City*, 4 (3), 317–340.

Singer, M. (2002). "True north". *The New Yorker*, 18 February, 118–123.

Skinner, H. and Gould, M. (2006). *Branding on ambiguity? Place branding without a national identity: marketing Northern Ireland as a post-conflict society in the USA*. Paper presented at CIRM, Manchester Metropolitan University, 6–7 September.

Smith, R. D. (2002). *Strategic planning for public relations*. Mahwah, NJ: LEA.

Sonmez, S. F., Apostolopoulos, Y. and Tarlow, P. E. (1999). Tourism in crisis: managing the effects of terrorism. *Journal of Travel Research*, 38 (1), 13–18.

Specht, A. (2006). Natural disaster management. In: J. Wilks, D. Pendergast and P. Leggeat (eds) *Tourism in turbulent times: towards safe experiences for visitors*, pp. 123–142. Amsterdam: Elsevier.

Stafford, G., Yu, L. and Armoo, K. (2006). Crisis management and recovery: how Washington, DC, hotels responded to terrorism. In: Y. Mansfeld and A. Pizam (eds) *Tourism, security and safety; from theory to practice*, pp. 291–311. Burlington, MA: Butterworth-Heinemann.

Stafford, L. (2005). Mission: tie Atlanta's strengths into a brand. *Atlanta Journal Constitution*, 11 September.

Stephens, L. (2001). *"The San Fernando Valley: the festive valley"*. Retrieved on 14 December from http://www.valleyofthestars.net/Library/Papers%20&%20Treatises/Pepperdine_Festive_SFV.htm.

Stocker, K. P. (1997). A strategic approach to crisis management. In: C. L. Caywood, *The handbook of strategic public relations & integrated communications*, pp.189–203. Boston, MA: McGraw Hill.

Stoner, R. C. (1992). *Practical promotion: strategies for improving services and image*. Washington, DC: ICMA.

Strauss, A. L. (1961). *Image of the American city*. New York, NY: Free Press.

Suyama, K. and Senoh, T. (2006) *Osaka brand renaissance: a new approach for place branding*. Paper presented at CIRM, Manchester Metropolitan University, 6–7 September.

Swarbrooke, J. and Horner, S. (1999). *Consumer behavior in tourism*. Oxford: Butterworth-Heinemann.

Sya, L. S. (2004). *"Malaysia – inviting"*. Retrieved 4 October from http://www.brandchannel.com.

Szondi, G. (2007). The role and challenges of country branding in transition countries: the Central and Eastern European experience. *Place Branding and Public Diplomacy*, 3, 8–20.

Tal, E. (1993). Promoting Jerusalem: a thin line between love and hate. *Otot*, 155, 42–43. (In Hebrew).

Tarlow, P. E. (2001). *Event risk management & safety*. New York, NY: Wiley.

Tarlow, P. E. (2005). *Tourism tidbits*, 27 November.

Tarlow, P. E. (2006). A social theory of terrorism and tourism. In: Y. Mansfeld and A. Pizam (eds) *Tourism, security and safety; from theory to practice*, pp. 33–48. Burlington, MA: Butterworth-Heinemann.

The Marker. Various dates.

The New York Times. Various dates.

Tilson, D. J. and Stacks, D. W. (1997). To know us is to love us: the public relations campaign to sell a business-tourist-friendly Miami. *Public Relations Review*, 23, 95–115.

Tsfati, Y. and Cohen, Y. (2003). On the effect of the "third person effect": perceived influence of media coverage and residential mobility intentions. *Journal of Communication*, 53 (4), 711–727.

Tuchman, G. (1978). *Making news*. New York, NY: Free Press.

van Dijk, T. A. (1988a). *News as discourse*. Hillsdale, NJ: Lawrence Erlbaum.

van Dijk, T. A. (1988b). *News analysis*. Hillsdale, NJ: Lawrence Erlbaum.

van Dijk, T. A. (1996). Power and the news media. In: D. L. Paletz, *Political communication in action*, pp. 9–36. Cresskill, NJ: Hampton Press.

Vandewalle, I. (2006). *Branding Liverpool '08: local, national, and international perceptions of the Liverpool '08 brand*. Paper presented at CIRM, Manchester Metropolitan University, 6–7 September.

Vatikay, Y. (2000). Advertisements during the 1970's. *Kesher*, 27, 78–87. (In Hebrew).

Wahab, S. (1996). Tourism and terrorism: synthesis of the problem with emphasis on Egypt. In: A. Pizam and Y. Mansfeld (eds) *Tourism, crime and international security issues*, pp. 175–186. Chichester: Wiley.

Waitt, G. (1995). Media representation of forestry and soil issues in the Australian urban press, 1990–1991. *Australian Geographical Studies*, 33 (2), 299–307.

Walker, D. (1997). *Public relations in local government: strategic approaches to better communication*. London: Pitman Publishers.

Walmsley, D. J. (1982). Mass-media and spatial awareness. *Tijdschrift voor Economicische en Sociale Geografie*, 73 (1), 32–42.

Webster's Dictionary. *"Patriotism"*. Retrieved on 6 November from http://onlinedictionary.datasegment.com/word/patriotism.

Weimann, G. (2000). *Communication unreality: modern media and the reconstruction of reality*. Thousand Oaks: Sage.

Weimann, G. and Nevo, B. (2001). *The Singaporean enigma*. Jerusalem, Israel: Zivonim. (In Hebrew).

Wheeler, K. M. (ed.) (1994). *Effective communication: a local government guide*. Washington, DC: ICMA.

White, C. M. (2006). *When the media are used to create a crisis: lessons in what not to do*. Paper presented in ICA, Dresden, Germany.

Winkler, S. (2006). *"Expertise: issues-management"*. Retrieved on 21 June from http://www.ogilvypr.com.

Wolfsfeld, G. (1988). *The politics of provocation: participation and protest in Israel*. Albany, NY: State University of New York Press.

Wolfsfeld, G. (1991). Media, protest and political violence: A transactional analysis. *Journalism Monographs*, 127, 1–61.

Wolfsfeld, G. (1997). *Media and political conflict: news from the Middle East*. Cambridge: Cambridge University Press.

Wolfsfeld, G., Avraham, E. and Aburaiya, I. (2000). When prophesy always fails: Israeli press coverage of the Arab minority's Land Day protests. *Political Communication*, 17 (2), 115–131.

Womack, B. (1981). Attention maps of 10 major newspapers. *Journalism Quarterly* (summer), 58, 260–265.

World Tourism Organization (2006). *"Crisis guidelines for the tourism industry"*. Retrieved on 13 October from http://www.world-tourism.org.

Yates, M. (2006). Project Phoenix: a benchmark for reputation management in travel & tourism. In: J. Wilks, D. Pendergast and P. Leggeat (eds) *Tourism in turbulent times: towards safe experiences for visitors*, pp. 263–276. Amsterdam: Elsevier.

Yaziv, G. (1994). *Social dictionary*. Tel Aviv: The College of Management.

Yediot Acharonot. Various dates.

Yochtman-Yaar, E. and Ben-Rafael, E. (1987). The changing position of the kibbutz in the Israeli society. In: Y. Gorni, Y. Oved and I. Paz (eds) *Communal life: an international perspective*, pp. 447–453. Ramat Efal: Yad Tabenkin and Transaction Books.

Young, C. and Lever, J. (1997). Place promotion, economic location and the consumption of image. *Tijdschrift voor Economicische en Sociale Geografie*, 88 (4), 332–341.

Zimet, D. (2006). Branding Turkey. *Menahalim*, October 9, 42. (In Hebrew).

Index

Terror attacks, 20, 25, 63, 80, 81, 96,
102–4, 110, 116, 118, 125, 126, 137,
138, 140, 143, 144, 148, 149, 151,
158–9, 168, 171–2, 177, 180, 181,
185, 189, 191, 196–9, 205,
207, 210
Texas, 141, 175
Thailand, 24, 30, 57, 138,
153, 165
The Simpsons, 29
Tiberias, 183
Titanic, 166
Toronto, 50, 128, 154
Tour operators, 149, 201, 208, 209
See also Travel agents
Tourism industry, 8, 66, 88, 96, 138,
150, 185, 196, 201, 207, 208
Tourist attractions, 15, 16, 22, 47, 106,
114, 117, 119, 138, 140, 145, 149,
181, 198
Trait grading, 22–3
Travel agents, 46, 119, 150, 199,
201, 208
See also Tour operators
Tsunami, 81, 138, 141–2, 150, 151
See also Natural disasters
Tulsa, 140
Tunisia, 116, 137, 143, 158
Turin, 17, 19
Turkey, 23, 29, 53, 137, 140
Tuscan, 155

Unemployment, 4, 9, 15, 143, 148
UNESCO, 169
Unique selling proposition, 15
United Kingdom, 10, 138, 153,
180, 209
See also Britain; England
United States, 5, 8, 10, 12, 25, 34, 41, 47,
49–51, 60, 96–7, 110, 125, 128, 131,
133, 140, 143, 145, 156–9, 165, 170,
176, 181–3, 185, 200, 201
See also America

Unstructured survey, 21, 23
See also Attitude surveys; Structured
survey

Vancouver, 14
Venice, 114, 120
Verkosta, 163
Vichy, 176
Victims, 91–6, 102–4, 112, 205
Vienna, 14
Violence, 13, 15, 27, 29, 31, 39, 63, 72,
84, 107, 108, 113, 125, 140, 142, 143,
153, 156, 207
Virgin Islands, 61
Visual Symbol, 56, 60, 65
See also Logo

War, 80, 131, 168–9, 171, 172, 176,
180–2, 185, 189, 198, 199
Civil war, 11, 171
See also Conflict
Washington (State), 51, 56
Washington, DC, 34, 38, 113, 127, 159,
172, 181–2, 195
Washington, DC Convention &
Tourism Corporation, 181
White Settlement (Texas), 175
Wildfires, 165
See Forest fires; *See also* Natural
disasters
Wisconsin, 47
World Tourism Organization, 60, 95,
141, 142, 150, 151
World Trade Center, 96
World Wide Web, 50, 63
See also Email; Internet
Wroclaw, 50–1

Yellowstone National Park, 165–6
York, 3
Yorkshire, 164

Zurich, 14